Hmong

Hmong
HISTORY
OF A PEOPLE

Keith Quincy

EWU
EASTERN
WASHINGTON
UNIVERSITY
P·R·E·S·S
Cheney

Library of Congress Cataloging-in-Publication Data

Quincy, Keith.
    Hmong, history of a people / Keith Quincy. — 2nd ed.
        p.   cm.
    Includes bibliographical references and index.
    ISBN 0-910055-24-6
    1. Hmong (Asian people)—History.   I. Title.
DS555.45.M5Q56   1995
950'.0495—dc20
                                                        95-41342
                                                           CIP

The text of this book was set in a digitized version of Caslon.
Book design by Terry Bain. Cover design by John Smith.

To my wife, Anna Moore Quincy

Contents

ILLUSTRATIONS

PICTURES

MAPS

Introduction

cAmericans first learned of the Hmong during the Vietnam War, which was really two wars. The larger, official war in Vietnam overshadowed the equally devastating war in Laos, where twenty thousand Pathet Lao (Laotian communist guerrillas), trained and backed by forty to sixty thousand North Vietnamese soldiers, sought to topple the government and establish a communist regime.

The North Vietnamese committed so many troops to Laos because their principal supply line, the Ho Chi Minh Trail, was mostly on Laotian soil. As the u.s. had a strong interest in interdicting traffic along the trail, it dramatically increased military aid to the Royal Laotian Government, eventually subsidizing the entire cost of Laos's armed forces. It proved to be an unwise investment. Staffed with inept and unashamedly corrupt officers, the Royal Laotian Army suffered repeated and humiliating defeats at the hands of the Pathet Lao and the North Vietnamese. Fearful of a communist victory in Laos, and barred by Geneva agreement from committing American troops to Laos, the u.s. authorized covert operations by the CIA to create an alternative indigenous fighting force capable of turning back the communists.

The CIA's clandestine army grew quickly from a rag-tag collection of several hundred montagnard guerrillas to an air-mobile army of nearly forty thousand. Most of the soldiers in the secret army, as well as the army's commanding general, were Hmong. In the early years, when public opinion supported America's military involvement in Vietnam, newspaper accounts depicted the Laotian Hmong as determined freedom fighters pitted against numerically superior Laotian communist forces and several divisions of North Vietnamese soldiers. However, once public opinion turned against the Vietnam War, reports of the fighting in Laos acquired a hard, cynical edge. Hmong serving in the CIA's clandestine army were no longer described as freedom fighters, but as mercenaries.

The Hmong's public image improved after Laos fell to the communists in 1975. Newspaper accounts elevated them from paid mercenaries to loyal u.s. allies who had suddenly become victims of a vindictive communist regime. Reports of communist oppression of Hmong civilians, and the use of chemical warfare against Hmong rebels, along with accounts of a mass exodus of Hmong fleeing to refugee camps in Thailand, appeared in the international press and blossomed into feature articles in *National Geographic*, *Geo*, and *Readers Digest*.

Unfortunately this last image of the Hmong as victims has dominated America's perception of the Hmong. Although it has insured a certain degree of sympathy for their plight, it has not contributed to an understanding of the Hmong as a unique race with a rich heritage. Indeed, the involvement of the Hmong in the Laotian war was only a single historical incident in the long saga of the Hmong as a people, which is why the Laotian war is covered only briefly in the last part of this book. A more comprehensive account of the CIA-sponsored Hmong army, as well as a chronicle of the Hmong rebellion following the communist takeover of Laos, occurs in *Harvesting Pa Chay's Wheat*, the forthcoming sequel to this book.

There are slightly more than six million Hmong worldwide. Most live in China. The Hmong in Laos, northern Vietnam, Thailand, and Burma, are all descendants of Hmong who migrated from China into Southeast Asia. Hmong are montagnards, though they have not always lived in the mountains. Nor was their original homeland China. They dwelled in central Siberia before migrating to northern China, where they competed with the Chinese for the rich soil along the banks of the Yellow River.

The Chinese made war on the Hmong and drove them south into the region encompassing present day Hupeh and Hunan provinces. Relations between the Hmong and Chinese vacillated between uneasy truce and armed conflict for centuries, with the Hmong suffering many devastating defeats. In the fourth century A.D., the Hmong established an independent kingdom that for a time rivaled the power of the Chinese empire. The Chinese destroyed the Hmong kingdom in the tenth century, and reduced thousands of Hmong to virtual slavery. Hmong who escaped this fate fled the Hupeh/Hunan region for the mountain zones of Kweichow, Szechwan, and Yunnan. They lived beyond the reach of the Chinese and enjoyed relative peace and independence until the eighteenth century, when the emperors of the Manchu dynasty waged a war of extermination against the Hmong of Kweichow and southern Szechwan. A century later, the Yunnanese Hmong suffered a similar fate.

Because of relentless persecution, thousands of Hmong fled China for northern Vietnam, Laos, Thailand, and Burma. Following the Second World War, the Hmong of northern Vietnam and Laos allied themselves with the French and fought against the Vietnamese communists. When the u.s. replaced France, the Laotian Hmong cast their lot with the Americans. Prior to the communist victory in Laos, nearly a third of the Laotian Hmong perished in combat, or died from starvation and disease caused by the fighting. After the communist takeover, thousands more Hmong died in concentration camps, perished in rebellions, or were killed trying to escape to Thailand. Of those who did escape, more than eighty thousand resettled in the u.s. It is for these Hmong, and especially their children, that this book is written.

AUTHOR'S NOTE

By tradition, Hmong first and middle names follow the clan name. Throughout the book, however, Hmong names are presented with the surname (clan affiliation) appearing last, the exceptions being names of historically famous Hmong known to the West in their traditional, and sometimes contracted, form; thus Vang Pao remains Vang Pao instead of Pao Vang, and Touby LyFoung does not appear in the text as Touby Foung Ly. Occasionally the original Hmong is added in parentheses, using the Smalley-Bertrais Roman Phonetic Alphabet (RPA) to avoid confusion where an alternate transliteration is possible.

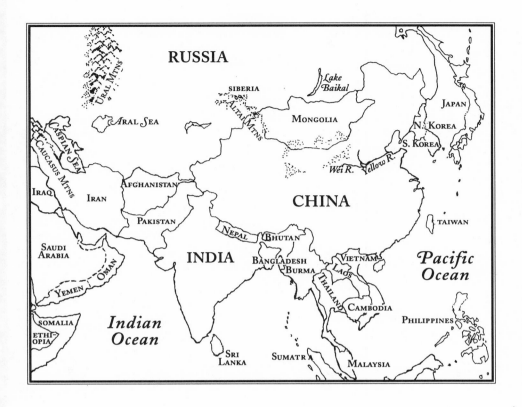

CHAPTER I

Ch'ien-Lung's Revenge

*T*HE YEAR WAS 1776. After a three-year campaign in the field, General Akoui entered Peking at the head of his victorious army with 250 prisoners in tow. Though weary, the general had good reason to be pleased that day. Among his prisoners was Sonom, the twenty-one-year-old Hmong king of greater Kin-tchuen, as well as the young king's immediate family and the principal members of his court.

The Manchu emperor, Ch'ien-lung, had demonstrated his appreciation by traveling ten miles from the imperial capital to greet the returning general. For even though Akoui's victory was minor in comparison to many of the empire's other triumphs, it was one the emperor had anticipated with relish. Now with the Hmong king in his grasp, Ch'ien-lung would have his revenge. It would be swift and terrible.

Throughout Ch'ien-lung's reign, China had been in continuous turmoil, much of it directly attributable to his expansionist foreign policy which resulted in the greatest increase of the empire in Chinese history. Burma, Nepal, and Turkestan were conquered and made protectorates, while China's hold on Tibet and Mongolia was strengthened. These successes had their cost, not only for conquered populations but for Chinese citizens who groaned under burdensome taxes and resented their Manchu rulers who were, after all, Manchurians and not Chinese. Things were even worse for the non-Chinese minorities who were treated by both the Manchu and Chinese as foreigners in their own land. There were uprisings on the Turkestan frontier and rebellions at home, not only in Shantung province but in Honan. There the "Society of the White Lotus," organized earlier during the Ming dynasty and now unified by a common hatred of the Manchurian usurpers, encouraged and organized numerous insurrections.

Then there were the Hmong. Compared to these other uprisings, the Hmong rebellion was of minor importance. Yet it was
especially irritating because Ch'ien-lung was forced to use a sledge-
hammer to swat a fly. Discounting the casualties, including a member of Ch'ien-lung's own family, the financial burden alone was
staggering. In the end, the cost of suppressing the Hmong would
mount to over 70 million taels (approximately $500 million), twice
what it cost to conquer all of Turkestan.

General Akoui was in fact the last of a number of generals sent
by the emperor to subdue the two rebellious Hmong kingdoms of
lesser and greater Kin-tchuen (near present day Suichiang). In 1767
the Governor of Szechwan province, Le Tsong-tou, informed the
emperor that the Hmong had come down from their mountains
and behaved like "brigands and bandits," pillaging towns and villages. The governor assured the emperor that appropriate measures
had been taken and no further trouble was anticipated. Almost as
soon as Ch'ien-lung received this first communiqué, however, Le
Tsong-tou was busy drafting a second. It told of the harsh measures
he had taken against the Hmong, including numerous executions.
It also related how this resulted in the Hmong of greater and lesser
Kin-tchuen joining forces and closing the passes through their territory, effectively severing all traffic to the southwest.

Le Tsong-tou did not have to spell out the seriousness of this.
With the passes closed the defense of Burma and Nepal, and indirectly all of Tibet, would be compromised. In addition, Hmong
interdiction of trading caravans passing through their territory
meant an inevitable decline in the revenue from the lucrative trade
that had taken years to cultivate in the southwestern protectorates.
The governor's letter closed with an anxious appeal for imperial
troops to put down the rebellion and reopen the passes.

The expedition was a miserable failure. Not only were no passes
reopened, the Chinese were unable to so much as enter Hmong
territory. The expedition's commander was summarily executed on
his return to Peking. His replacement was more cautious and, from
all accounts, reluctant to engage the Hmong in battle. This left
diplomacy as the only alternative. Gifts were brought to the Hmong

who came down from the heights and received them with enthusiasm, then promptly disappeared into the mountains with the peace offerings before the Chinese could open talks. While such conduct might be subject to various interpretations, the commander in charge preferred to read it as a sign of open submission to the emperor's authority. And so it seemed until hostilities broke out five years later.

Two envoys were sent from the Peking Court to open negotiations with the Hmong and to exhort them to come to their senses and obey the emperor. Not only were the emissaries treated badly, the two Hmong princes dared in their presence to describe the emperor's rule as criminal. To attack imperial armies was one thing, but to speak of the emperor in such a way was unheard of. In theory, the authority of Chinese emperors was based on a supposed mandate from heaven. To slander an emperor was therefore blasphemy. When informed of this Hmong sacrilege, Ch'ien-lung flew into a rage and vowed on the spot to spare no expense in suppressing the Hmong rebellion. He would do more. He would exterminate them.

Though the idea was extreme, it lacked originality. Earlier emperors, who had also grown weary of repeated Hmong uprisings, invariably gravitated toward a policy of mass extermination. This was as much a response to the underlying cause of Hmong rebellions as it was a reaction to the rebellions themselves. A principal reason for Hmong rebelliousness was their resistance to sinicization. It was the Hmong's refusal to accept Chinese culture as their own, a culture which the Chinese had come to equate with civilization itself, that both puzzled and infuriated state authorities. It puzzled them because they could not understand why the Hmong did not want to become civilized. It infuriated them because this persistent refusal was viewed as an assault on the sanctity of Chinese culture and construed as evidence that the Hmong were a race of incorrigible criminals who not only posed a threat to law and order but who constituted a threat to civilization itself. Such a line of reasoning not only made a policy of extermination acceptable, it turned genocide into a moral crusade.

Determined to eradicate the Hmong, Ch'ien-lung dispatched three armies under the command of General Ouen-fou. Not only did Ouen-fou carry superior arms, with nearly 120,000 infantry and cavalry under his command, he enjoyed a ten-to-one advantage in numbers over the Hmong, made even greater by the sure knowledge that the rebels would not have time to join their scattered troops and face him as a united force.

Even so, it is likely the general's face reflected grim determination rather than confidence as he led his troops. Bent and braced against the howling wind, they stretched out single file behind him for nearly a mile, up the narrow mountain pass that would take them to the edge of Hmong territory. A spur of the great Tibetan plateau, the mountains of Kweichow and Szechwan slope from an average altitude of 6,000 feet in the east to 4,000 feet in the west, with scattered peaks that rise as high as 9,000 feet. Viewed from an airplane, the terrain resembles the surface of a waffle iron: the peaks of the limestone mountains are flat from erosion and each mountain is ringed by deep gorges. The occasional valley is so deep and shut in on all sides by steep inclines that it can be crossed only by taking the little paths, no more than goat trails, which run along the slopes.

To this one must add the unhealthy climate. Temperatures vary greatly from one district to another and often drop or rise unpredictably in the space of a few days or even hours. At any given time it might snow or rain. Powerful winds suddenly gust and then disappear. If one had to predict the weather, rain would be the best bet since it rains nearly two hundred days out of every year. During this protracted rainy season, malaria and other fevers breed with abandon. But Ouen-fou had more to worry about than miserable weather and nearly impassable terrain. For he was aware, as many Chinese generals before him had learned firsthand, that the Hmong are unsurpassed guerrilla fighters.

Nearly thirty years earlier another Manchu general, Fu Nai, detailed the Hmong's fighting ability with unconcealed frustration. When they "approach our camps they are never together but are divided into little groups of three or five men who hide in the trees and rocks, and are so accomplished at concealment that one never sees them. Then they ambush us so suddenly that we are unable to protect ourselves and on each occasion suffer many wounded."

Yet, to Ouen-fou's surprise and relief, he met only light resistance. Once safely through the first mountain pass, he ordered the two other generals under his command to hold back their forces and guard against a possible assault from the rear while he advanced through the next pass with the remaining troops. Again no resistance was encountered. The pass eventually narrowed and then sloped down into a deep gorge. Ouen-fou may have paused to consider the wisdom of entering the gorge. It was an ideal spot for an ambush. He could have returned and joined his main force, or sent messengers to direct them to join him. But he did neither. Since his scouts reported no sign of the rebels, the general waved his troops on.

Once all the Chinese were inside the gorge, Hmong materialized from behind rocks and from inside the crevices and fissures that ran up the face of the rock walls that hemmed in the Chinese. This time there was no weak resistance, nor were the Hmong few in number. Hmong warriors stationed on cliff edges rolled boulders down on the hapless Chinese, while other Hmong moved in force to close off all the escape routes.

Then as quickly and mysteriously as it had begun, the fighting suddenly ceased. The Hmong withdrew to the perimeter, attacking the Chinese only when they tried to escape. These assaults were so devastating that the Chinese gave up all thought of flight. Disheartened soldiers busied themselves gathering what firewood they could find and sat clustered in knots for warmth. As the days passed, food and water grew scarce. A few desperate infantrymen tried to escape under the cover of night, scratching and clawing their way up one of the cliffs that led to freedom. Those below discerned their fate from the screams that echoed through the gorge.

When the Hmong judged the Chinese sufficiently weakened by thirst and hunger to be able to offer only weak resistance, they

7

launched an all-out attack. Not one Chinese soldier escaped. Nor did the dead Chinese receive a decent burial, for neither of the two remaining generals bothered to mount a serious search for their commander. Probably they guessed his fate and did not wish to share it. Whatever the reason, they soon left the region and returned to Peking.

The true fate of General Ouen-fou and his men would not be learned until several years later from Hmong prisoners captured in another, more successful, campaign. Meanwhile, it was as though the earth had swallowed up nearly fifty thousand men.

It is unlikely that the emperor, once informed of the mysterious disappearance of Ouen-fou and his entire army, entertained any false hopes of the general's eventual return. Other commanders serving under other emperors had disappeared in much the same way after venturing into Hmong territory, and none had ever returned. Ouen-fou's disappearance disappointed Ch'ien-lung. He would have preferred to make an example of Ouen-fou. Instead, he vented his anger on the other two surviving generals, executing one and exiling the other.

The emperor had tasted enough of defeat. What he needed was an extraordinary general, someone not only renowned for his tactical acumen but also possessing bulldog tenacity when leading campaigns in the field. After canvassing his officers, Ch'ien-lung settled on General Akoui, a brilliant strategist who had recently distinguished himself in campaigns in Burma and was therefore no stranger to maneuvers in mountainous terrain. By one account, Akoui was also a "cold-blooded man and single-minded in his dedication to a task, fearing nothing, not even the displeasure of the emperor, if fulfilling his duty required it."

Ch'ien-lung permitted Akoui to select his own troops and granted the general full discretion in carrying out the campaign against the Hmong. But Akoui did more than carefully select his troops; he gathered information. He learned that while the Chinese had often defeated the Hmong in open terrain with the advantage of superior numbers and arms, these things proved a handicap in the mountains where a large army had to travel single file over narrow trails and heavy artillery could be transported only with great effort.

Yet Akoui needed superior numbers and arms to defeat the Hmong, for not only were they superb soldiers, Hmong guerrillas were especially skilled in the arts of ambush and quick retreat. Against such an enemy a large force was essential, as was the willingness to suffer steady and draining casualties in numerous skirmishes. Without adequate supplies, however, a large army could not long survive in the field. And experience had shown that on the Kweichow-Szechwan frontier, supply lines were difficult to keep open.

There was an additional problem. Akoui had learned from his informants that the Hmong had erected massive strongholds at strategic locations overlooking every major pass. These strongholds could only be taken by siege. And for this Akoui needed heavy artillery, cannons weighing hundreds of pounds and capable of shattering stone walls several feet thick.

Akoui's solution to the first problem was to do without supply lines entirely. His army would carry everything it needed. This required nearly as many coolies as Akoui had soldiers. His solution to the second problem was equally bold. The heavy cannons required for mounting effective sieges were left behind in Peking. In their place Akoui carried iron ingots to enable him to forge cannons on the spot when needed. He also divided his army into several divisions so that he could enter the Hmong territory from many directions at once in a coordinated assault. To insure that the defeat of the Hmong of greater and lesser Kin-tchuen would be final, Akoui planned to hold troops in reserve and use them in a rear-guard action to prevent Hmong troops from escaping through unguarded passes.

Akoui's forces were attacked the moment they entered Hmong territory. While the Hmong were quickly forced to retreat from the open field, they offered stiff resistance once they were in their mountains. Though the seasoned general was able to secure the first pass he entered, it was only after a furious battle in which Hmong women fought alongside their men. Yet, if Akoui had become master of the pass, he had also become its prisoner, for the Hmong had him hemmed in. While Akoui set up camp, the Hmong kept themselves busy building stone fortresses on the surrounding crests.

Although the Manchu general enjoyed the advantage of having put the Hmong on the defensive, he nevertheless realized that he would suffer heavy losses in any attempt to scale the cliffs to assault their fortifications. Prudence dictated patience. Three long months were spent in search of an alternate route up the mountain. The search was in vain for none existed. However, in the end Akoui's patience was rewarded.

From October to February much of Kweichow is draped in a dense fog. It fills the valleys, then rises upward until it engulfs even the mountain crests. By December the fog is so thick that the sun shines through only a few days each month. Perhaps this bit of information was among the many facts Akoui had gathered about the land and accounts for his willingness to remain locked up in the pass. In any event, once the fog materialized, Akoui was quick to make good use of it. Under the protection of this cover, a large force was sent scaling up the cliffs to take the Hmong by surprise. It was the sort of strategy the Hmong themselves would have admired had it not proved so costly to them.

Realizing that they were hopelessly outnumbered, the Hmong fought in retreat, holding each fortification until the flood of Chinese soldiers became too great to hold back. One by one their fortifications fell. But not all at once, nor even overnight. While Akoui was quick to press his advantage, the ferocity of the Hmong slowed the inevitable advance. Within a year and a half the tenacious general had penetrated no more than forty miles into Hmong territory, but that was far enough to bring him to the capital of lesser Kintchuen. He placed the Hmong city under siege.

The Hmong had been caught unprepared. No Chinese army had ever penetrated so far into their mountains, let alone captured the capital of lesser Kin-tchuen. Confident that Akoui would prove no exception to the rule, the Hmong had laid away no stores of food, and the principal source of water, a well, lay outside the walls of the capital. A smaller well inside the walls served for a while, but the underground stream that fed it ran slow, and even before the supply ran out, the water turned green and putrid.

Disease spread quickly throughout the population. Seng-Ke-Sang, the king of lesser Kin-tchuen, was one of the first to fall ill and die. The king's death was received as a bad omen by the Hmong trapped inside the city's walls. If they did not act, and act soon, disease and starvation would claim many more lives. Surrender was an option but not an attractive one. Memories of Chinese atrocities committed against Hmong captives were still vivid, and General Akoui gave every indication of being more cold-blooded and ruthless than the average Chinese commander. If surrender was out of the question, then an attempt to break through the enemy's lines was the only alternative left to them.

The breakout was not orderly, but it was effective. Scattering in all directions, the Hmong of lesser Kin-tchuen caught the Chinese off-guard, and by the time Akoui reestablished control over his army, the majority of the Hmong had escaped to freedom. The few hundred taken captive were summarily executed. Akoui's only consolation was that after entering the deserted city, he found the body of the dead Hmong king. He ordered the head of the corpse cut off and placed in a basket and sent to Emperor Ch'ien-lung to certify the death of Seng-Ke-Sang. Akoui then set off after the remaining rebels who were headed in the direction of greater Kin-tchuen. He razed every town and village along the way, destroying forts and anything that might prove of any use to the retreating Hmong, who might rally and attempt to return by the same route.

When Akoui finally reached the border of the second Hmong kingdom, the young Hmong king, Sonom, was there to meet him. Again, Hmong women fought alongside their husbands, fathers, and brothers. Boulders crashed down on the Chinese as they marched through the pass that led to Leouei, the capital of greater Kin-tchuen. The Chinese were ambushed from all sides. Chinese soldiers vainly tried to scale the cliffs and breach the enemy's line of defense. Hundreds fell to their death at the feet of their comrades. Despite the heavy casualties, Akoui refused to retreat. The battle raged on for days. Finally the Hmong retreated with Akoui in pursuit. The Manchu general patiently secured one position after another until he reached Leouei and placed it under siege. The siege lasted nearly eight months, and Akoui used this time well. He joined his scattered divisions into a main force and stationed troops at key passes to block all escape routes once the capital fell into his hands. He was carefully preparing for what he erroneously believed would be the final battle.

Starvation and disease eventually took its toll on the Hmong trapped inside the city's walls. Realizing the hopelessness of the situation, Sonom led the main body of his soldiers out of the capital through a secret passage. Luckily, they encountered only one of Akoui's columns on the outskirts of the city and successfully broke through the line to make their escape. Alerted of the breakout, Akoui quickly launched an assault on the city. He met only weak resistance and by the time he breached the city's walls he found the capital nearly deserted. Furious, he set off in pursuit of Sonom and what was left of his army. Akoui kept up the chase for ten days, but no Chinese could match the pace of a Hmong in the mountains. His troops exhausted, Akoui broke off the chase and returned to Leouei where he gathered his soldiers and set off at a more leisurely pace for Karai, the last remaining Hmong fortress in the region.

As Akoui had anticipated, Sonom and the last remnants of the Hmong army were holed up in the fortress. Akoui prepared for a long siege. The smoke of blazing forges darkened the sky as new cannons were made. Tents were set up, fortifications erected and, most important of all, troops dispatched to the other side of the mountain to prevent Sonom's escape. The general intended this siege to be the last.

Akoui used this lull before the storm to write a dispatch to the emperor detailing the events of the past months. Sadly, he listed the many distinguished officers who had fallen in battle, among them the emperor's own son-in-law, Prince Mongu. Akoui described the siege and conquest of Leouei and assured the emperor that the destruction of what remained of the Hmong rebel force was near at hand.

Within a few months the Hmong conceded the hopelessness of

their position. With only a few hundred soldiers left, and food and water running out, it would only be a matter of time before they died of starvation or disease. Sonom summoned a general council. It was agreed by all that surrender was unthinkable. The discussion therefore turned to the best way to die. The preferable course was to insure that as many Chinese as possible would share their fate. It was decided that at the last moment when Akoui's cannons had battered down the fortress walls and the Chinese were streaming in, Karai would be put to the torch. The remaining Hmong along with the Chinese who had breached their defenses would be buried in the collapsing rubble. The destroyed garrison, a massive burial mound, would remain as a monument to Hmong resistance.

And so it might have been had not Sonom's mother begged him to spare his younger brother and sister. The young king did not have the heart to refuse. On the off chance that Akoui might be inclined toward mercy, a messenger was immediately sent to the general's camp to request that Sonom and his entire family be spared and that the Hmong king be allowed to rule over his old kingdom. In return, Sonom would agree to rule under the authority of the emperor and in his name. It was a gamble at best, but Sonom knew that in the past Chinese emperors had often settled with tribal minorities on similar terms.

Though there was a precedent, the request was ill-timed. Several armies and a score of generals earlier, the emperor might have given the demand serious consideration. But by now the Hmong had simply cost Ch'ien-lung too much. And, of course, there was the matter of calling him a "criminal," a sacrilege Ch'ien-lung was not about to allow to pass unpunished.

Akoui knew this, for the emperor had not sent him on a mission of pacification but on one of annihilation. Of course, Akoui had no intention of revealing this to Sonom. The final assault on Karai would likely be a bloodbath for both sides, and Akoui had lost too many men already. Stalling for time, Akoui informed Sonom that this was the sort of request only the emperor could grant and that it would therefore be necessary to send to Peking for instructions. However, to build up Sonom's hopes the general told him that he would personally recommend leniency. Apparently heartened by these words, Sonom set aside all thought of the destruction of Karai and waited expectantly for news from Peking.

When the emperor received Akoui's communiqué, he correctly presumed that the rebellion was as good as over. His spirits raised, he took the occasion to publicly praise the general whose exploits he described as unmatched in the empire. He announced to all present at the court that, from this day on, Akoui had permission to wear the ruby button, the ceremonial badge of a foreign prince. He also made Akoui a Count of the Empire and granted him permission to wear the gold embroidered robe of four dragons which only titled princes of the emperor's own family were permitted to wear. Having honored Akoui, the emperor retired to give the general the reply he had requested. In essence, he told Akoui to promise Sonom anything so long as it would guarantee his capture.

Upon receiving the emperor's instructions, Akoui pondered how best to approach Sonom so that he might be persuaded to surrender his troops and abandon Karai. Apparently he concluded that a promise to return his kingdom to him to be ruled in the name of the emperor might backfire. Sonom might simply remain in the fortress and wait for the Chinese to withdraw before attempting to return to Leouei. Whatever his reasoning, Akoui promised Sonom only this: that should he surrender the entire royal family would be spared and his court and his soldiers could expect fair treatment. Sonom took the bait and surrendered his forces to the general who not only treated the royal family with respect on the trip to Peking but allowed Sonom the personal liberty to visit his troops and confer with his officers. Akoui did not want Sonom to realize the real fate that awaited him in Peking, for the Hmong king could always commit suicide and cheat the emperor of his final revenge.

The scales did not fall from Sonom's eyes until he was brought to the emperor who had summoned his chief ministers specially for the occasion. While Sonom knelt before Ch'ien-lung, an official of the court detailed the high crimes the Hmong king had committed against the empire in general, and against the emperor in particular. The reading of the sentence immediately followed.

Sonom and his entire family, including the young prince and princess and ten of Sonom's close advisors, were to be tied to posts, gagged and then cut into pieces. As a final insult and a standing warning to all would-be rebels, their heads were also to be cut off and exhibited in cages with their names and titles attached.

The sentence was carried out immediately. If the emperor had counted on the additional pleasure of seeing Sonom and his family beg for mercy, it is likely that he was sadly disappointed. For hundreds of years the Hmong had resisted Chinese repression. Victories were few, defeats many. Hmong prisoners rendered the only homage to the sacrifices of their ancestors available to them: to the very end they never weakened, never afforded the Chinese the satisfaction of witnessing a Hmong beg for mercy or shrink from the executioner's sword.

After the execution of the royal family, nineteen of the remaining Hmong were simply decapitated. The rest, slightly more than two hundred of a rebel force that had numbered ten to twelve thousand, were given to Chinese officers as slaves. Even this was not enough to satisfy the emperor's desire for revenge. Officials accompanied by soldiers were sent to Kweichow and Szechwan to comb the countryside in search of Hmong civilians, most of whom were simple farmers who had taken no part in the rebellion. Thousands of them were impressed into labor gangs and transported to various parts of the empire as slave labor for public works projects. If this was meant as an object lesson for would-be Hmong rebels, it failed to do the trick. Hmong rebellions would continue. Unfortunately, so would Chinese repression. There were some Hmong, however, who had found a way to break this endless cycle.

In 1746, thirty years prior to Sonom's execution, several hundred Hmong had abandoned China forever and crossed into Vietnam to begin a new life. During the following century thousands of other Hmong would migrate to Vietnam, Laos, Thailand, and Burma. Settling high in the mountains, far away from the densely populated lowlands, they would experience peace for the first time in centuries.

CHAPTER 2

Origins

*T*HE FIRST WESTERNERS to make contact with the Hmong in China were Catholic missionaries. This occurred early in the seventeenth century. The missionaries quickly learned there were two groups of Hmong, the "raw" and the "cooked" (*sheng* and *shu*). These were Chinese labels, not Hmong. The cooked Hmong were those who had assimilated into the Chinese culture and settled in the lowlands, living among the Chinese. The raw Hmong lived up in the mountains and had never accepted Chinese ways. The Chinese described them as wild barbarians who would cut a stranger's throat at the slightest provocation. While this terrifying description deterred most missionaries from attempting to make contact, a few hardy souls threw caution to the wind and sought them out.

It was not easy. For one thing, the Chinese did not always know exactly where to find them. Only lowland Hmong, who sometimes traded with their highland brothers, knew their exact location, and they were reluctant to guide strangers to these hidden redoubts. Then there were the hazards of the journey. The mountain routes were serviceable for montagnards accustomed to tightrope walking over mountain crests and adept at grasping vines for support while ascending nearly vertical trails that zigzagged up mountain sides. For ordinary lowlanders, however, the trip was both harrowing and exhausting.

The few missionaries who did secure guides and endured the trek were richly rewarded, for the people they found were unlike any they had ever seen in China. Contrary to the popular image of the raw Hmong as a race of bloodthirsty brigands, the missionaries found them to be a gentle and generous people. The Chinese were right about one thing: the raw Hmong did not follow Chinese ways. They did not even use chopsticks, but ate with spoons like Europeans. Their children played many of the same games as European children: hide-and-seek, shuttlecock, marbles, and spinning tops. And particularly striking was the fact that many of these "raw" Hmong looked like Europeans; red or blond hair was not uncommon, and more than a few had blue eyes.

While such encounters naturally invited questions about Hmong origins, the missionaries did no more than the Chinese to provide answers. This is not to say that Chinese historians had nothing whatsoever to say about the Hmong. Quite the contrary. The Hmong play a predominant role in early Chinese history where they are described as an ancient people who occupied the fertile Yellow River basin long before the Chinese themselves migrated into the area. Though Chinese historians must have considered the possibility that the Hmong had migrated into China, there is no mention of it in their ancient histories. Instead these texts simply characterize the Hmong as the first enemy of the Chinese. The Hmong figure most predominantly in the narrative accounts of the numerous military campaigns mounted against them over the centuries following the establishment of the first dynasty.

And so matters stood until the beginning of this century when Father F. M. Savina was sent by the Society for Foreign Missions, headquartered in Paris, to spread the word of God to the Hmong of Laos and Tonkin (northern Vietnam). As a priest, Savina was naturally dedicated to the divine mission of saving Hmong souls; but Savina was a scholar as well, fascinated by Hmong culture and history, and committed to unraveling the mystery of their origins.

Savina not only mastered their language but spent years developing a romanized Hmong script, for the Hmong had no written language of their own. He also studied their religion and customs and recorded their legends which had been handed down from generation to generation for thousands of years, many presumably unchanged except for minor variations. For perspective he studied anthropology, comparative religions, and linguistics, constantly factoring what was known about other peoples, ancient and modern, into what he knew about the Hmong.

By 1924 he felt confident enough to publish his views on the origins of the Hmong in his *Histoire des Miao*. Savina emphasized three facts about the Hmong which he believed were the keys to their origins: their physical appearance, their language, and their legends.

BLOND HAIR AND BLUE EYES

In appearance the Hmong are, Savina writes, "pale yellow in complexion, almost white, their hair is often light or dark brown, sometimes even red" or "corn-silk blond," and a few even have "pale blue" eyes. All of this, he argues, "disbars them from belonging to any other race of China." Savina concluded that these northern European traits were not only evidence of a mixed racial background "somewhere between the white and yellow races," but, more importantly, suggested that the original homeland of the Hmong lay outside of Asia.

Modern anthropologists have also noted the presence of European traits in Hmong populations, though instead of light skin and hair, they stress facial features such as the absence of an epicanthic eyelid fold, narrow faces, and aquiline noses. Recent studies of Hmong in Laos and Thailand have led some anthropologists to classify them as the most Caucasian population of Southeast Asia.

While most Hmong today are light skinned, few have blond hair or blue eyes. If such Hmong are now a rarity, long ago they may have been the rule rather than the exception. In legends of old China told by Laotian Hmong, the distant ancestors of the Hmong are depicted as "white," with pale skin and light hair. This was before the Chinese crushed a major Hmong uprising and ordered mass executions. According to Nao Yang Vue: "because Hmong with light skin and fair hair were easy to single out from the general population, most were killed." Nao Yang claims that the few "white" Hmong who survived lived a precarious existence, for the Chinese continued to search for them even after the Hmong migrated to Indochina.

For eighty-year-old Cher Sue Vue this is more than legend. He still retains a vivid memory of the time during his childhood when the Chinese crossed over the border into Sam Neua province in

northeastern Laos looking for white babies. "At that time there was only one white baby in our village. The infant's parents were warned before the Chinese arrived, and they carried him into the forest where they hid until the Chinese finally left."

While we can never know for sure whether most Hmong were once blond and blue-eyed, the predominance of Caucasian features in contemporary Hmong populations strongly suggests they were not originally Asians. Savina believed the location of their homeland prior to migrating to China could be determined by an examination of their language and legends.

LANGUAGE

The Hmong language is monosyllabic and tonal and extremely simple in structure. There is no conjugation of verbs, no declension of nouns. The vast majority of words have only one vowel and few words end in consonants. Excluding special inflections used to ask questions or express surprise, most Hmong words can be pronounced using one of eight basic tones. Despite the simplicity of Hmong syntax, the subtlety of Hmong tones makes it a difficult language for non-native speakers to master.

Savina did master the language, though. And because the Hmong had no written language of their own, he developed a romanized Hmong script modeled after the simplified Vietnamese script *Quoc Ngu* developed in the seventeenth century by the French Jesuit, Alexandre de Rhodes. Not only did this script make it possible to preserve the legends of the Hmong in their own language, it also permitted a detailed study of the phonetic and syntactical structure of their native tongue and the classification of Hmong within the languages of the world.

Savina classified it as a form of Ural-Altaic, one of the three major language groups of the Caucasian race. He believed that a similar language was spoken long ago by a subgroup of the Caucasians who inhabited central Asia and western Russia, the same region where ancestors of the Hmong must have lived before migrating east into Asia.

However, modern linguists assert that Hmong is not related to Ural-Altaic or any other major language group. The only language with which it has any affinity is that spoken by the Yao montagnards of southwest China, though there is no evidence that the two languages are actually related.

LEGENDS

Savina believed that the Hmong legends, even more than the Hmong language, provide near irrefutable evidence of the Hmong's non-Asian origins. These legends, he insisted, reveal an earlier homeland outside of China. They also tell of a long migration north from this homeland into Siberia where the Hmong dwelled for an indeterminate period before migrating southward into northeast China.

Selective and necessarily incomplete, Savina's account of the Hmong legends emphasizes the parallel between Hmong, Babylonian, and biblical legends. He concludes that the Hmong "must be viewed as having had their primitive origins on the banks of the Tigris and Euphrates, from whence they left for the north, either through the Caucasus or through Turkestan." These legends include a Hmong account of the creation of the world, a history of the human race, and a history of the Hmong people, both before and after they arrived in China.

Creation

In the Hmong creation legends, according to Savina, God created heaven and earth in seven days. The earth was first covered with water until God created ten suns to dry it up. The process took seven years. When the first bit of land appeared, God created the first man from a pinch of earth, gave him a soul and the power of speech and sight and the ability to walk on two legs. When this first man dreamed, a woman appeared to him, and when he awoke he found her lying beside him, a gift from God. The two became man and wife and had many children.

In those days God talked directly to man, and whenever humans needed his help they simply asked for it, though at first they needed very little divine assistance because God had created plants and animals in abundance for their use. The earth was then beautiful to behold; plants grew flowers as big as baskets and yielded equally impressive fruit. This guaranteed plenty of food to eat and, over all, an easy life.

The first complaints to God were about the ten suns which had not gone away after evaporating the seas that had once covered the earth. Indeed, the suns were slowly transforming the earth from a paradise into a desert. But God refused to take the suns away.

In those days trees were gigantic and a number were cut down and fashioned into arrows that were shot at the ten suns. All but one of them was destroyed. The remaining sun fled and hid for seven years, and for these seven years the earth was plunged into darkness. Though the sun was repeatedly entreated to return, it always refused. At the end of the seventh year a rooster crowed and, at the seventh crowing, the sun was overcome with curiosity and came out of hiding. This, so the legend goes, is why roosters have combs, for it is a gift from God for bringing back the hiding sun. It is also why roosters crow before sunrise: they are calling the sun who hides at the end of every day.

Original Sin

In the beginning humans were immortal. But one day a young woman picked and ate a white strawberry which God had forbidden anyone to touch. The same young woman also drank from a spring which God had forbidden anyone to ever approach. Angered, God condemned all humanity to an eventual death and expelled the people from their paradise to a less fertile land where they had to labor for their food.

God was not without mercy. He taught men and women how to farm the land, how to hunt, and how to make clothes to wear, for until this time they had no need of clothes and went about naked. Though humans were no longer immortal, for a time they still lived a very long life, sometimes reaching 800 or 900 years of age; but the strain of hard work eventually shortened their life span.

The Flood

The loss of immortality was followed by another disaster. It began to rain, not just at one place but all over the world. It rained for forty days and nights until nearly every living thing was drowned.

Shortly before the deluge, two brothers who worked the same field were angered when they discovered that someone was coming during the night and undoing all the work they had completed during the day. They found a hiding place one evening and waited for the culprit. It was an old man who wasted no time filling in the furrows they had spent all day digging. The eldest brother wanted to kill the old man on the spot, but the younger brother wanted to question him and discover the reason for this peculiar behavior.

The old man told them that he filled in the furrows because their work was futile. A flood would soon cover the earth with water and drown all living things. It was then that the two brothers realized that the old man was God in disguise, and they asked him what they might do to escape this fate. He advised the eldest brother, who had a violent temper, to build an iron boat. To the younger brother, however, he advised the construction of a wooden boat large enough to carry his sister and himself and a male and female of every species of animal along with two seeds of every kind of flower, tree, and grain.

The two brothers did as God advised, and it was shortly after this that it began to rain. When water covered the land the iron boat sank, but the younger brother's wooden boat floated and with the rising water rose toward heaven.

When the rain finally ceased God sent nine dragons, accompanied by two huge black cranes, to dry up the land. It was the task of the dragons to drill an immense hole in the earth through which all the water would drain. The two cranes were kept busy gathering up all floating trees that might plug the hole.

Even after the water finally receded, the sister and brother were forced to remain in the boat because the earth was covered with a thick layer of mud that had the appearance and consistency of chicken excrement. The two survivors were rescued from this sea of mud by a giant eagle who swooped down and carried them to a narrow piece of dry raised land. The eagle, himself near death from starvation, was also saved from death by the two humans who, in gratitude for his help, gave him pieces of their own flesh, taken from behind the head, armpits, and knees. These hollows have remained in these places ever since.

Children of Incest

As soon as the land had dried enough for the brother and sister to walk upon it, they planted seeds and tended their fields. The brother was younger than his sister, who was near womanhood. When the brother matured he indicated his desire to marry, but his sister refused such a grave sin. Nevertheless, he persisted, noting that she was, after all, the only woman in the world. She finally consented to allow God to decide the issue. They carried the halves of a millstone to the top of a hill and rolled them down. When they descended to the bottom they found the two halves joined. They threw a needle and thread into the air, and when they picked them up they found that they were also joined. The sister then agreed to the marriage.

The infant born of this union was formless, without arms or legs and, in some versions of the legend, shaped like an egg. The perplexed parents cut it open, believing the infant was inside. When pieces of the infant's flesh touched the ground, each piece was transformed into a normal child. Seeing this, the parents cut the infant into very small pieces so as to create as many new babies as possible. By this act they repopulated the world.

Tower of Babel

One legend on which Savina placed special importance was the "Tower of Babel" story. It recalls a time in the distant past when the earth had become densely populated and construction was begun on a giant stairway to heaven. When the structure finally rose so high it poked through the clouds, hundreds of thousands crowded on the stairs in a rush to enter heaven. This angered God who struck them with lightning and reduced the stairway to rubble.

Prior to this event, all people spoke one language. After it, each family spoke a different language. Unable to communicate with each other, families began living apart. Because of this, mankind was divided into different races, each with its own language.

The Great Migration

One of these families contained the first Hmong. As this family expanded, overpopulation became a concern and the Hmong decided to leave their homeland and search for more fertile land. They traveled a great plateau to reach a northern place where days and nights lasted six months, the water was frozen, and snow hid the ground. Only a few trees grew and they were small. The people, too, were short and squat, clothed in furs. When the Hmong left this region, they came to Honan, which was the first Hmong home in China.

In China a dispute over land arose between the Hmong and neighboring races. The matter was brought before the king who settled the disputed in the following way: a delegate from each race would set out at dusk and return at sunrise, and the ground covered would belong to his people. The representative of the Hmong moved into the hills and by dawn was on the top of a high mountain. From that time onward the Hmong have lived on the crests among the clouds.

SAVINA'S INTERPRETATION

While Savina conceded that all primitive peoples have creation legends, and many have legends of a catastrophic flood, he insisted that the "story of the Tower of Babel and the confusion of languages is unique to the inhabitants of Chaldea," a region that encompasses present day Iraq and Syria. Indeed, Savina found the parallel between Hmong and biblical accounts of creation, original sin, and the flood so striking as to rule out mere coincidence. How, he asked, could the Hmong have come by such legends unless they had once lived, or are descended from a people who once lived, in ancient Chaldea?

Drawing heavily on the ancient history and archeology of his day, Savina identified these people as the Turanians, an ancient Caucasian people who populated the Iranian plateau, invaded Iran, and spread across the plains situated between the Tigris and Euphrates rivers. It was here in Chaldea, prior to the period when the Turanians were forced out of the region by Aryan invaders from southern Russia and Turkestan, that the flood and Tower of Babel legends were born.

Displaced by the Aryan intruders, the Turanians returned to the Iranian plateau and, around 5000 B.C., began a steady migration into Russia, Siberia, Mongolia, Manchuria, and Korea. The ancestors of the Hmong, Savina concluded, were a subgroup of these migrants. They were the band of Turanians who trekked north across western Turkestan until they reached the base of the Caucasus mountains and headed northeast into the frozen land of Siberia, pushing as far north as sixty degrees latitude. After their sojourn in Siberia the ancestors of the Hmong migrated south and settled in northeast China which, according to both Hmong legend and Chinese history, placed them in Honan near the bend of the Yellow River sometime before 3000 B.C.

Actually Savina was more confident about the location of the Hmong homeland than he was about the migration route from there to China. He conceded that it was equally likely that they crossed the Caucasus mountains into Russia before heading for Siberia, or they may have moved northeast from the Iranian plateau, over the Tyan Shan and Altai mountain chains, and then followed the Ob River into northwestern Siberia.

Savina also proposed alternative routes for the Hmong migration from Siberia to China. They may have gone directly south through Mongolia and, after reaching the Yellow River, followed it until they reached its bend in Honan. Or they may have come down through Manchuria. However, Savina believed that the most likely route was directly south through western Siberia to the edge of Mongolia where the Hmong would have been able to pass between the Tyan Shan and Altai mountain chains, through the "pass of Dzungaria," the corridor through which so many others would later cross into Asia from the west. From there the Hmong could have easily continued east along the base of the Altai mountains until reaching the edge of the Gobi Desert. Turning south they would have quickly reached the Wei River. And by following the course of the Wei until it joins the Yellow River, the Hmong would have found themselves but a short distance from upper Honan and the fertile Yellow River basin.

CAVEATS

Savina's account is fascinating, a true adventure story. But the archeological interpretation of prehistory has changed considerably over the past sixty years and much of what was considered valid in Savina's day is now rejected as either false or overly simplistic. The more serious problem is that the parallel between Hmong and biblical legends so crucial to Savina's interpretation of Hmong origins has not been corroborated.

No one besides Savina has identified a Hmong Tower of Babel legend, or for that matter one dealing with the confusion of languages or one depicting original sin. True, the Hmong do have a legend that refers to a stairway to the sky, but it is made up of mountains, each one taller than the previous. This mountain stairway leads not to heaven but to the home of Ndu Nyong (*Ntxwy Nyoog*), the god of death, an evil god who is the enemy of all mankind.

It is also true that the Hmong have legends about a golden age, a Garden of Eden if you will, but it is a disobedient wife who is described as the cause of its end, not a woman eating a forbidden fruit.

As for the loss of immortality, Hmong legend treats it as a simple fact. Shue Long Vue, a Laotian Hmong, summarizes the legend in

27

this way: "At one time in the world there was no death, though people often got very sick, especially as they got older. Then one day a man was turned into a tiger and when he got very old he died. This was the first death among mankind. After that no man was immortal."

Only Savina has identified a Hmong flood legend which describes the building of an ark aboard which the male and female of every species of animal and plant was placed. In the standard account a drum or gourd saves the brother and sister from drowning, and the most that they carried with them on board were some seeds.

What is interesting about the Hmong flood legend is the dragon sent to dry up the land after the water had drained away. Chinese flood legends from the Shantung region, near where the Hmong are supposed to have first settled in China, relate how Pa, the lethal heat goddess who sometimes assumed the shape of a dragon, was sent by the gods to dry up the land after the flood.

The Shantung flood legends undoubtedly reflect historical fact, for in ancient times the bend of the Yellow River was subject to massive flooding. This bit of history, rather than the periodic flooding of the Tigris and Euphrates rivers which gave rise to the Babylonian and biblical flood legends, is quite sufficient to account for the existence of the Hmong flood legend.

The discrepancies between the Hmong legends collected by Savina and those reported by others, and those current among the Hmong today, can probably best be explained by Savina's missionary activity. The Hmong he interviewed were also part of his flock and familiar with the standard bible stories. Wanting to please, they simply incorporated aspects of many of these stories into the telling of their own legends and inadvertently led Savina astray.

HMONG ORIGINS: ANOTHER LOOK

Though imperfect, Savina's account of Hmong origins merits attention. If it is unlikely that the ancestors of the Hmong once made their homes on the banks of the Tigris and Euphrates rivers, it is not unreasonable to imagine they are related to a people who long ago migrated from the west into Eurasia and, later, into Siberia. This would account for the Caucasian features so prominent among the Hmong today. It would also explain the Siberian legend common to the Hmong of China and Southeast Asia. In this legend the Hmong inhabited a distant land where days and nights were six months long, where lakes froze and people wore furs. For Hmong who have never seen snow or ice, the legend tells of "rigid water" and "fine white sand."

Then there is Hmong shamanism, which Savina underplayed since it undermines his claim that the Hmong are "primitive monotheists." The Hmong practice a pure form of shamanism. The shaman is not a witch doctor who uses rituals and magic spells to influence events; he deals directly with the spirit world. After falling into a trance, his soul leaves his body and enters the realm of souls, phantoms, genies and ghosts where he combats the evil spirits who cause misfortune, illness, and death. Shamanism originated in Siberia, further evidence that the Hmong once lived there. If they did, they were probably related to the predominantly Caucasian population that had begun to migrate to central Siberia from Eurasia in large numbers nearly seven thousand years ago.

A warming trend set in at the end of the last glaciation and reached its peak sometime around 5000 B.C. The rise in temperature opened up northern Europe, Eurasia, and Siberia to migrations from the south. By 3000 B.C., southern and central Siberia had become solidly Caucasian up to the borders of Mongolia.

The only exception to this general pattern occurred in the Minusinsk Basin, west of Lake Baikal on the northern edge of Mongolia. There Siberian Mongolians from the surrounding forests completely supplanted the Caucasians. By the beginning of the Christian era, other Mongolians from the south moved up into central Siberia and transformed the population of the Siberian steppe from Caucasian to solidly Mongolian by the beginning of the Christian era. By this late date, however, the Hmong had already left Siberia and were well established in China, along with other Caucasians who left behind well-preserved mummies recently unearthed at Xinjiang in northwest China.

This also substantiates, though by a different route, Savina's assertion that the original homeland of the Hmong is to be found in southwestern Eurasia. If the Hmong formed a subgroup of the Caucasian population of Siberia before migrating to China, their original homeland could have been somewhere on the Iranian plateau or in southern Russia where many Caucasians once resided before moving north into Siberia.

Despite their western origins, it is doubtful that the main features of Hmong culture, which has survived relatively unchanged over the centuries, were fixed prior to the time the Hmong dwelt in Siberia. That culture reflects a life spent on the Siberian steppe, and later adapted to a montagnard existence. It is a pastoral rather than nomadic culture. Though the Hmong have wandered for centuries over the face of China and southeast Asia, it was oppression that kept Hmong hill farmers on the move, not a wanderlust inherited from the hard-riding nomads of the Siberian steppe who terrorized the settled populations of Russia and China until massive walls were erected to hold them back.

While the Hmong taboo against eating horse meat has been used as evidence that the Hmong once rode with these Siberian horsemen, the historical evidence makes this unlikely. It was not until the beginning of the Christian era that the economy of the Siberian steppe changed from pastoral to nomadic. This was at least a thousand years after the Hmong arrived in China. The consensus among contemporary historians of ancient China is that the Hmong became part of Chinese history no later than 1200 B.C. and perhaps as early as 3000 B.C., which is the date given by ancient Chinese historians. The Hmong did eventually become skilled horsemen, but only much later in the seventeenth century when the Hmong of Kweichow and Szechwan began to breed mountain ponies for use as war horses and acquired a reputation as the best horsemen in the empire. The taboo against eating horse meat was likely developed during this period.

Even before the Hmong took to horses, they struck as much fear in the hearts of the Chinese as had the dreaded nomads of Siberia. The Chinese erected the Great Wall to protect China's northern borders from marauding Siberian nomads. Fifteen hundred years later, a scaled-down version of the Great Wall was constructed on the Hunan-Kweichow border to hold back advancing Hmong armies.

CHAPTER 3

Hmong in China

ARCHEOLOGICAL EVIDENCE

*A*S EARLY AS 2500 B.C., migrants from Siberia had penetrated most of northeastern China, gaining footholds in Manchuria as well as in present day Hopei and Shantung provinces. The Hmong were perhaps the most adventuresome of these Siberian immigrants because they continued the trek southward into the interior until they reached the bend of the Yellow River in upper Honan.

This was the home of the Yangshao Chinese, hill tribesmen who dominated the region between 4000 and 3000 B.C. The Yangshao practiced swidden or "slash and burn" farming. They cleared virgin land of trees and underbrush, burned the debris and used the ashes as fertilizer for seeds deposited in stick-holes. They also raised pigs as the principal source of their protein. Yangshao houses consisted of stamped earth floors, an indoor hearth, and a thatched roof supported by stout vertical posts.

It is likely the Hmong borrowed liberally from the culture of their first Chinese neighbors, which not only enabled them to adapt to their new environment but prepared them for the future when Chinese oppression would force them to retreat into the high mountains and become montagnards. Indeed, Hmong montagnards today live much as the ancient Yangshao, raising pigs, clearing virgin forest for their fields, and dwelling in simple ridgepole huts not unlike those inhabited by the Yangshao.

The Yangshao were eventually absorbed by the Lungshan Chinese who were rice farmers. Since some groups of Hmong practiced rice farming in the distant past, it is possible that the Hmong also borrowed from the Lungshan. The Lungshan were displaced by the Shang Chinese who established the earliest Chinese dynasty identifiable by archeological records. The Shang dynasty lasted from 1500 to 1000 B.C., during which time it successfully subdued its neighbors and used many as slaves for constructing massive grave sites for Shang royalty.

Excavation of these burial sites in the early 1930s at Anyang unearthed non-mongoloid skeletons mixed in with mongoloid remains. Some of these non-mongoloid skeletons may have belonged to Hmong slaves who manned the work gangs that built the tombs, or perhaps Hmong (or other Caucasian Siberians) belonged to Shang royalty. However, complete results of these finds have yet to be published. The Chinese may be embarrassed by the implication that their distant ancestors were not all Chinese.

No doubt, the Shang who used cowrie shells as money exercised some influence over the development of Hmong culture: to this day the women of the Cowrie Shell Hmong still sew these shells in linear or semicircular rows on the backs of their blouses.

If the Hmong borrowed freely from Chinese culture when they first arrived in China, they also vigorously resisted complete assimilation, which made their life in China difficult. In time the Chinese became many and the Hmong remained few. The Chinese demanded integration into their way of life as a precondition for decent treatment. Eventually the Hmong were forced to retreat to the mountaintops where the freedom to live as they pleased became the prime consolation for the hard life of the montagnard.

LEGENDARY ACCOUNTS

From both archeology and legend we learn that, in the beginning at least, the Hmong and Chinese enjoyed friendly relations. The Chinese and Hmong offer different accounts of the erosion of this good will. The Hmong speak of Chinese duplicity, while the Chinese talk candidly of power politics and identify the defeat and suppression of the Hmong as the event that unified China into an empire.

Hmong Legends

One Hmong legend actually describes the Chinese and Hmong as brothers. The Hmong was the older and stronger brother. When their parents died the two brothers separated and eventually lost all trace of each other. Yet they both continued to visit their parents' graves once a year to pay their respects, though they did so at different times so that they never met. Then one day the Hmong brother noticed that someone had been worshipping at his parents' graves before him. He wondered who it might be and returned regularly to see if he could catch the intruder. The next time the Chinese brother showed up, the Hmong brother grabbed him and asked what he was doing there. The Chinese brother asked him the same question. It was then that they realized they were brothers. After this the two brothers and their descendants drifted apart. According to the legend, the Chinese completely forgot about their brothers, but the Hmong did not.

Another Hmong legend tells of two great kingdoms, one Chinese, the other Hmong. The land of the Hmong lay to the north of the Yellow River, that of the Chinese to the south. The two realms were constantly at war, and during one period of Hmong ascendancy the Chinese emperor maneuvered to link the two races by blood with a marriage between his daughter and the son of the Hmong monarch. The child born of the union grew into a spoiled and ambitious prince. On his thirtieth year, he accepted an invitation to visit his Chinese grandfather. The grandeur of the imperial palace was a stark contrast to Hmong society where both rulers and ruled lived in humble surroundings. Chinese opulence fanned the Hmong prince's ambition and made him an eager recruit to the emperor's plot to overthrow the Hmong. The young prince was trained in the iron ball killing technique. No larger than a child's marbles, the polished spheres could kill in the hands of a master. When he was able to fling them over fifty yards with force and accuracy, the prince was judged ready.

When the prince returned home, no one noticed the leather pouch which he had hidden away for the right moment. The Hmong king was struck down one afternoon as if by magic, and lay dying in a pool of his own blood. All activity ceased while the Hmong nation gathered for the funeral rites. Since they would last several days, the Hmong were easy prey for the Chinese army that had been secretly assembling on the Hmong frontier, waiting for the assassination. The prearranged plan was that once the Chinese conquered the Hmong, the assassin prince would be placed on the throne, bypassing his father who was next in line. Though the Hmong were caught by surprise and quickly defeated, they were not conquered. They chose to abandon their kingdom rather than to be enslaved by the Chinese. Fleeing south across the Yellow River into Chinese territory, they reached the safety of the southern frontier. The assassin prince was not among them.

When it came time for the Hmong to select a new sovereign, they passed over the father of the assassin and chose Mong Kao Lee, the daughter of the slain king. In her honor they called their former homeland by her name, Mongoli or Mongolia. And so it fell to Mong Kao Lee to guide the Hmong on their southern trek in search of a land where they could remain free.

The journey south led them over many mountain chains. Still accustomed to life in the lowlands, the Hmong were ill prepared for the rigors of the montagnard life. Many mountain tribesmen turned hostile when the Hmong crossed their territory. As in many Hmong legends, when things seemed hopeless something magical occurred to set them straight.

One day Chang Leng Vu went into the forest to look for herbs. He was startled by a voice coming from above in a tree. When he looked up he saw a chicken with one of its legs trapped in a tangle of branches. Much to his surprise, when the chicken saw him looking up it spoke. "If you release me from these branches," the chicken said, "I will grant you any wish." Chang Leng Vu climbed the tree and released the chicken who immediately flew away, his flapping wings cracking the air like thunder. A few minutes later the chicken returned, but in the form of a man. He had returned to reward the Hmong for helping him.

Chang Leng Vu did not want to waste his one wish foolishly. After pondering the matter he said, "I want only a souvenir to memorialize the remarkable event of coming upon a talking chicken who could also turn himself into a man, a souvenir from you which, when I am in trouble, will enable me to call upon you to grant my one wish." The request was granted and Chang Leng Vu received a small metal coin. It was a magical coin which, when waved three times, would glow and send a message to the magic chicken to come and help whomever possessed it.

Armed with the magic coin, Chang Leng Vu persuaded the Hmong to migrate across hostile territory. They had not gone very far before bandits attacked. This caused some to lose faith in Chang Leng Vu. To regain the trust of his people, he marched up to the stronghold of the bandits and warned them that should they harm the Hmong again they would pay with their lives. As proof of this he waved the magic coin three times. It glowed bright red, shooting shafts of light wherever he pointed it. The bandits retreated into their fortress, trembling with fear as the sky darkened and the sounds of thunder rolled over them. It began to rain. The wind howled and grew in force. It yanked trees up by their roots, blew down houses, and sucked up a number of bandits screaming into the dark sky. All the while, Chang Leng Vu stood before the gate of the bandits' stronghold, the wind and rain whirling around him, and shouted repeatedly to all who would hear: "Allow the Hmong to pass unmolested or you will suffer more storms, more calamities."

It was by means of Chang Leng Vu's magic coin that the Hmong migrated southward into the Chinese frontier where, for many centuries, they lived in peace and beyond the reach of the Chinese. Other Hmong legends expand on this account and relate that the Hmong migrated south from Honan to the lake zone of Hupeh and Hunan and from there spread out into Kweichow and Szechwan.

Chinese Legends

Chinese legends tell the story from a different perspective. It begins in the distant past, around 2700 B.C., during the reign of the legendary Emperor U-Wang who ruled as a tyrant. At this early date the Hmong (called the "Miao," or the savages, by the Chinese) were sufficiently powerful to merit a voice in government. One of their nobles, Tche-you, served as a minister to the emperor. Though he had served the emperor well, the day came when he could no longer stomach the way U-Wang mistreated the Hmong. He unified the scattered Hmong tribes into a rebel army and engaged U-Wang's troops near Peking and routed them. Fearing for his life, U-Wang withdrew to a stronghold south of the capital.

The emperor's defeat was welcome news to the Chinese nobility who had also suffered under his reign. They selected a popular young nobleman and renowned warrior, Huan-yuan, as their leader. Huan-yuan led their combined armies and defeated U-Wang in successive engagements. The emperor was captured and executed.

The nobility were eager to reunify China under imperial rule, and the only obstacle that stood in their way was the Hmong, whose easy victory over U-Wang had led them to envisage even greater things. Talk of an independent Hmong nation was common in the Hmong tribal councils. If something was not done quickly, the Hmong might turn from talk to action. Other tribal minorities chafing under Chinese rule might easily be whipped into a rebellious mood and join the Hmong in a bloody, and perhaps even successful, revolt.

The nobles therefore urged Huan-yuan not to disband his forces but to continue the campaign on Hmong territory. The fighting was fierce, and losses were heavy on both sides, but Huan-yuan was a brilliant general. The Hmong were defeated and Huan-yuan made emperor. He was also given a new name—Hoang-ti, the Yellow Emperor.

According to the legend, Hoang-ti's battlefield experience with the Hmong convinced him that they were a ferocious and savage people, too primitive to be effectively administered by ordinary laws. He therefore established a separate criminal code for the Hmong, substituting mutilation for incarceration as the principal form of punishment. Minor offenders were to be branded on the face with a hot iron; more serious crimes were punished with castration, or chopping off the nose or ears, or execution.

While this legend no doubt reflects actual conflicts which occurred very early between the Hmong and the Chinese, as well as Chinese suppression of the Hmong at an early date, Hoang-ti never existed. He was a convenient fiction created by wandering Chinese scholars providing a much sought after service to Chinese nobility.

Beginning in the fifth century B.C., Chinese feudalism began to come apart at the seams. One emperor after another proved incapable of maintaining order or of controlling errant nobles who ruled as they wished in the face of vain protests from Peking. Although the emperors had lost de facto power, they nevertheless continued to exercise considerable authority; in the eyes of nobility and peasant alike, the emperor alone, with or without power, was still the only legitimate ruler of the realm. Hence, while many a noble longed for the crown, which seemed ripe for the plucking, most could not claim rightful succession to the throne. They had power, but lacked legitimacy. It was in the attempt to rectify this problem that noble families began to employ wandering scholars who presented themselves as experts on royal genealogy. For the right price, an ambitious governor or lord could acquire a most impressive family tree that proved he was descended from an earlier imperial family. And should he be lucky enough to capture the throne and unify China under imperial rule, he could claim legitimacy through descent from an earlier dynasty.

Hoang-ti had up to that time been only a lowly agrarian god in southern Shansi. But with the stroke of a calligrapher's brush, he was transformed into the forefather of nearly every noble family who had the misfortune of not being related to either the present or past dynastic families. In an effort to add luster to the concocted lineages, and to indirectly diminish the significance of existing royal families, Hoang-ti was passed off as the first emperor of China, a true patriot who not only unified the Chinese but routed the Hmong barbarians, their traditional enemy.

HISTORICAL ACCOUNTS: SHANG TO HAN

The events described in the Hoang-ti legend probably occurred sometime between 1600 and 800 B.C., for part of the legend is that Hoang-ti, in an effort to maintain control over the Hmong, reorganized their tribes into settlements of "eight families around a com-

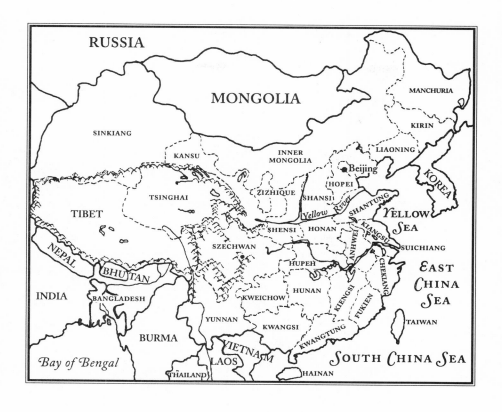

mon well." This was a prominent feature of land tenure during the dynasty of the Shang, and was continued, with some modifications, under the Chou dynasty.

Shang Dynasty
(1600–1028 B.C.)

The Shang were more or less at continuous war with their tribal neighbors, including the Hmong. Defeat at the hands of the Shang, and forced integration into the eight-family system, compelled large numbers of Hmong to abandon their traditional lifestyle as migrant swidden farmers for the sedentary life of the feudal peasant.

The Shang dynasty was centered in Honan, but toward its close its territory extended all the way to western Shantung, southern Hopei, central and south Shansi, east Shensi, and parts of Kiangsu and Anhwei. The Hmong shadowed this expansion; by the beginning of the Chou dynasty they were to be found in nearly every area of the old Shang empire.

Chou Dynasty
(1028–257 B.C.)

When King Wu, the first king of the Chou dynasty, struggled for dominance with the last emperor of the Shang, the Hmong immediately volunteered their support. The Chou proved faithless. After the Shang defeat, the Chou banished a large number of Hmong to San Wei, a mountain region in southern Kansu inhabited by combative montagnards led by a warrior chieftain with the imposing name of "White Wolf."

The Chou maintained power on the frontier by garrisoning troops near trouble spots. To guarantee adequate food supplies, peasants from controlled areas were forced to resettle near frontier garrisons. Perhaps the Chou recalled Hmong courage and military prowess in battles with the old Shang armies and decided that only tough Hmong farmers could be expected to survive in the land of the White Wolf. If this was the intent it backfired. The Hmong drifted into the mountains out of the reach of the Chou garrisons. Fearing they might join other mountain tribes in a revolt, the Chinese sent mandarins to live among the Hmong to learn their ways and discover how they might be more easily governed. Few mandarins penetrated very far into Hmong territory, for the timid scholars feared the Hmong whom they believed to be more ferocious than the wild beasts of the region.

Having learned nothing useful about the Hmong, Chou authorities adopted the tried and true course of material rewards. The Hmong were offered choice farm land in the valleys and entire villages were constructed for their convenience, all in an effort to draw them out of their mountains. But the Hmong so valued their new freedom that none accepted the offer, and the fields and villages remained empty. By the seventh century B.C. these same Hmong were joining forces with the Turks, Mongols, and semi-nomadic Tibetan tribes of the Wei River basin in attacks on Chou garrisons.

The fate of these Kansu Hmong remains a mystery. For after a hundred years they were never again mentioned by Chinese historians. The majority may have been absorbed by the expanding Chinese population well before the beginning of the Christian era. There is, however, one Chinese legend which relates that the Kansu Hmong eventually abandoned the area, followed the course of the Wei River into northern Szechwan and from there entered Tibet where, presumably, they continue to live today, hidden away in some distant mountain retreat.

Though a large number of the Hmong from the lake region were exempted from the forced migration to San Wei, they were hardly to be envied. Chou oppression continued unabated. Revolts were frequent enough to tax the tolerance of imperial officials who responded by intensifying the repression until it assumed the dimensions of an extermination campaign.

For a time the Hmong held their own against the Chou and even enjoyed some early victories. But these were soon followed by a string of devastating defeats. In 826 B.C., General Fang-chou engaged the Hmong with three hundred thousand troops and three thousand war chariots. The Hmong did not have a chance. They held the field as long as possible and then retreated for their lives. Additional, though not so crushing, defeats followed. Soon the Hmong began to migrate from the area en masse. By one account a number fled east, reached the ocean, and sailed to the South Seas. Others migrated into Kiangsi; some moved south through Hunan into Kwangsi, establishing settlements along the way. However, the great majority fled southwest into the highlands of Szechwan and Kweichow where they were beyond the reach of the Chou. The Keh-Lao and other montagnards tried to drive the Hmong back across the Hunan-Kweichow border. Most of the Keh-Lao were decimated.

Ch'in Dynasty
(256-207 B.C.)

In 256 B.C., the last Chou emperor bowed to the military might of the feudal state of Ch'in, centered in Shansi and Kansu provinces. The Ch'in sought to bring all of China under their rule by extensive militarization. After neutralizing opposition in the interior, they positioned troops in the north to hold back the warrior nomads who periodically invaded the empire. Seeking a permanent solution, they began construction on the Great Wall.

Han Dynasty
(206 B.C.-A.D. 220)

Ch'in success in pacifying the northern frontier enabled the Han dynasty to direct its attention south. By A.D. 25, Han troops were conducting operations as far south as Chiao-Chih Chun, an ancient kingdom that encompassed Kwangsi province and Tonkin (northern Vietnam). The expedition was led by General Ma-yuan who easily routed the Hmong of Kwangsi, then pushed on to Tonkin where he enjoyed equal success against Vietnamese montagnards and Kwangsi Hmong who had migrated into the region some years earlier. After a campaign of terror, Ma-yuan erected a bronze column on the Tonkin border that bore the inscription: "All Tonkinese who pass this column will be known." To the Han, the column represented the southern limit of the civilized world. For super-stitious Tonkin tribesmen, ignorant of the meaning of the column's inscription, the monument was received as a material manifestation of a guardian spirit; they eventually surrounded the column with boulders to shelter it from the ravages of wind and rain, believing that as long as it stood their people would flourish.

Twenty-two years after the Tonkin expedition, the Han sent an-other general, Liu-Shang, to quell a Hmong uprising in southern Hunan. According to the Chinese historian, Yih-Fu, this rebellion had "ravaged the . . . administrative districts" in the region. Liu-Shang drafted troops on the coast near the mouth of the Yangtze River and sailed upstream to the lake region where he disembarked and set off for southern Hunan, "full of contempt" for the Hmong whom Ma-yuan had so easily defeated in Kwangsi. His army en-countered enormous difficulty penetrating Hmong territory. Communiqués to the Han capitol of Loyang abruptly ended; the entire military force simply disappeared.

The battle-hardened Ma-yuan was called up to replace the van-ished general. At the start, the campaign had all the earmarks of a veritable rout. The Hmong were defeated in the open field and forced to withdraw, with the aged general dogging their retreat. Then Ma-yuan made the mistake of allowing himself to be closed up in a gorge, where 20,000 of his men were lost to sickness and he died himself. In retaliation, General Tou-chang was sent, not to engage the Hmong in battle, but to attack defenseless towns and villages. Unarmed civilians were killed, homes burned to the ground, and everything of any value pillaged. This savagery continued on and off for another three years until the Han emperor Liu Hsiu finally deemed the territory pacified.

Subsequent acts of suppression were small-scale and few in num-ber. The Hmong made good use of this welcome calm in their stormy relations with the Chinese to reoccupy lost territory. By the second century they commanded much of Hunan and Kweichow, and had established a beachhead in southern Hupeh. They also pushed north along the banks of the Han River, penetrating deep into northern Hupeh where they were later joined by Hmong from eastern Szechwan displaced by migrating Tibetan nomads. Hmong began to filter into their former Honan homeland, some continuing as far north as Shensi and as far east as Anhwei.

Between 403 and 561, there were forty Hmong uprisings in areas formerly under Chinese control. These were not bandit raids typical of other tribes, but genuine attempts to capture and exercise political power in Hmong occupied territory.

Hmong Kingdom
(A.D. 400-900)

By the middle of the sixth century even the Chinese were forced to concede the existence of a Hmong kingdom which, in one form or another, had been functioning since the beginning of the fifth century. The kingdom had evolved from a loose federation of tribes into a hereditary monarchy.

The king of the Hmong was not an absolute monarch. The independent spirited Hmong would never tolerate anyone, and especially a Hmong, exercising absolute power over them. In fact, the office of king was to some degree elective. On the death of the Hmong monarch a successor was chosen from among his sons by all men capable of bearing arms. Nor was this a hollow election with few candidates. Then, as now, the Hmong practiced polygamy and the king was expected to have many wives and, thus, many sons from whom to choose.

There was another, more pervasive, way in which Hmong politics displayed democratic or, more correctly, republican features. The Hmong monarchy functioned very much like a federated state in which most of the real power devolved to local units. Villages were organized into districts, with each district containing twenty villages. Every district had its own chief who was elected by all men capable of bearing arms and who could be removed through special election should he prove incompetent or corrupt. The district chief appointed a village headman for each village under his jurisdiction, the wisdom of the appointments standing as an indication of his capacity to rule.

Though a headman was appointed rather than elected, unhappy villagers could, and apparently quite often did, complain to the district chief when they felt their village headman ruled badly, for the district chief's power of appointment included the power to remove appointees for misconduct or incompetence.

Popular assemblies were another check on misconduct. They occurred both at the village and district level. Headmen were expected to call such an assembly when any important decision was to be made, such as cooperative work projects involving the laying out of new fields or the construction of roads and waterworks. Again, all men capable of bearing arms voted, and the majority vote decided the issue. Villagers could also convene the assembly on their own to deal with charges of malfeasance lodged against their headman. In such instances, if the majority agreed misconduct had occurred, it became a formal complaint that had to be presented to the district chief.

Popular assemblies were also convened at the district level for deciding important issues affecting the welfare of the district. As at the village level, this might involve issues such as the building and maintenance of roads and waterworks, but it might also include issues left off the village agenda, like the time and place of the most important Hmong communal religious celebration, the New Year festival. This high level of participation in politics meant that most important political issues were decided at the local level. Not only did districts and villages make policy, they provided the funds and administration to implement it. Consequently, though issues of national defense were decided by the king, his power to decide was severely limited by the need for consensus at the local level for implementing decisions once they were made. It was the right of each district to determine through its popular assembly the extent of its contribution in soldiers, arms, and supplies to the enterprise.

The king's dependence on the voluntary support of hundreds of popular assemblies functioned as a serious constraint on military

HMONG
KINGDOM
A.D. 400-900

MONGOLIA

LIAONING

KANSU

INNER MONGOLIA

Beijing

HOPEI

SHANSI

ZIZHIQUE

TSINGHAI

SHENSI

SHANTUNG

Wei River

Yellow River

•Sun-wei

HONAN

KIANGSU

ANHWEI

HUPEH

Chang River

SZECHWAN

CHEKIANG

HMONG
WALL

KIANGSI

KWEICHOW

Lip'ing•

HUNAN

FUKIEN

YUNNAN

KWANGSI

KWANGTUNG

BURMA

TONKIN

LAOS

Mekong River

SOUTH CHINA SEA

adventurism. Despite the ill-deserved reputation for bellicosity the Chinese have given the Hmong, they were then, as they are now, a peace-loving people, slow to anger and even slower to fight unless forced to do so out of desperation. If, however, their lives or freedom are in danger, they will quickly rally around a leader to defeat their enemies. The Hmong king could therefore count on popular support if the realm was truly threatened, but not otherwise.

The Hmong legal system was also administered at the local level. While custom governed crimes and their penalties, the determination of guilt or innocence was left to the village. Should any party find the decision wanting in wisdom, the verdict could always be appealed to the district chief, or even a popular assembly, though to prevent frivolous meetings the person who requested such an assembly had to provide food and lodging for all who attended.

That the Hmong kingdom existed at all was symptomatic of the disarray that plagued China from the third through the sixth century. For almost two hundred years the nation's monetary system was in a shambles. Coins were minted in copper, which became scarce, leading to a sharp contraction in the money supply. Barter became the rule, and commercial activity languished. Politics mirrored the economic collapse. The central government was no more. Independent warlords competed for power, some enjoying momentary success, like Sima Yan who crushed all opposition and then crippled his army by melting down his soldiers' weapons to mint coins for the revenue required to rebuild the central government. In the fourth century, Mongolian nomads invaded China from the north; Tibetan warriors streamed in from the southwest.

The Hmong kingdom reached the zenith of its power and prestige in the last half of the sixth century. China had collapsed into an uneasy feudalism with different factions struggling to gain control and reunite the empire. Since the Hmong exercised de facto control over much of Hupeh, Hunan, and Kwangsi, they enjoyed considerable bargaining power with the rival factions. Hmong were appointed to high positions in the courts of competing dynasties, each seeking the Hmong as military allies in struggles with their rivals.

This political leverage evaporated in 618 when Li Yuan captured the throne and established the T'ang dynasty. The T'ang launched a campaign to reconquer all territories lost to the Hmong. Though their generals proved unequal to the task, a great deal of Hmong territory was brought under administrative control, leading to a dual system of government: local matters were left for the Hmong to decide as they wished, but taxes had to be paid to the empire, and Chinese living in Hmong territory were subject only to Chinese law.

Then, in 907, the Hmong kingdom was threatened with total annihilation. The Chinese adventurer Ma Yin led a rebel army and annexed most of Hunan as the independent state of Ch'u. The Hmong rose up against him and were devastated. Though Ma Yin's army was eventually overwhelmed by imperial forces, the military might of the Hmong was at an end. Within fifty years the Sung dynasty launched a series of campaigns to bring Hupeh and Hunan under tight control. During the fighting the Hmong king and all of his generals perished.

A Hmong legend recounts these last days. Tchu Kyou Toua Hang ruled over the Hmong. Old and weary of war, he was in the field with his armies to face the Chinese invaders. The Hmong put up a fierce resistance against insurmountable odds. Had it not been for the king's only daughter, Ngao Shing, the Sung would have had an easy victory.

Ngao Shing was not only incredibly beautiful, she was endowed with supernatural powers exercised through the medium of a magic flag. When the Hmong were being assaulted from all sides, it was she who marched forward, waved her magical flag, and called forth a terrible storm that forced the Chinese to retreat.

The Chinese general Ty Ching sued for peace, pledging that his forces would withdraw if the Hmong surrendered the magic flag. Tchu Kyou Toua Hang and his advisors met to consider the offer. They concluded Ty Ching was laying a trap. Once he had the magic flag the Hmong would be slaughtered. They delivered a fake flag, black and white with the emblem of a dragon surrounded by flying birds: an exact duplicate of the original in every detail except that it lacked magical powers.

Ty Ching delivered the flag to the emperor, who tested its authenticity by casting it into flames, for it was rumored that the magic flag could not be burned. The flames consumed the flag, and Ty Ching was placed under arrest and condemned to death. After much pleading by relatives, the general's sentence was commuted to life imprisonment and then to a full pardon.

Ty Ching was free but disgraced. To regain his honor he led a new expedition against the Hmong. However, this time he did not run headlong into battle. He meant to trick the Hmong as they had tricked him. He entered Hmong territory under a flag of truce, passing himself off as an emissary from the emperor who sought the Hmong as allies. Tchu Kyou Toua Hang consented to the provisions of the alliance which included the marriage of Ngao Shing to the emperor's son, the next in line to the throne.

Tchu Kyou Toua Hang delivered his daughter to the Chinese, but she refused to go through with the marriage. Ngao Shing was imprisoned and tortured, yet still refused to consent. Weak and ill, she soon died. The Hmong still possessed her magic flag, but without Ngao Shing it was useless. Ty Ching quickly defeated the Hmong, killed Tchu Kyou Toua Hang, and drove the Hmong out of their kingdom.

The fall of the great kingdom was a major turning point in Hmong history. It was the end of their golden age. In time the Hmong would have other kings, called "kiatongs" or little kings, but none would ever exercise substantial power or rule over all of the Hmong. Longing for a return to their golden age, the Hmong became resolute irredentists, waiting for a messiah to deliver them from the Chinese and restore their ancient kingdom; by legend, he will be divinely inspired with magical powers sufficient to defeat the enemy, no matter how numerous nor how strong. The sway of this messianic vision can be inferred from the ferocity of subsequent Hmong uprisings, not only in China but in Vietnam and Laos where thousands of Hmong later migrated to avoid Chinese repression.

The Sung campaign to destroy the Hmong kingdom was part of a larger campaign to subdue all ethnic minorities in China. Everywhere it followed the same pattern. Sung legions flexed their muscles, ethnic rebels scattered, and engineers appeared to erect military garrisons to protect Chinese squatters brought in by the thousands to tip demographics in favor of the Chinese. Hunkered down in the ruins of their lost kingdom, the Hmong could fight or flee. Most fled, migrating west into Kweichow and Szechwan. A smaller number marched southeast into Kwangsi and Kwangtung.

Dispersed and powerless, the Hmong were once again a tribal people, linked by a shared language and customs but isolated geographically into separate groups. A Hmong legend claims that present day Hmong tribes were invented by the Chinese after the collapse of the Hmong kingdom. The Chinese ordered the Hmong to wear clothes of different colors. Some were required to wear black cloth and were called the Black Hmong; those who used white cloth were called the White Hmong. This is the origin of the five principal Hmong tribes in China today: White, Black, Flowery, Red, and Blue. The explanation for this strange policy is that the Chinese hoped such distinctions would eventually lead to actual divisions among the Hmong, making unified action difficult.

It never came to pass. Their tribes have never been as important to the Hmong as their clans, which bind all Hmong to past generations through patrilineal descent. As with their tribes, the origin of Hmong clans is something of a mystery, though legend attests there were originally between eight and twelve bearing Chinese names. Whatever their origin, from the tenth century on, clan affiliation grew in importance, creating mutual rights and obligations enjoyed or owed to members of the same clan. While this created divided loyalties, it never fully inhibited joint action against a common enemy or put an end to Hmong rebellions.

Ming Dynasty
(A.D. 1368-1644)

After their flight into the mountains the Hmong enjoyed comparative peace, for the Sung were preoccupied with strengthening
China's commerce instead of its military might. The dynasty's growing military weakness eventually invited invasions from the north.
By the early twelfth century, all of northern China fell under Manchurian control. In the late thirteenth century, Mongols ousted the
Manchurians and conquered the rest of China. During the conquest, Kublai Khan led a Mongol army into Kweichow to subdue
its population. It was a short campaign and the Mongols did not
penetrate very far into the mountains; most Hmong in the province
were left undisturbed.

In the short span of seventy years the Mongols' brief Yuan dynasty began to unravel. Mongol princes warred against each other
while Chinese peasants rebelled. Softened by decades of inactivity,
the once invincible Mongol military was routed by a peasant army
led by a Buddhist monk named Zhu Yuanzhang, the first emperor
of the Ming dynasty. The Ming ruled China with an iron hand and
expanded foreign trade. Burma, which had fallen to China under
the Mongols, was selected as the primary outlet for trade with all of
Southeast Asia. To this purpose China annexed Yunnan to insure
access to Burma's borders, and initiated work on a transport road
across Kweichow to provide a direct route to Yunnan. Of course,
before the road could be completed the region had to be pacified.

First military zones were created and then administrative districts. Local tribal chiefs were incorporated into the administrative
hierarchy with the title of "Tu Si." Once appointed, they held the
position for life, and could pass it on to their heirs. As long as the
Tu Si faithfully collected taxes and preserved order, the Chinese did
not interfere with tribal affairs. In time, the Ming strengthened the
authority of the Tu Si, transforming them into virtual warlords.

In Kweichow only Lolo (another tribal minority) were granted
the title of Tu Si, though Lolo lords often appointed Hmong as
sub-officials charged with maintaining peace among their own

51

people. The increased autonomy granted to the Tu Si led to abuses and often tyrannical rule. The Hmong in particular were much oppressed by Lolo lords and frequently revolted against their authority. With each revolt the Hmong grew bolder, much to the alarm of the imperial court.

In 1459 General Fang-Yn led an army into Kweichow to restore order. He enjoyed an early victory, but the defeated Hmong carried out numerous raids against isolated military posts before Fang-Yn could gather enough troops from Szechwan to mount a massive campaign against them. Fang-Yn established over two thousand garrisons in the Kweichow-Szechwan region from which he launched repeated raids on Hmong villages and military strongholds. In the end he succeeded in capturing or killing over forty thousand Hmong.

Yet within fifty years the Hmong were again attempting to reassert their independence, and revolts and rebellions continued sporadically until, by the end of the sixteenth century, not a year passed without the Hmong engaging in some kind of armed uprising. Not only were the Hmong exercising greater boldness, they were occupying new land across the Kweichow border into Hunan. To block their migration, the Ming erected a scaled down version of The Great Wall on the Hunan-Kweichow border. The "Hmong Wall" was ten feet high and stretched a hundred miles with military posts at intervals along the Chinese side. No Hmong were permitted to cross over, even to trade with Chinese villagers on the other side.

Manchu Dynasty
(A.D. 1644-1911)

By 1640 the Ming dynasty was at the nadir of its decline. Provinces ignored its mandates. Tax revenues were so low the government had insufficient funds to mount a defense against Mongol invaders who made directly for Peking. Sensing the imminent collapse of the dynasty, various notables in the provinces jockeyed for political power with hopes of eventually ascending to the throne. One of them, Li Tzu-ch'eng, gained control of Shensi province, declared himself emperor, and marched on Peking. The last Ming emperor committed suicide before Li Tzu-ch'eng got to him.

Li Tzu-ch'eng struggled to right the tottering empire, but the old Ming bureaucracy refused to cooperate, and provincial governors turned their backs on him. Meanwhile, the Manchurian (Manchu) horde pressed on. Only the forces of Wu Sangui blocked their advance, and the Ming general's allegiance to the new regime was threadbare; before the two armies closed, he went over to the enemy side and joined the march on Peking. Wu Sangui had hoped to share power with the Manchu, but after Peking fell into their hands, the Manchurians made it clear they intended to rule China on their own. Wu Sangui had to settle for a military promotion and the formidable assignment of bringing all of western China under Manchu control.

By 1661 this task was completed. It was an impressive achievement that fanned Wu Sangui's ambition. Twenty years of collaboration with the Manchu had convinced him that their power was all smoke and mirrors. Only Chinese inability to mount a united offense kept the Manchu on the throne. Wu Sangui decided to rally the Chinese and drive the Manchu out of China. Unfortunately, having devoted most of his distinguished military career to the suppression of the western provinces, he could hardly count on them for support. Wu Sangui moved his troops eastward, traveling along the Yangtze, to secure patronage from the gentry. But once the fighting heated up, the gentry lost their nerve and withdrew their support. Wu Sangui retreated south, setting himself up in Kwangsi near the southern border of Kweichow. He held out against the Manchu until his death. His grandson, Wu Shih-fan, took over the leadership of the resistance until 1681, when it was crushed by the Manchu.

One of Wu Shih-fan's generals, Hwang Ming, fled from Kwangsi to Kweichow with a hundred soldiers. They were given refuge by the Hmong of Lip'ing on the eastern border of Kweichow. The following year another defeated general, Ma Bao, fled with his troops to Kweichow. He passed through Hmong territory on his way to Yunnan. Ma Bao and his men were forced to leave their weapons with the Hmong before continuing their journey. These included rifles, gunpowder, armor and cannons.

In gratitude for their hospitality, Hwang Ming and his soldiers instructed the Lip'ing Hmong in the use of these weapons and taught them how to manufacture their own. This is the origin of the famous Hmong Blunderbuss, or flintlock rifle, which until very recently was used by the Hmong throughout Indochina.

Hmong warriors previously had wielded only crossbows, swords, knives, and spears, a crude arsenal when compared to rifles and cannons, yet often sufficient to terrorize the better-equipped Chinese. Hmong poisoned arrows were particularly feared, for to be struck by one meant instant death. The Hmong were ferocious in battle, particularly the Jiu-Gu Hmong of central Kweichow. Protected by a metal helmet, a cuirass of thick buffalo hide overlaid with copper plates, and iron mail covering their arms and legs, the Jiu-Gu fought with a shield in one hand, a spear in the other, and a knife between their teeth.

If poisoned arrows and Jiu-Gu warriors struck fear in the hearts of Chinese infantrymen, one can only imagine the alarm raised when Hmong equipped with modern rifles began to venture into territory occupied by Chinese, terrifying the inhabitants and defeating all who opposed them. This coincided with a major change in Manchu policy toward tribal minorities and made war between the Hmong and Chinese inevitable.

The Manchu scrapped the old Tu Si system and placed ethnic territories under direct administration by the Chinese civil bureaucracy. Not only did this maximize political control, in Kweichow and Szechwan it enabled greater exploitation of the rich deposits of coal, silver, and copper, and vast stands of timber which tribal chieftains had failed to develop. To insure adequate food supplies for the operation, Chinese farmers were brought into the two provinces under military protection and allowed to take possession of the best land. To help cover the expense of increased government activity, taxes were increased in the two provinces.

In Kweichow, the taxes proved ruinous for Hmong farmers. To avoid the forfeiture of their land in lieu of unpaid taxes, many turned to Chinese merchants who lent them money at an exorbitant rate of five percent per month. Many Hmong lost their homes and land to these creditors.

The Manchu justified such practices as the cost of bringing culture to the natives. Prince Ortai, the governor of Kweichow and Yunnan provinces, stated the government's position in an official report that was widely circulated: "the Miao are really an admirable people and deserve civilization and good government. We ought to give it to them and become their rulers."

Insurrections were frequent. In 1727 Ortai seized on a minor uprising as a pretext for an all-out war against the Hmong. General Zhang Kwang Si led the campaign in Kweichow, which commenced with the sacking of Bazhai, a Hmong town in the center of the province. Zhang Kwang Si then moved on Guiyang, the provincial capitol. Advancing from the south, he was forced to cross the Lien River to enter Guiyang. Arriving in the dead of night, he slaughtered Hmong boatmen and commandeered their boats. By daybreak, Guiyang was under Chinese control. The following year, Zhang Kwang Si marched on Lip'ing. A Hmong army of ten thousand, fully armed with rifles and cannons, advanced to engage him. Battle casualties were high on both sides, but the Chinese prevailed. Prince Ortai ordered the captured weapons melted down, cast into an iron pillar eleven feet high, and placed on an island in a river that ran just south of the battle scene as a monument to the Chinese victory.

Much to Ortai's consternation, the Hmong rebelled again, this time in the southwest corner of the province. Hmong descended from the mountain forest and massacred the inhabitants of four towns. The raiders demolished government buildings on three rivers and blocked all river traffic. Peking called up troops in the surrounding provinces to mount an offensive on three fronts. The fighting was furious and the Hmong suffered heavy casualties. But the Chinese sometimes suffered heavy losses as well. On one such occasion the Hmong drew them into a pass ringed with rock falls. The Chinese were crushed below, the survivors fleeing before the Hmong could descend from the cliffs and finish them off.

This was only one small victory amid a general rout. Over-whelmed, a large number of Hmong surrendered. They were summarily executed. This did not have the desired effect. Scattered Hmong tribes joined forces and constructed stone signal towers at one-mile intervals along the mountain ridges. The remains of these towers, in which fires were set to warn of advancing Chinese, still stand today. The rebels took a blood oath to fight to the death. They killed their wives and children and faced the imperial army as men with nothing to lose. Fighting like demons, they captured several passes and, for a time, cut all Chinese supply routes.

News of these heroics infuriated the Manchu emperor Shih Tsung. After calling on the reserves, Ortai had assured him there would be an end to the insurrections. In a caustic letter Shih Tsung observed that with "thousands of soldiers in action for months . . . there is hardly any contact possible between the territories . . . and it is nearly impossible to get supplies to the wounded in the field." The emperor dismissed Ortai and replaced him with Zhang Kwang Si. The general mobilized his forces, reopened the passes, and cornered the rebels on a high plateau. The Hmong soon ran out of supplies and neared starvation. In an act of desperation they tried to fight through the enemy's lines. The Chinese assaulted them on all sides. Twenty thousand Hmong were killed. Another twenty-seven thousand were taken prisoner, and half of them executed. Zhang Kwang Si then unleashed his forces on hapless civilians. The soldiers sacked over twelve thousand Hmong villages, drove thousands of farmers off their land and confiscated their property. When it was all over, the Chinese counted the Hmong rifles that had fallen into their hands. There were nearly fifty thousand in all. The Hmong had obviously applied what they had learned from General Hwang Ming who fifty years earlier repaid their hospitality by instructing them in the manufacture of Chinese firearms.

The region remained pacified until the rebellion of the two kingdoms of greater and lesser Kin-tchuen. Following the defeat of Sonom and his people by General Akoui in 1776, another twenty years passed before the Hmong appeared in force on the Kweichow-Hunan frontier to raze towns and terrorize Chinese peasants. The uprising was in response to stepped up immigration of Chinese into the area, euphemistically called "guest people" by the government. Defended by militiamen, the immigrants quickly crowded Hmong off their land. Two Hmong chieftains, Shih San-Pao and Shih Liuteng, organized a guerrilla force and scattered the local Chinese militia. Peking sent an army to crush the insurrection. The presence of imperial troops only induced more Kweichow Hmong to revolt.

The campaign dragged on for eleven years. On occasion the Hmong gained the upper hand. Wu Ba Yue, a Hmong chieftain from the border region, defeated imperial troops in several engagements. Flushed with these successes, he urged his partisans to follow him to Peking to dethrone the emperor. Not knowing the distance to the Chinese capitol, or its precise direction, he sent out scouts to discover a route to Peking. A short time later he was captured and executed.

The slow pace of the pacification was partly due to the corrupt leadership of the Manchu general staff. Fu-k'ang-an, a close relative of Ch'ien-lung, was in charge of the early stages of the campaign. He diverted military funds to enrich his officers and to soften the normal hardships of living in the field. There were false accounts of victories over the Hmong, when in fact the army had conceded the field, allowing the rebels to devastate the countryside while officers and their staffs withdrew to the safety of walled towns, which were seldom attacked by Hmong guerrillas. Reports of high enemy casualties were routinely padded by counting civilian dead as slain enemy. Despite his efforts to dodge the Hmong, Fu-k'ang-an was killed in battle. A short time later, forces were transferred to Hubei to quell an unrelated rebellion, leaving behind only twenty thousand troops to face Hmong rebels. Another three years passed before reinforcements arrived, turning the tide against the Hmong.

The reinvigorated Manchu army established agricultural colonies throughout Kweichow to protect Chinese peasants from Hmong marauders. Newly created militias patrolled Hmong villages. In 1806 engineers arrived to rebuild the Hmong Wall, which had become a ruin from decades of neglect; the engineers also constructed more than a thousand new military posts. Hemmed in, patrolled and monitored, the Hmong finally laid down their arms. To insure the peace would last, provincial authorities required them to surrender all weapons. Thousands of rifles, crossbows, spears, and armor passed from the Hmong to the Chinese.

With the Hmong defenseless, Chinese once again flooded into the area. Hmong lost their farms to squatters enjoying military protection, or to Chinese creditors who confiscated their land for unpaid debts, reducing a large number of Kweichow's Hmong to impoverished tenant farmers or sharecroppers. The final insult was a concerted effort to force assimilation. Civil authorities required Hmong children to attend Chinese schools to learn to read and write and to absorb Chinese culture. To hasten the process, the government prohibited Hmong from observing traditional celebrations and ceremonies, and pressured Hmong fathers to allow Chinese men to wed their daughters.

Many Hmong found such conditions intolerable and migrated from Kweichow to the mountain areas of neighboring provinces. Some Black Hmong settled in southern Hunan and northern Kwangsi. White Hmong migrated north into Szechwan, and numbers of Flowery Hmong made the trek west to Yunnan to link up with existing Hmong communities in the province.

HMONG AND HAW

As it turned out, Yunnan was not a good choice. A large proportion of the Yunnanese were Muslims, descendants of Chinese converted to Islam by Arab traders who first entered Yunnan with their caravans over a thousand years earlier. Known as the "Haw" in Yunnan and as the "Panthays" in Burma, they were mostly merchants and traders. Though prosperous, they were excluded from polite society. The non-Muslim Chinese sometimes dragged the Haw from their homes, beat or killed them, and looted their shops. Any appeal to Yunnanese authorities for protection was futile, since government officials were as prejudiced and hostile toward the Haw as the general population.

In 1818 the Haw rebelled. They did so again in 1826 and 1834.

Each time they were defeated. The worst, and last, Haw rebellion, the Great Panthay Rebellion, began in 1855 and lasted until 1873. Because of Peking's preoccupation with the more serious and widespread Taiping Rebellion, and the ability of the Haw to purchase modern European weapons from the British in Burma, the Haw were eventually able to take control of the entire province. Their leader, Tu Wen-hsiu, declared Yunnan an independent Muslim state. And so it remained until 1872, when Peking sent sufficient troops to regain control of the province.

The majority of Yunnan's Hmong sided with the Haw. And like the Haw they paid dearly for their rebellion. Once the imperial army cut the supply routes to Yunnan, the rebels had to contend with starvation and bubonic plague, as well as an invading army.

The tide turned against the rebels, and the Chinese responded with the kind of savagery they had previously reserved for the Hmong alone. In 1871 the rebel city of Chengkiang in southern Yunnan capitulated after enduring a long siege. The capitulation agreement called for the citizens to be treated with mercy. But once the city gates were unlocked, the Chinese, under the command of Shao Ta-jen, rushed in and began to slaughter the inhabitants. Haw soldiers resisted and then retreated. Many escaped, but the women, children, and elderly left behind were cut down without mercy. When night fell, the bodies of nearly six thousand victims covered the streets of Chengkiang.

In all, a million Yunnanese perished before China regained control of the province. Following the Haw defeat, Chinese soldiers confiscated Haw property and prohibited the Haw from opening shops or engaging in trade. Repeating the atrocities at Chengkiang, soldiers attacked Hmong villages and slaughtered men, women, and children indiscriminately. Though many Hmong and Haw had already left the region, even larger numbers now formed a river of migrants, flowing southward toward Indochina.

They were not the first Hmong to migrate to Indochina. Since the late 1700s, Manchu oppression had pushed the Hmong to migrate southward, following the mountain chains across the border into northern Vietnam.

CHAPTER 4

Settling in Indochina

EARLY CROSSINGS

*I*N THE LATE 1740S a small number of Kweichow Hmong, refugees of the massive military campaign waged against the Hmong in that province between 1727 and 1740, crossed over the Chinese border and entered Indochina. They settled in two places about 150 miles apart on the northern Vietnamese border. One was at Dong Quan, a village fifty miles inland from the Gulf of Tonkin. The other was located near the limestone mountain region of Hoang-Su-Phi.

Fifty years later more Hmong entered Vietnam, but this time they were a much larger group of around six thousand. They crossed the border and occupied the mountains above the Tai village of Dong Van, just a few miles from the point where the three borders of Yunnan, Kwangsi, and Vietnam intersect. For a time, relations between the Hmong and the Tai lowlanders were strained, occasionally erupting into violence. But as the Hmong seldom ventured from their highland villages into the fertile Tai valleys below, apprehensions over claim jumping subsided and the Tai accorded the newcomers a grudging tolerance.

LAOS

Sometime between 1815 and 1818, another Hmong settlement sprang up west of Dong Van on the northern tip of the Fan Si Pan mountain range. The settlers were probably a splinter group from the Hmong community near Dong Van who left their comrades to search for better land. When they arrived at the Fan Si Pans, they marked out their villages, built homes, cleared fields, and planted their first crops. But within a few years the homes were empty, the fields choked with weeds, and the Hmong nowhere in sight.

It was all the doing of one man, a Chinese opium merchant named Ton Ma. On one of his stops to collect opium from the new Hmong community, he told the people of the lush, uninhabited mountains of Xieng Khouang province in eastern Laos. He also offered to guide a contingent of the Fan Si Pan Hmong to this promised land on his next trip to Xieng Khouang. Ton Ma's motives were not entirely altruistic for the province possessed some of the world's best opium growing areas. But, then, the Hmong were opium growers, so there was profit to be made on both sides.

Pa See Lo, the recognized leader of the Fan Si Pan Hmong, assembled the village chiefs and elders to discuss how best to proceed. The decision was that a small party under the leadership of Kue Vue would undertake an exploratory expedition to Laos. If all was as Ton Ma had described, others would follow.

The place Ton Ma led them to was just a few miles inside Laos near a town the Laotians called Nong Het. Kue Vue and his men explored other areas nearby but none impressed them as much as the terrain near Nong Het. Ton Ma had not deceived them. The mountains and high plateaus were nearly uninhabited and densely forested. The thick vegetation would mean extra work when clearing fields for planting, but after it was burned the cut timber and thick underbrush would provide abundant fertilizer for the already rich soil.

After Kue Vue and his men returned to northern Vietnam and informed their comrades of what they had found, the question was no longer whether a portion of the village should migrate to Laos, but whether the entire community should do so. It was decided that one large group, again led by Kue Vue, would first settle in Nong Het and, if all went well, the rest would follow. These homesteaders traveled as the Hmong have always traveled, carrying everything they owned on their backs, driving their livestock before them, walking the crests of the mountains until they reached their destination.

Within a few years they established ten villages around Nong Het, and in honor of the Chinese trader who had made it all possible, they named one of the rivers that flowed nearby the Ton Ma.

This no doubt pleased their sponsor who was a frequent visitor to Nong Het during the opium harvest. In later years when the harvests were large and his visits correspondingly longer, he built a winter residence close to the river that bears his name.

The success of the Hmong at Nong Het, coupled with Ton Ma's prodding, convinced Pa See Lo to lead the remaining Fan Si Pan Hmong to the area. Pa See Lo had an additional reason for the final evacuation of the remaining Hmong from the Fan Si Pan mountains. Ton Ma promised him that he would be made kiatong ("little king") of the Nong Het Hmong when he resettled.

Everything would have been perfect if it had not been for the tigers. The increase in the size of the Hmong community required the clearing of land for new fields and villages. Some of the sites chosen happened to fall well within the hunting grounds of tigers unfamiliar with and, therefore, unafraid of man. By one account the tigers were so numerous that guards had to be placed around workers clearing new fields to forestall attacks. A few of the tigers regularly raided villages, carrying away not only livestock but old women and young children. During one attack, an old woman guarding the family's livestock was carried off. The entire village set off in pursuit, beating gongs and blowing horns, hoping the noise would frighten the tiger and make him drop the old woman. They found her dead in the forest. Instead of carrying the corpse back to the village, the old woman was left were she lay and a trap set for the tiger. Villagers braced and aimed flintlocks at a spot where the tiger would have to cross to get at the old woman's remains. Next they stretched strings across the approach and tied them to the weapons' triggers. The trap worked. After that chickens, goats, and pigs were used as bait. Within a matter of months, tigers no longer posed a threat to the Hmong of Nong Het.

With the threat of tigers removed, the Nong Het Hmong enjoyed several years of uninterrupted peace until their kiatong, Pa See Lo, was murdered by Chinese bandits during an abortive raid on his village's opium cache. The death of Pa See Lo necessitated the selection of a new kiatong and the vote went to another member of the Lo clan, Xia Sue Lo.

Recruiting new kiatongs from the Lo clan became something of a precedent that remained unchallenged for several decades. By the early 1850s this political consensus was strained by two events. New migrants, mostly members of the Ly and Moua clans, demanded more representative politics. Then there was the matter of the arrival of a Ly kiatong from China who refused to renounce authority over his own clansmen.

The Ly kiatong came from southern Szechwan where the Panthay rebellion had claimed thousands of Hmong lives. For many of the Szechwan Ly, the choice was migrate or die. The old patriarch of the Szechwan Ly had remained behind to hold off the Chinese, while his four sons led a southern retreat toward Indochina. Before they departed, their father transferred his authority as kiatong of the Ly clan to Nghia Vue Ly. A full year passed before Nghia Vue Ly and the remnants of his clan finally reached Nong Het. The arrival of another kiatong posed obvious political problems for the Nong Het Hmong. Which of the two possessed ultimate authority? A compromise was reached. Nghia Vue Ly would exercise authority over the Ly, and the Lo kiatong would represent the remaining Hmong. But it was not long before the Moua clan objected to the arrangement and soon they, too, had their own kiatong, Chong Kai Moua. Though authority was divided, the Lo kiatongs continued to enjoy greater prestige and influence than either the Ly or Moua kiatongs.

Word of the success of the Nong Het Hmong attracted other Chinese Hmong to Indochina. Not all chose Laos, however. A large number headed for northern Vietnam. As the Vietnamese would later characterize the event, they entered Vietnam like an invading army.

VIETNAM

In 1860, toward the end of the Taiping Rebellion in China, more Hmong crossed the border in the company of Chinese, probably Haw Muslims from Yunnan and possibly even a number of de-

feated Taiping rebels. The group was first sighted in the frontier region of Dong Van, Yen Minh, and Quan Ba. Organized as a military force, they easily routed the Vietnamese soldiers guarding the border passes and then headed south, following the course of the Song Chay River toward Hanoi.

The Vietnamese Mandarins in districts near the river town of Tuyen Quang sent troops to block the Hmong advance, but they were quickly overwhelmed and relentlessly pursued all the way to Tuyen Quang, where they rallied the support of the local citizens and attempted to repel their pursuers. The Hmong launched two major assaults before the city fell into their hands. Flushed with their victories, the Hmong continued south and entered the delta region.

A mountain people, the Hmong do not do well in tropical climates. Illness, probably malaria, began to take its toll and slow their advance. This provided officials in Hanoi the breathing space to organize a resistance. All troops in the Red River delta were called up and placed under the command of Governor Son Tay. The hastily assembled army, including a unit of war elephants, intercepted the Hmong at Yen Binh, just sixty miles north of Hanoi. The Hmong held their own until the war elephants were brought forward. They had never seen such beasts and were properly terrified. The Hmong hastily retreated into the mountains where the elephants were unable to follow. They traveled east to the Clear River, then north to the high plateau region of Quan Ba near the Chinese border, where they established several villages and remained undisturbed for years.

Other Hmong continued to cross over the Chinese border into Indochina. Like moths drawn to the glow of Nong Het, many chose to settle in Laos, but others, undaunted by the earlier Hmong defeat at Yen Binh, headed for the established Hmong settlement of Quan Ba in northern Vietnam.

It was near Quan Ba on Mount Phuoc that a mysterious Hmong named Sioung began each day with sacrifices to the genies and spirits of the forest, after which he spent several grueling hours in gymnastic exercises. After months of hard practice he was able to jump incredibly high off the ground, a feat which convinced him he was at last ready to fulfill what he believed to be his destiny and become the long awaited new king of the Hmong.

Sioung descended Mount Phuoc and entered a Hmong village. The curious villagers watched as he piled up benches into a make-shift tower. To their amazement, the stranger reached the top bench in one leap. Sioung announced to the astonished villagers below that he was the king of the Hmong. He said that the genies who gave him the power to perform such an incredible feat had also insured his success by planting magic beans which would grow into men instead of plants. They would be his soldiers and help him defeat his enemies.

News of this remarkable event spread rapidly throughout the hill tribes in the area. Many of the Hmong, longing for a messiah, were taken in by Sioung's gymnastics and hailed him as their king. But other montagnards, like the Nung and Man, were also impressed. It was not long before Hmong, Nung, and Man began showing up at the village, some bearing gifts, others simply wishing to show their respect and others just eager to have a look at the mysterious Hmong whose leaping ability was even more impressive now since he had replaced the makeshift tower of benches with a taller one made out of stones.

Many of the Hmong who acknowledged his sovereignty eagerly awaited his instructions. Sioung's first royal proclamation was the announcement of his new name. It was to be Choen-Tien. And his first command was that his subjects were to build him a palace. Much to the consternation of the Buddhists at Dong Van, the gold inlays and carved wood for Sioung's palace were obtained from raids on their pagodas. When the palace was completed, Sioung ordered his subjects to construct a tower on the palace roof. The tower's name was to be Long-Wei, Seat of the Dragon, and its principal function was to enable Sioung to be closer to heaven so that he could more easily converse with the genies and other spirits.

His residence completed, Sioung directed his attention to the problem of establishing his authority over the border region around Quan Ba. This necessitated an army, which he raised from the villages of the Hmong, Nung, and Man. He recruited Hmong black-smiths to forge flintlocks. Others collected the necessary saltpeter, sulfur, and charcoal to make gunpowder. He distributed arms and ammunition to his troops, who wore white turbans as uniforms. One hundred flags representing Sioung's new kingdom were made and dispatched to the military posts throughout his realm.

Soon Sioung's authority was recognized by all the tribesmen in the area, save for the Tho who would not submit. Furious at their refusal to recognize his divine right to rule, Sioung led a military expedition against them. His first assault was on the Tho village of Lang Dan. The Tho put up a weak resistance and were driven off, watching from the hills as their village was pillaged and then destroyed.

A much larger Tho village near Quan Ba was the next target. There Sioung met with greater resistance. This did not save the Tho village; it merely cost the Tho more lives. After razing the town Sioung sent a band of his men to intercept the fleeing Tho before they could reach the provincial capital of Ha Giang and appeal to the Vietnamese Mandarin for help. When his soldiers caught up with them, the terrified Tho scattered in all directions. Some escaped but most, over a thousand, were killed. Sioung's repression of the Tho continued for twelve more years.

The victories at Lang Dan and Quan Ba increased the Hmong king's reputation among the various tribes so that he no longer felt there was any need to direct his troops in the field. This task he assigned to his officers. Sioung remained in his palace, coming out only in the morning, afternoon, and at sunset to stand on his tower so that his subjects could venerate him.

Out of simple prudence, Vietnamese officials from neighboring districts paid their respects to the Hmong king. They had no desire to invite his anger. It was a small price to pay to keep his troops out of their districts.

Sioung took as his wife the youngest daughter of a tribesmen named Tao Yao. Shortly after the marriage, Sioung killed his bride. Tao Yao was furious but dared not complain out of fear for his own life. He was forced into action, however, when Sioung informed him that he intended to marry his other daughter. Tao Yao immediately packed up his family and quietly made his escape to China.

Once in safer surroundings, Tao Yao's desire for vengeance quickened. He found ten men renowned for their courage, strength, and guile and employed them as assassins. In due time they arrived at Sioung's palace and presented themselves as skilled artisans in need of work. They spent several weeks doing odd jobs inside the palace until some trouble with the Tho led Sioung to dispatch most of his troops, including the majority of the palace guards, to put down the rebellion. When the few remaining guards took a break for dinner, the assassins entered the king's inner chambers and killed him.

Sioung's kingdom dissolved with his death. Among the Hmong, political authority once again returned to their freely chosen village chiefs. The Tho were no longer persecuted, though long before Sioung's death most had already migrated to the lowlands where they were beyond the reach of the Hmong king, and where tropical disease, like malaria, which had decimated the Hmong in their 1860 invasion of the Red River delta, provided additional insurance against Hmong attacks.

In 1911 another Hmong, bent on reviving the fallen kingdom, passed himself off as another Sioung. He even took his name. Trading on the reputation of the real Sioung, he whipped the Hmong into a rebellious mood. Now, however, the Hmong had to contend with the French, as well as the Vietnamese. The second Sioung was captured and imprisoned. He died in jail, disillusioned.

The political vacuum created by the death of the first Sioung was partially filled by Shue Cha, chief of a Hmong village in the limestone mountain region near Hoang-Su-Phi. His rise to power was not as dramatic as Sioung's, but it was steady. Within forty years he controlled most of the territory around Hoang-Su-Phi, as well as an area of equal extent on the other side of the Chinese border. In 1894 the Chinese formally recognized his authority by granting him the title of Tu Si, a provincial administrator with full power over the tribal minorities in his district. Without opposition from either the French or Vietnamese, Shue Cha applied his new-found authority in the Vietnamese as well as the Chinese portion of his kingdom.

The French, in particular, did not interfere because Shue Cha's support was crucial to the maintenance of a French monopoly in coffin wood. Hmong lumberjacks harvested the abundant coffin wood trees and, under Shue Cha's orders, delivered the timber only to the French. For the first time since their entry into Indochina, some Hmong were enjoying a modest degree of affluence. Also for the first time, they were taxing the French. Shue Cha levied a duty on every stick of lumber the French purchased from the Hmong.

The renown of Shue Cha spread all the way to Laos, where the Hmong began to invest him with magical powers. It was claimed that he could change himself or others into different forms. Following his death, stories began to circulate that he had not actually perished but had only changed his form.

In one such tale Shue Cha changed himself into a tiger to obtain meat for some hungry Hmong. He told them that when he returned with the meat, they would have to hit him or he would remain a tiger forever. But on his return, he so frightened them that they ran away. After that he roamed the forests, a legendary and feared creature, a Hmong bogeyman, who occasionally raided Hmong communities and carried off the most beautiful young woman of the village.

RELATIONS WITH OTHER TRIBAL MINORITIES

With a few exceptions, the Hmong who settled in Laos and Vietnam maintained friendly relations with their montagnard neighbors. Sioung nearly exterminated the Tho tribesmen who refused to acknowledge his authority. And in Laos during the latter half of the nineteenth century, the Hmong of Xieng Khouang province engaged in a bloody war with the Kha (also known as the Khmu), montagnards like themselves who considered the Hmong interlopers and unwisely demanded tribute from them as a condition of settlement in Kha occupied territory.

Descendants of the first inhabitants of Indochina, the Kha were driven from the fertile lowlands into the mountains by repeated waves of conquering invaders. In Laos, shortly after the establishment of the kingdom of Luang Prabang, the Kha were actually enslaved by the Lao Tai, the descendants of Tai invaders from southern China. Though the Kha were no longer officially slaves by the end of the nineteenth century, they still occupied the bottom rung of the Laotian social ladder.

The arrival of Hmong offered the Kha hope of improving their social status, for the Hmong gave early evidence of a gentility bordering on servility. Here, or so it seemed at the time, was a people who could be abused with relative impunity. The Kha informed the Hmong that they were trespassing on Kha land and would have to pay a tribute or leave. Though the Hmong consider all unoccupied land free for the taking, they nevertheless acquiesced to Kha demands. They did not want trouble. This concession went to the Kha's heads, and they began to treat the Hmong as they themselves had been treated: with contempt.

Equally disturbing, the Kha discovered the delights of Hmong opium. For nearly two centuries, opium has been the Hmong's only cash crop, the principal reason they cultivate the poppy. While the Hmong appreciate the medicinal benefits of opium, they consider the recreational use of the drug a bad habit and view addiction as a serious character flaw. And it was for this very reason that the Hmong reacted to the growing number of Kha opium addicts with disgust and also with alarm because the Kha began demanding tribute in opium rather than in agricultural produce and livestock. Threatened with a loss of their only source of income, the pliant Hmong suddenly stiffened their backs and refused to pay. The Kha responded with violence. The Hmong gathered up their flintlocks and crossbows and went to war.

The Kha had made the mistake of equating Hmong amiability with weakness. After suffering devastating defeats, many Kha fled Xieng Khouang province and settled in the mountain region near Luang Prabang. Those who remained behind found that the Hmong were quick to forgive past injuries and eager to maintain friendly relations with any group, provided it was willing to do the same.

CHAPTER 5

Hmong Society

THE HMONG VILLAGE

*T*HE HMONG GENERALLY lived at higher altitudes than Laos's other montagnards, usually above 3,000 feet and sometimes as high as 5,000 feet. At this altitude they faced few competitors for the available land; it also placed them beyond the reach of the tropical climate and lowland diseases that so often devastate montagnard populations. Hmong villages varied in size from a few families to twenty or thirty, and were usually constructed along the same plan. High mountains surrounded the slopes on which the Hmong built their houses. This was entirely practical. It placed the village near a stream and guaranteed an adequate water supply. If a stream was not nearby, villagers erected a bamboo aqueduct to carry upstream water to the village. The slopes also provided much needed drainage to reduce the chance of flash floods during monsoons. And the surrounding mountains served as a buffer against heavy winds and rain.

Homes were simple affairs built on whatever flat surface a chosen slope provided or, if none existed, on a terraced plot carved out of the slope. The frame of the square Hmong house consisted of stout poles driven into the ground. Split rail planking (or in some cases split bamboo) formed the siding. Since the Hmong lacked the proper tools, tight fits between adjoining planks were uncommon and finished walls showed many gaps and cracks through which cold winter winds blew. Clusters of palm leaves fastened to a latticework of bamboo poles served as the roof.

A thorough stamping of the earthen floor made it firm and kept dust down to a minimum. Planks fastened to the rafters provided storage space for pots and pans, dry goods, clothes and blankets. Simple partition walls separated bedrooms from the living room and cooking area.

Furnishings were equally Spartan: a bench or two and a few

stools for sitting. A small stove near the front door was used for cooking family meals; a larger stove toward the back of the house was for boiling corn into mash for pigs, or for cooking large meals for ceremonial occasions. No house was without its altar, usually erected against the back wall so that it faced the front door.

The size of the house depended on the size of the family, which might vary from three or four to over twenty individuals. If the family was just getting started, the basic plan described above would suffice. However, more often than not, several generations lived together under one roof, necessitating the addition of extra rooms and extending the floor plan to accommodate them.

Shelters for livestock were built close by, and in many cases were direct extensions of the house. This included stables for horses and cattle, sties for pigs, and coops for chickens. While the inevitable accumulation of animal waste was usually washed away with the first monsoon, it usually caused serious health problems in the interim between monsoons and gave Hmong villages a very distinctive odor. Infant mortality was understandably high, as were outbreaks of communicable diseases, such as typhoid fever, amebic dysentery, and bubonic plague. It was not uncommon for entire villages to pack up and move when disease occurred.

Despite the unsanitary conditions, there was a strong interest in certain aspects of personal hygiene. A clean face and white teeth were much admired, so much so that when the French introduced the Indochinese to toothbrushes the Hmong were among the first to use them. On ceremonial occasions when Hmong dressed in their finest, one could be assured that elaborate tribal costumes covered bathed skin. Paying hygiene any greater respect than this required considerable effort which, from the Hmong's perspective, did not justify the benefit, especially since they had almost no grasp of the connection between poor hygiene and disease: a fact which may have been partially due to the incredible physical vitality of the average Hmong. Excluding tropical diseases to which centuries of mountain living had made them particularly susceptible, unsanitary conditions that would inevitably lead to sickness and death for most people took less of a toll on the hardy Hmong. Moreover, as we shall see, the Hmong held very definite ideas about the causes of illness and death, and poor hygiene did not figure in. Of equal importance was the simple fact that Hmong villages were always temporary. There was little incentive to invest the time and energy in building better homes or constructing sewage systems when it was understood that whatever was built would invariably be abandoned, often within three years.

Things were different three hundred years ago when the Hmong of Kweichow and Szechwan lived in permanent villages. Then there was an incentive to construct fine houses, at least as far as one's income allowed. The Black Hmong of eastern Kweichow were among the wealthiest Hmong in the region, and their homes reflected it. They were not ramshackle affairs but sturdy wooden structures with sawed timber siding and heavy beam frames fitted to a base that sat on ten-foot-high pilings. In some villages the Hmong constructed kilns in which they fired decorative tiles for their roofs. One entered these houses up a broad staircase and through a veranda that ran along three sides of the dwelling. In the main room stood a large stone fireplace where the cooking was done. It was also where family and friends gathered, seated on benches near the fireplace, to warm themselves and socialize at the end of the day.

In more recent times, Southeast Asian Hmong have occasionally built homes that rival those of the Black Hmong of Kweichow. But this was only in settled villages where housing was meant to be permanent. Bliayao Lo, the leader of the Lo clan in northeastern Laos until his death in 1935, lived in a large two-story stone house. At one time it accommodated over fifty people. Constructed near the turn of the century, it was still in good condition fifty years later. Unlike most of the other Hmong in the area, Bliayao Lo was not a migrant farmer. He was a wealthy rancher with nearly a thousand head of cattle.

Nao Ying Yang, a Hmong from the same region, grew up in an equally impressive home built by his grandfather, and rebuilt by his father in 1954-1955. Like Bliayao Lo, Nao Ying Yang's father was a prosperous rancher. He was also a successful farmer, whose bumper harvests (the result of using the manure from his four hundred head of cattle as fertilizer for his corn fields) justified the construction of a huge storage barn. The two-story Yang home had twenty rooms and was constructed from sawed timber. Eighty feet long and twenty-five feet wide, it was large enough to house over seventy people.

After World War II, when an increasing number of Laotian Hmong either switched from swidden to paddy farming or found employment in the civil service, the establishment of a permanent residence became more common and created an incentive for a number of Hmong to improve their housing. Some even constructed their homes in the Lao fashion, on stilts. And a few of the wealthier Hmong built European-style houses.

FARMING

The Hmong kept livestock near the home but cultivated fields away from the village, at least a half-mile to prevent livestock from grazing on them and no further than a two-hour walk away. When they exhausted all arable land within this radius, villagers abandoned the area and moved to a new site.

Since the Hmong practiced swidden farming, these moves were frequent. Except for the ashes left by burn-off, cleared fields were neither fertilized nor irrigated. This meant that the soil was often depleted within a few years and unusable for another twenty or thirty, for mountain soil does not regenerate quickly. Hmong generosity, coupled with a liberal concept of property rights, created additional pressures on arable land. New groups of Hmong, especially if they belonged to the same clan, were usually welcomed into the community. And since land became property only when used, all unoccupied land was free for the taking.

Generally, when it came time to move, a new village was established no farther than a day's walk away. But, if a number of villages existed in the area and most of the nearby arable land had already been exhausted, there was no other choice than to seek out virgin land on the slopes of another mountain. When this was necessary a few families were sent on ahead with provisions to hold them until

their first crop. If all went well these scouts would report back and the remainder of the village would join them. Unfortunately, the discovery of choice land often attracted other villages to the new site, quickly transforming what would have been productive land for a few into exhausted fields for the many.

Numerous small moves added up. In Thailand, where Hmong migration patterns have been documented, the pace of migration averaged about six miles per year. At that rate, between birth and death an individual might live in twenty different villages and cover several hundred miles, all by foot carrying everything he owned on his back. It was difficult under such circumstances for the Hmong to call any place home or even to develop loyalties to a particular country, especially as some may have been born in China, migrated into Vietnam, and spent their later years in Laos or Thailand. As with their ancestors, the Hmong reserved their loyalties for family, clan, and race.

Though swidden farming condemned the Hmong to a migrant existence, it had its advantages. It did not require altering the existing landscape. Farmers did not need to terrace hills or dig canals and aqueducts. And it required few tools; a Hmong farmer could get by nicely with simple axes, hoes, and planting sticks.

The preparation of fields for planting usually began in February and sometimes continued into April. Old fields were simply cleared of brush and weeded, but new sites required more work. Farmers cleared trees and underbrush, collected the refuse into piles, and left it to dry. By March it was ready for burning.

Planting began after the ashes were spread over the fields for fertilizer. The main crop was corn which, unlike many crops, thrives in the mountains. While a portion of the corn harvest wound up as cornbread, most of it fed livestock, especially pigs. Besides corn, the Hmong planted yams, cucumbers, pumpkins, radishes, beans, ginger, sugar cane, bananas, peaches, eggplant, melons, tobacco, and opium.

Of all these crops, opium required the most labor and made the greatest demands on the soil. While corn grew lush and tall for years, the opium poppy thrived for only a few seasons. Though it accelerated depletion of the soil's nutrients, opium was the only cash crop, and the Hmong had cultivated it for centuries.

OPIUM CULTIVATION

The Hmong have two legends recounting the origin of opium. In one a beautiful Hmong girl with many suitors remained a virgin longer than was customary, and the young men who sought her favors became impatient. One morning while working in her garden she was attacked by one of the suitors and raped. Though she struggled, she was also overwhelmed by pleasure. The joy she experienced in her humiliation drove her mad. She took one lover after another. At first she was discriminating in her taste, but soon she began to seduce any man who happened along, rich or poor, young or old, single or married. Her sexual excesses so destroyed her health that she fell ill and died. Before her death she made a vow to be reborn as a flower whose sap would excite passion as had her caresses and yield pleasures greater than even she had given. And so it happened that an opium poppy grew from her grave. The flower's pod oozed a white sap whose perfume called forth memories in all who inhaled it of the pleasure experienced by all the young woman's lovers. The balm of the sap also induced dreams in which the young woman appeared to reveal the secret of harvesting opium and how to prepare it for smoking.

The second legend simply states that opium came to China from a place called England. Indeed, no word for opium exists in the Hmong language, and they call it by a Chinese name, "ya-ying," which means tobacco from the west. This reflects historical fact, for it was the English who created the opium market in China, expanding yearly trade for the drug in China from a few tons in the mid-eighteenth century to a massive 2,400 tons by the early nineteenth century.

The robust market for imported opium encouraged opium farming inside China. As opium grows best at high altitudes, the Hmong were well placed to cultivate it profitably. They were also experienced opium farmers, having grown it for centuries for medicinal purposes. They knew which kind of soils, determined by color and taste, produced the greatest yield of poppy sap; and they were adept at extracting sap from the opium pods.

In Laos, the Hmong usually planted opium in their corn fields in late summer after the corn had been harvested. By January, the pods of the opium poppies were the size of walnuts and ready for harvesting. This was a labor-intensive chore, requiring a full month of dawn-to-dusk labor by a skilled adult to harvest the sap of just one-half acre of poppies. Only with the help of every able-bodied family member, including children as young as seven, could a farmer hope to harvest a sizable crop, which was the goal of nearly every Hmong farmer once the market for the drug began to grow.

The work was tedious. Starting early in the morning, a worker tapped one poppy pod after another with a triple-blade knife, incising both sides of each pod. By afternoon the milky white sap from the tapping had solidified into a rubbery amber mass and the scraping could begin. Harvesters placed the scraping in containers or wrapped them in leaves. After the sap was collected, workers formed it into balls, which they kneaded and pounded into bricks. The bricks were then wrapped and stored until they could be sold to opium merchants.

Not all of the harvest entered the narcotics market. Hmong farmers held back a small portion for the home. Some of it they processed into powder for oral use to reduce fevers and combat stomach cramps. The remainder was turned into smokable opium to be used as a pain killer for severe injuries or as an analgesic to alleviate the suffering associated with the chronic diseases of old age. Creating smokable opium was a simple process. A farmer boiled raw opium in a pot, the ratio of the water being about ten to one, then filtered the mixture and reboiled it several more times until it was reduced to a hard mass. This he broke into small chunks which could later be transformed by a flame into a soft fuming gob, inserted into a pipe and smoked.

In Laos, as in China, opium merchants were mostly Chinese who either lived in or near a Hmong village or were itinerant merchants who made the rounds of Hmong villages after the opium harvest. Since the yearly harvest for a single farmer seldom yielded more than a few pounds of raw opium, a small caravan could easily transport an entire village's output, or even that of several villages, to market. It was customary for opium merchants to pay in advance (almost always in silver, either in ingots or French piasters) for future harvests. The advance payment was crucial to persuade Hmong farmers to neglect their traditional subsistence crops for the labor-intensive cultivation of the opium poppy. While this made the Hmong dependent on local markets for the provision of many necessities, it raised their overall standard of living.

While the Hmong considered the economic benefits from growing opium to far outweigh the evils of drug addiction for their own people, they nevertheless acknowledged it to be a serious problem. Even if they did not view addiction as a sin, they considered it a debilitating vice and a sign of weak will, especially in a young person. If recent surveys can be considered representative of long term trends, Hmong addiction rates have been lower than average in China and southeast Asia and atypically concentrated among the elderly, principally victims of chronic pain who became addicted after prolonged use of the drug to combat the suffering associated with rheumatism, tuberculosis, or cancer. While this was tolerated as perhaps a necessary evil, young healthy adults who became addicted were often treated as social pariahs. Invariably they were poor family providers and, if they were bachelors, had great difficulty finding a bride.

Despite their condemnation of opium addiction within their own communities, it is unlikely Hmong farmers suffered pangs of conscience for supporting the habits of legions of non-Hmong addicts, especially since, by the mid-1800s, the opium market was either legalized or directly managed by Asian governments. Indeed, in the late 1800s local Chinese authorities in Kweichow province forced the Hmong to pay taxes in raw opium. Sanctioned by law and sustained by strong markets, Hmong opium farmers had no more difficulty justifying their crops than Kentucky farmers today who, with the sanction (and subsidies) of government, grow tobacco that sustains the nicotine addiction of millions of Americans.

For some time the opium market in southeast Asia lagged behind the ever expanding narcotics market in China. This began to change in the early nineteenth century when famines plagued China. The coastal provinces of Kwangtung and Fukien were hit particularly hard; for the rest of the century peasants from these provinces left the country in large numbers. Some immigrated to America and Mexico where labor for huge railroad construction projects was in short supply. But most emigrated to southeast Asia where the British and French were expanding their empires and needed cheap labor to erect dams, complete irrigation projects, and build railways.

Large numbers of these immigrants were opium addicts who formed the nucleus of a new and vigorous opium market evidenced by a precipitous rise in opium imports to the region. The development was not unopposed. In Thailand three kings in succession fought the growth of drug trafficking. The undertaking was doomed from the start. Harsh penalties, including execution, were enacted, but they affected only the native population and resident Chinese. The British who brought the opium into the country were beyond the reach of the law. Conceding defeat and eager to increase sagging government revenues, King Mongut legalized the trade and granted the Thai opium franchise to wealthy Chinese in the late 1850s. Eventually the Thai government stepped in to assume full responsibility for retail sales while the British continued to manage imports.

The French moved nearly as fast as the English to spread opium addiction in southeast Asia. As soon as the French gained control of an area they integrated their official opium monopoly into the colonial administration, which meant the trafficking was not just tolerated but organized and backed by the prestige and power of the French government.

From its inception the rapid expansion of opium trafficking alarmed Vietnamese emperors. They objected to it on both moral and economic grounds, although the economic side of the question was the most pressing due to the constant drain of silver into the vaults of the French opium monopoly, reducing the supply of Vietnamese silver and inflating its value. However, efforts to restrict illicit opium trafficking were abandoned in the late 1850s after the French launched a successful military invasion, first against Hue and then against Saigon. In order to acquire the necessary revenue to pay for the large indemnity demanded by the French as punishment for Vietnamese resistance, the Vietnamese emperor reluctantly endorsed an opium franchise in the Tonkin region.

The French colonial administration not only managed the import of Indian and, later, Chinese opium, it established official retail outlets for the drug as well as government-run opium dens which, by 1918, numbered in the thousands. Managers of the state-run opium refinery, erected in Saigon near the turn of the century, spent years perfecting a fast-burning smoking opium with an eye to increasing demand, an aim that was also served by the importation of large amounts of Yunnanese opium. Far less expensive than the Indian variety, Yunnanese opium made addiction possible for even the impoverished lower classes of Indochina.

Colonial revenues from the southeast Asian opium trade were enormous, at one point amounting to forty percent of all revenues.

Even in bad times opium revenues seldom dropped below twenty percent. Indeed it was opium that placed the French experiment in imperialism in Indochina on a profitable footing from the start, and provided justification for more intensive colonization of southeast Asia. From their foothold around Saigon the French moved north and west, eventually conquering all of Vietnam, Cambodia and Laos. While a good deal of the necessary infrastructure was financed out of opium revenues, the pace was so rapid and so poorly managed that deficits began to mount. One response to the deficits was to expand the opium trade.

In 1878 public opinion forced the British parliament to pass the Opium Act which severely restricted England's participation in the opium trade and limited British sales of opium to registered Chinese and Indian addicts. In British Burma, where addiction had spread beyond the Chinese minority to the native population, trafficking among the Burmese was also strictly prohibited. Britain's 1908 agreement with China to phase out the importation of Indian opium was followed by a second agreement in 1911 which aimed at speeding up the process. By 1915 most Chinese provinces were barred to all foreign opium and England's complicity in international drug trafficking was at last drawing to a close.

This did not appreciably alter the supply of narcotics, since other nations quickly moved in to take up the slack. This included not only France but many former British colonies such as Burma, Pakistan, Iran, Afghanistan, and Thailand. Within a few decades, however, France achieved the dubious distinction of having successfully replaced England as the world's foremost trafficker in opiates.

Just prior to the outbreak of the Second World War, France imported nearly sixty tons of opium annually from Turkey and Iran to supply the more than one hundred thousand addicts who formed the nucleus of the Indochinese opium market. The war severed this supply line. With the Japanese occupation of Indochina, all shipping to the region was interdicted by the British navy. The French turned to domestic opium production to replace lost imports. By the late 1960s, Hmong farmers in Laos supplied the raw opium for nearly seventy percent of the world narcotics market in heroin, morphine, and smoking opium.

While the Hmong of Laos and northern Vietnam had been selling their raw opium to the French for decades, they did not produce enough to meet the needs of the opium monopoly. To increase Hmong production, the French raised the official purchasing price for raw opium and placed Hmong notables on the Opium Board to guarantee delivery of all available opium harvested by Hmong farmers.

Hmong opium production skyrocketed and continued to increase even after 1946 when, in response to international public opinion, the French dismantled their opium monopoly. The monopoly was gone, but not the French-sponsored opium traffic which went underground. Until the mid-1950s, the French continued to encourage Hmong opium production to raise revenue to support their war against the Vietnamese communists. Even after the French departed Indochina, the traffic in opium continued to grow with much of the raw opium that supported it coming from the Hmong. French narcotic syndicates allied with Vietnamese gangsters and corrupt South Vietnamese officials used Hmong opium to supply not only the southeast Asian narcotics market but the growing market in Europe and the u.s.

NOT ALWAYS MIGRANTS

Though slash-and-burn agriculture required a migratory lifestyle, the Hmong saw this not as a problem but as a part of their heritage. Their mobility contributed to their sense of freedom. If their non-Hmong neighbors mistreated them, or if a government abused them, they could always vote with their feet. Not being tied to the land, they could refuse assimilation into the dominant culture of their host country. It was their trump card, and for centuries it had served them well.

This is not to say that the Hmong preferred the migratory lifestyle they had evolved during centuries of oppression. Given the opportunity, the Hmong of Southeast Asia might very well have developed a way of life similar to that enjoyed by their Kweichow brethren during times of peace.

Denied access to the rich soil of the Chinese lowlands, many Kweichow Hmong abandoned swidden farming and transformed the steep slopes of their mountains into terraced fields buttressed by stone retaining walls, some as high as twenty feet. They built bamboo aqueducts to divert mountain streams to irrigate their crops. In eastern Kweichow, Hmong raised fish in rice fields and bred them in special ponds on the outskirts of villages. They sold the carp, tench, and perch raised in these ponds to neighboring villages.

A thriving timber industry, also in eastern Kweichow, owed part of its success to the Hmong commitment to conservation. After an area had been clear-cut, they planted new trees to replenish the forest. Consequently, pine, cedar, and oak, as well as Chu trees used by the Chinese to make paper grew in abundance. The Ming dynasty constructed its imperial buildings from Hmong timber. The Kweichow Hmong also marketed Japanese pine for making the best coffins.

Famous for felling trees on steep slopes and maneuvering them down the mountainsides, Hmong lumberjacks ferried the logs downstream to Chinese dealers. These dealers linked the logs into huge rafts and floated them to sawmills across the border in Hunan.

Hmong boatmen sailed up and down these same rivers, which were often the only efficient means of transporting goods. Known as the Dragon Boat Hmong, they were famous for their ability to navigate dangerous rapids, which increased in number and severity the further one traveled upstream. Moving downstream, they ferried loads of wood oil, hides, and timber as far east as the Hunan lake region. To celebrate their skills, every year in May they staged boat races in slim dugouts, each with a finely carved dragon's head rising above the bow.

Then as now, Kweichow was rich in silver, and the Hmong in the province were accomplished silversmiths, a skill they have preserved. It is seldom that a Hmong village of any size in Vietnam, Laos, Thailand, or Burma does not possess at least one accomplished silversmith who can be counted on to fashion the silver jewelry Hmong wear during festivals, especially a bride on her wedding day.

The Hmong of Indochina have seldom enjoyed such a stable relationship with the land, but swidden farming did have its benefits. After the clearing and planting was completed, they enjoyed nearly a month of uninterrupted leisure away from the fields. While some of this time had to be devoted to much needed repairs on the family home, horse and cattle stables, and pig sties, most of it was set aside for hunting.

HUNTING

Superb marksmen with either crossbow or flintlock, the Hmong considered nearly everything from mice to elephants fair game, though the most prized quarry were deer, elephant, wild pig, and rhinoceros. Because of their passion for hunting, all game close to the village quickly disappeared and with it the sounds one normally associates with the forest. Nights in an established village were therefore uncommonly quiet.

In the mid-1930s the German anthropologist Hugo Bernatzik lived several years with the Hmong of Thailand. An avid hunter, he was very much impressed by Hmong daring and skill during the hunt, especially as their only weapons were crossbows and flintlocks, primitive weapons when compared to Bernatzik's high powered European hunting rifle.

Though the Hmong used poison on their arrows, it was not the deadly toxin of old China. Extracted from the sap of certain trees and then boiled into a rubbery mass, the poison was slow acting and took considerable time to disable or kill a large animal. Like the crossbow, the flintlock was a short-range weapon, and though a well placed shot might kill a large animal, more often than not it simply wounded, which meant that the Hmong could usually count on being attacked by their prey. For this reason they seldom ventured forth alone on these hunts. If one Hmong was charged, another leaped in to distract the attacker. Often it was necessary for everyone involved to run for cover, a fact driven home to Bernatzik after he examined the four-inch deep holes punched into a tree trunk by a wounded gaur (a larger and more ferocious cousin of the American bison) trying to get at several Hmong huddled behind the tree for protection.

Despite their crude weapons and the dangers they faced, the Hmong were highly successful hunters, even with the elephants and rhinoceros that roamed the mountain forests. Bernatzik met one Hmong who had in his lifetime killed two rhinoceros and over twenty elephants. In the case of the elephants, the shots were fired from only a few yards away, a feat that was due not only to the hunter's stealth but to his cleverness in nullifying the elephant's keen sense of smell by smearing elephant dung over his body.

Between planting and harvest the main occupation was caring for livestock, weeding the crops, and collecting animals caught in traps set around the fenceless fields. These catches not only augmented the Hmong diet, they greatly reduced crop damage caused by wild birds, pigs, rodents, and deer.

LIVESTOCK

The Hmong raised pigs and chickens, oxen and horses, though few families could afford to own an ox and even fewer a horse. Oxen served a dual purpose. They were used as draft animals and were sacrificed at funerals. Horses, on the other hand, were used only for hauling and the transport of goods.

Though highly valued, they were not the same quality of animal as the famed Hmong horses of seventeenth-century China, which were considered by the Chinese to be the best in the empire. These legendary mounts could scale mountains like goats and descend them at a dead run. They were also great jumpers and were often jumped over wide ditches for sport and, if we are to believe Chinese accounts, for the selection of officers in the Hmong cavalry. This test consisted of galloping one's mount up the side of a mountain and then dashing down to the bottom where a large ditch filled with blazing logs awaited them. It was here the truly superior mounts were separated from the rest, for only they did not break stride before leaping through the flames to the other side. These horses were seldom sold, but when a sale was made it was at an astronomical price, and the buyer was usually a Chinese official who needed an extraordinary gift to ingratiate himself with his superiors.

Though pigs and chickens were the principal source of protein in the Hmong diet, they were not raised primarily with an eye to nutritional needs. Their main purpose was sacrificial. As a matter of simple economics, this was not an efficient use of livestock. At any one time special ceremonial or sacrificial needs might wipe out the entire breeding stock of pigs or chickens. While all might eat well on such occasions, there would be little if any meat added to the diet for several months afterward. But shamanist beliefs played a pivotal role in Hmong culture. Pigs or chickens, or both, were sacrificed to appease ancestors, to aid the dead at funerals, to aid shamans in curing illnesses, and to celebrate births, weddings, and the New Year festival.

CHAPTER 6

The Spirit World

*I*N HMONG COSMOGRAPHY, the creator and ruler of the world is Hua Tai (*Hua Tais Ntuj*). Unlike the Christian God, Hua Tai has little interest in the affairs of man. Indeed they bore him. He lost interest in mankind, in all their bickering and feckless ways, almost as soon as he created them. One of his lieutenants, though, had compassion for man. He is Yer Shau (*Yawm Saub*). As the Hmong portray him, Yer Shau is not only God's personal representative to mankind, he is also half man, half God. He is godlike in the sense that he sees and knows all, but he is like a man in that he has material substance and lives in a house. And as a man he is more like the Hmong than any other race of men. He tends a garden and raises pigs. He is an earthy fellow who likes to eat and drink and have long discussions with friends. Also like the Hmong, he is polygamous.

It was Yer Shau, and not Hua Tai, who saved mankind from the great flood. It was also Yer Shau who saved mankind from Ndu Nyong (*Ntxwj Nyoog*), the god of sickness and death. Appropriately called "The Savage One," Ndu Nyong is the king of the demons who harass the Hmong and bring them misfortune, sickness, and death. He lives in a fortress at the top of a mountain chain where he spends his time devouring living things. His greatest pleasure is to consume thousands of Hmong at a setting, tearing at their flesh and drinking their blood like some wild beast.

Actually, what he devours is one of their souls. The Hmong believe an individual has more than one soul. Some claim the number to be three, others seven or more; disagreement over the exact number does not cause much consternation, for the Hmong are not bothered much by fine points of theology. One of these souls, envisaged in the form of a pig or ox, resides in Ndu Nyong's huge corral where he keeps his livestock, which includes just about anything he can lay his hands on. If Ndu Nyong happens to consume one of these souls, the physical individual also dies. Conversely, when the physical individual dies it is presumed that Ndu Nyong has consumed this corralled soul, which is why an ox is sacrificed at a Hmong funeral ceremony: the soul of the ox will take the place of the consumed soul, and the other souls of the deceased can live on through reincarnation—the implication being that should no new soul take its place, all the souls that constitute the perdurable essence of an individual would cease to exist. The imagery is instructive. Ndu Nyong holds every Hmong hostage. He can bring death at any moment.

Ndu Nyong is assisted in his war against mankind by a host of evil spirits (*dab*), who cause pain, sickness, and death. Long ago these spirits were not much of a threat to mankind. They were not invisible then as they are today, and they were extremely vulnerable. Having no skin, their vital organs were easily pierced by a spear or could even be plucked out by hand. This fatal weakness was exploited by men who killed the spirits for sport until they were near extinction. Heaven interceded, camouflaging the spirits with a magic dust that made them invisible. Now it was the spirits' turn to harass their former tormentors by causing them misfortune, illness, and death. Fortunately, humans are not completely without protection, for Yer Shau has provided them with shamans who have the power to combat Ndu Nyong and his demons in his own domain.

THE FIRST SHAMAN

Shamanism was first practiced by Siberian tribesmen and later spread south to China, southwest to central Asia, and east across the Bering straits to North America. The Hmong probably became shamanist during their sojourn in Siberia and continued to practice the religion when they migrated to China where shamanism was adopted by many other tribal groups and incorporated in the state religion by the early dynasties.

Such facts do not figure in the Hmong account of shamanism. According to Hmong legend, in the distant past mankind prospered and multiplied. This pleased Yer Shau, but when Ndu Nyong surveyed the scene it whetted his appetite. Without Yer Shau's approval or knowledge, he descended to earth and began devouring mankind. When Yer Shau realized what was happening, he sent two servants to earth to kill Ndu Nyong. But Ndu Nyong was able to elude them since he could fly and they could not. The two returned to Yer Shau to tell him of their failure. He ordered them back to earth, while he pondered the matter. In the meantime the two servants had a child. His name was Shee Yee (*Tsiv Yis*), the first shaman, also known as *Ndzo Ying*, "the inspired one." When his parents were called back to heaven, they did not take Shee Yee along. Abandoned and alone, he turned to the Hmong for help. Ironically, the future guardian of Hmong health and welfare was rejected by them when he begged to be taken in. The excuse for this atypical hardheartedness was that the child was as fat as a Chinese mandarin. Rejected by the Hmong, Shee Yee had no other choice than to appeal to the Chinese for aid, which he received from a Chinese Lord who put him to work in his stables.

When Shee Yee reached manhood, he spent his leisure walking the countryside around the Chinese Lord's palace. On one such walk he discovered a nest of large, leathery, white eggs. They were not like any eggs he had ever seen before. To his surprise, when he broke them open he found they were empty. Stranger still, when he returned to the same spot the next day, the eggs had miraculously become whole. Again he broke them open, and again they were empty. But this time, instead of leaving, Shee Yee remained out of sight and waited to see what sort of magic was being used to make the eggs whole. Shortly after dusk his patience was rewarded. An enormous shadow passed over him in the pale moonlight. When he looked up he saw a dragon swoop overhead and land near the eggs. After inspecting the damage, the dragon searched the ground, tearing up bushes and kicking up stones until it found what it was after. Shee Yee watched as the dragon uprooted a plant, separated the tubers from the stalk, crushed them in its talons and placed the pulpy mass in a bowl of water. The dragon slithered over to the eggs, raised the bowl to its mouth, and blew over it, spraying the water on the eggs. Immediately the eggs were made whole.

It was then that Shee Yee realized the significance of the event. Yer Shau had sent the dragon to earth so that he, Shee Yee, would find and break its eggs and discover the secret to curing the ill and bringing the dead back to life. When the dragon flew away Shee Yee emerged from his hiding place and hurried to gather as much of the magic herbs as he could carry before setting out to heal mankind of its illnesses and bring the dead back to life.

Shee Yee had good reason to make haste, for Ndu Nyong was now devouring so many humans that mankind was on the point of extinction. Indeed, when "The Savage One" divined what Shee Yee was up to, he flew into a rage and, unable at the moment to lay his hands on the shaman, attacked and killed the Chinese Lord's horses, which numbered in the thousands. Perhaps this was also meant to sidetrack Shee Yee because when the shaman's former employer begged him to restore the animals to life, he did not have the heart to refuse.

To make up for this delay, and to improve Shee Yee's chances in his battle with Ndu Nyong, Yer Shau gave him the power of flight or, more accurately, the next best thing: a winged horse, a Hmong Pegasus, to serve as his mount and to speed him on his way to raising the souls of the dead.

Before he left on this mission, the Chinese Lord insisted that Shee Yee be rewarded for reviving the slain horses. He was given two companies of Chinese soldiers to serve as his helpers in the great battle ahead. The carnage was horrible to behold. In an attempt to outstrip Shee Yee's healing efforts, Ndu Nyong slaughtered more humans than ever before. Yet Shee Yee was able to match him, soul for soul. It soon became clear to Ndu Nyong that he could never win the contest. He conceded defeat and pledged he would remain with Shee Yee as his servant.

This was not Ndu Nyong's real intention, however. He was only biding time until he could figure out a way to destroy Shee Yee, a task that became all the more pressing with the birth of Shee Yee's

first son. If the child reached adulthood, there would be no stopping the two. While Shee Yee was away healing the ill, Ndu Nyong murdered the infant, butchered him and used the pieces to prepare a meal which he served to Shee Yee on his return. The first shaman unwittingly consumed his own child. Grief-stricken after realizing what he had done, Shee Yee intended to kill Ndu Nyong but was stopped by Yer Shau who ordered him to simply maim "the Savage One" so that he would at last experience some of the pain he had caused so many humans. Shee Yee used his shaman tools to pierce Ndu Nyong's eyes and cast him out of his house to wander among mankind as a beggar.

Though blind, Ndu Nyong was nevertheless able to find his way back to his fortress in the sky. Less powerful than before, but still full of hatred for mankind, he gathered his evil spirits about him and renewed his campaign to cause pain, sickness, and death. There was still much work for Shee Yee to do. But because he had eaten his own son, the strength of his resolve to heal mankind was considerably weakened. He soon departed earth to live in heaven for eternity but promised to return in a year with his shaman's tools as a gift to mankind so that they could heal themselves. When he did return, no one was there to greet him. Furious, Shee Yee threw the tools to the ground and declared that the sacred healing instruments would never again have the full power, and would work only one out of ten times.

Still, the tools were of some use. One out of ten is better than nothing. Of course, other shamans who followed in Shee Yee's footsteps would have to enter the spirit world to make good use of them. For this they needed the neng spirits (*dab neeb*) as guides. These are the same spirits Shee Yee used in his fight with Ndu Nyong. It is to the shaman and his neng helpers that the Hmong turn when seeking protection from Ndu Nyong and his legions of malevolent spirits.

Though the Hmong believed wandering souls to be the cause of many illnesses, they also acknowledged the existence of organic disease which is best treated with physical rather than spiritual remedies. They were, and remain, pragmatists, and in many cases if someone could demonstrate the physical means to effect a cure for some disease, the Hmong employed it. Still, it was no easy thing for the Hmong to distinguish between a malady with a spiritual origin and an illness with a clear organic cause. To a westerner, if an arm is broken, a splint rather than a shaman is called for. To a Hmong this would be a careless diagnosis. For even a broken arm might be traced to a spiritual cause. How was the arm broken? Was it really an accident or was a spirit angered and seeking revenge by causing the fall that led to the broken arm? If a spirit was angered, the broken arm may not be the end of things. Other evils may befall the victim and therefore a simple splint will not be enough to really heal the patient. That the Hmong were prone to ask such questions indicates the extent to which they were willing, even when the problem appeared on the surface to be completely organic in nature, to contemplate problems in the spirit world as sources of human difficulties in the physical world.

While the head of a Hmong household was familiar with rites and ceremonies useful in dealing with or placating the spirits, only the shaman had the ability to leave his body, enter the spirit world, and deal directly with the spirits, demons, and genies. This was not an acquired skill but a gift from heaven. To receive the gift was also to accept a calling to heal the sick and prevent evil.

THE SHAMAN'S CALLING

The manner in which a Hmong received this calling was every bit as dramatic as that experienced by a Protestant Christian. There was the recognition that one had been specially selected to serve and there was also a sense of rebirth. The selection was made by the neng spirits. Sometimes they appeared in a dream and conveyed their selection to the dreamer, but most often they signaled this selection by making an individual seriously ill. Often when an illness did not respond to treatment, the affliction was thought to be the result of a visitation by neng spirits. If a shaman deemed this to be the case, he would perform a brief ceremony to invite the neng to stay with the individual, confirming the calling. If the diagnosis of the illness was correct, the individual usually fell into a deep trance and then completely recovered.

During this trance the individual might experience his soul leaving his body and entering the spirit world. As one shaman described the event, he was dead for seven days during which time his spirit traveled on a long journey to the palace of Shee Yee. During the journey he crossed a field of fire and jumped over a giant caterpillar and finally came to a door with slashing blades that cut the unworthy but allowed the just to pass through unscathed. Shee Yee himself wrote on his chest and back and placed the Book of Knowledge, the book containing the secrets of the shaman's healing art, on his chest. Then one of Shee Yee's helpers gave him the shaman's bell, rattle, and drum to use when he entered the spirit world again.

To receive the shaman's calling required dedicating one's life to healing the sick. It also meant that one possessed the unique ability to enter the spirit world and retrieve wandering souls. This included souls that had just left a body and remained nearby, perhaps outside the home or beside a trail, as well as souls that had left the world of man and entered the world of spirits, sometimes traveling as far as

Ndu Nyong's fortress. Only the shaman could pursue such a soul and bring it back.

It is also this ability that imparted special significance to the shaman as a representative of the Hmong to heaven. According to Hmong legend, man and God once communicated freely, but now only the shaman retains the power, if not to speak directly to God, to communicate with Shee Yee and, through him, Yer Shau who cares about mankind. It is this aspect of Hmong shamanism that has helped to sustain the Messiah myth, the belief that Yer Shau will one day send the Hmong a king who will rule over an independent Hmong nation. If the shaman could not communicate with the spirit world, the Hmong would have no way to appeal to heaven to send them their king, or to know of his impending arrival.

Despite the shaman's unique abilities, there were many things of a spiritual nature the Hmong felt competent to handle without a shaman's aid. Divination, or predicting the future, was one of them. The tools employed were simple: halved buffalo horns or the parts of sacrificed animals.

If the eldest son of the house planned to travel to a nearby village, the head of the household might throw two halves of a buffalo horn on the floor. Was the flat side of each up or down, or was one up and one down? If the configuration was wrong, he delayed the trip and tried the horns again until they came up right. Many adults in a Hmong village knew such divination techniques, as well as many others involving the examination of the tongues, feet, or bones of sacrificed animals (usually chickens), and so long as they proved effective to the purpose at hand there would be no need to consult a shaman.

Even if the trouble were a wandering soul, a shaman might not be needed. Souls could wander for various reasons. Evil spirits could entice them out of the body. Fear or unhappiness could cause them to leave. Whatever the reason, a wandering soul was considered a serious matter because if it did not return, the body would die.

However, if a soul had not wandered far, or if it left the body at a particular place due to fright, a shaman would not necessarily be required to retrieve it. Often when a child fell suddenly ill, the head of the household searched for an insect on the ground where the youngster had been recently frightened. If he found the insect, presumed to be harboring the frightened soul, he carried it home for a simple ceremony to return the soul to the child's body. Or he might place a chicken outside the house to scratch the ground in search of the lost soul which, when found, was tucked up under one of its wings. The chicken was then sacrificed, and the soul and the child reunited. Sometimes the head of the household built a bridge to help a wandering soul find its way home. He placed it over a stream or at a fork in the road where the soul might have lost its way.

On the other hand, family members always consulted a shaman when they believed that a soul had left the physical world and entered the realm of the spirits, which was invariably the presumption when an illness did not respond to conventional home remedies.

JOURNEY INTO THE SPIRIT WORLD

A shaman did not accept just any case. First he consulted the neng spirits, employing offerings of food to attract them and using divining tools to ascertain their intentions, not only regarding the cause of the illness and its seriousness, but also to determine if the neng spirits would be able, or willing, to help effect a cure. Often an improvement in the patient's condition signaled that the neng were favorable.

The ceremony to retrieve a soul was physically demanding and was often quite long, sometimes lasting several hours. First the shaman called the helper spirits to assemble for the hunt. When he was confident they had all arrived, the shaman straddled a bench and placed a black veil over his face. Shortly after this his body began to tremble and then he fell into a trance, a sign that he had entered the spirit world. Since the shaman engaged in considerable gymnastics, assistants stood close by, ready to support him if he lost his balance and fell.

After a few moments the shaman began to bounce on the bench as though riding a horse. And so he was. For he had called on the great winged horse of Shee Yee to carry him on his search. The journey was a dangerous one. He crossed a wide sea, the home of innumerable dragons with the ability to mesmerize passersby with their eyes, transfixing their victims before they leaped up and dragged them down into the depths. If a dragon had captured a wandering soul, the shaman descended into the water and rescued it, an act that might be signaled by one of the shaman's assistants placing a rock on his lap to help weigh him down and make the descent easier.

Once he crossed the sea, the shaman began the search for the lost soul in the forests and fields of the underworld. Like the Hmong's own mountains, the terrain was crisscrossed with thousands of footpaths used by wandering souls seeking the lair of Ndu Nyong. The abundance of trails made it easy for a wandering soul to take a wrong turn and lose its way. Some souls became frightened when lost and were eager to return to the world of man but could not find their way back. Other lost souls, steadfast in their resolve to remain in the spirit world but unable to find the way to Ndu Nyong, hid in a hole or under a rock to elude the shaman. Though the Hmong believed few wandering souls ever reached Ndu Nyong, the shaman nevertheless had to expect the worst. He covered as much ground as possible in the shortest time, overlooking nothing in case a soul had gone to ground to hide. Yet he never tarried long in one place, fearing that he might never catch up with a soul that had found the true path to Ndu Nyong's lair. And this is why he had spirit helpers, summoned at the beginning of the ceremony.

Numbered among these were, of course, his neng. There were also the two companies of soldiers which the Chinese Lord placed under Shee Yee's command and which Shee Yee made available to all shamans. Thousands of other beneficent spirits joined in whenever the cause was just. Some of the shaman's helpers beat the bushes to flush the lost soul; others scared away evil genies intent on interfering with the hunt. Helper spirits examined every hole and turned over every rock in search of the wandering soul. The pursuit continued, if necessary, to the very door of Ndu Nyong's fortress.

During the search the shaman, still supported by his assistants, might leap to the top of the bench and jump about. Witnesses to the ceremony could only guess at the meaning of these gyrations, and the dangers the shaman faced on his journey into the spirit world. Perhaps he was fighting off dragons or evil spirits, perhaps he was urging his winged horse to attempt giant leaps over mountains. For those with vivid imaginations, the gyrations of the veiled shaman suggested a frightening drama of good against evil, of armies locked in mortal combat, the fate of a soul hanging in the balance.

When he found the lost soul, the shaman was always careful not to frighten it. The object, after all, was to bring it back home and keep it there. He gently coaxed it out of its hiding place, assuring it that all would be well, that loved ones longed for its return. Just as gently, he led it back home. It was then that the shaman, as well as the lost soul, crossed over into the world of man. And it was only then that the shaman emerged from his trance, often exhausted from his efforts.

On rare occasions a lost soul would find Ndu Nyong and be granted reincarnation. At such times the patient faced certain death unless the shaman acted quickly. While still in a trance, the shaman urged his mount onward to search every village for the pregnant woman whose fetus had been granted to the lost soul by Ndu Nyong. When the woman was located, the shaman led the soul away and brought it home, allowing another soul to be reincarnated in its place.

Most often the shaman sacrificed a pig by slitting its throat before the healing ceremony began. The patient (if well enough to eat), the immediate family, and close relatives consumed the bulk of the sacrificed animal after the ceremony. The shaman received no more than the head as payment. Shamanism was a vocation not a profession. Even the most successful shaman, his success evidenced by the many jawbones hanging in his house, had to farm like any other Hmong to support his own family.

If the sacrifice of an entire pig was a considerable expense for most Hmong families, a family plagued with illness or a death (which required the sacrifice of an ox) might in a short time find its livestock reduced to a few animals. Even a family enjoying good health was expected to perform ritual sacrifices to ancestors or to appease various important spirits, such as the central post spirit and the door spirit. Such sacrifices were thought essential to safeguard the continued health of the family or to improve it if it was bad.

Considered simply as a health care system and not a religion, Hmong shamanism could be characterized as economically inefficient, as would any health care system that commanded the lion's share of a society's resources. Those least able to afford this sort of medical care paid the most in proportion to their total wealth. In many cases the consequence was to make wealthier families less wealthy for a time, but poor families poverty stricken perhaps forever. For a wealthy family with many pigs and oxen, heavy sacrifices depleted their stock but did not reduce it below the level required to build it up again. In contrast, a poor family left with one pig would never have more without purchasing or trading for additional pigs.

It is not entirely fair to blame all this on the Hmong religion. As already indicated, the Hmong are very pragmatic and trust results more than ideas. If less expensive medical care had been available, it is likely they would have used it. In recent years, Hmong have been quick to use modern medicine when accessible, though they return to the shaman if modern techniques fail. Nor should one forget that so many sacrifices were made because so much could go wrong. In a world of danger and uncertainty, it was foolhardy to trust things to fate. In a safer world the need to sacrifice would be less. I once asked an elderly Hmong émigré to the u.s. why the traditional altar was absent from his apartment. His answer was simple. In America there were no tigers, snakes, or enemy soldiers.

RITES OF PASSAGE

Birth, marriage, and death are major events in the life of the Hmong, as they are in all societies. For the Hmong they are also rites of passage. A birth signifies the reincarnation of a soul in a new body.

In marriage a Hmong assumes the full responsibilities of adulthood. And in death the individual's soul leaves this world to join the world of his or her ancestors to wait until it is time to be reborn.

Birth

Many Hmong believed that when a man died he would be reborn as a woman, and when a woman died she would be reborn as a man. It was a belief in cosmic justice, for the lot of the Hmong woman was always a hard one. The independent spirit of most Hmong women was also a factor, for it was not very difficult to imagine they had once been men. Whatever its sex, the birth of a child was a great event. In one sense it was a reunion, a reincarnated soul reentering the world of man. It also meant a family had a new member, and for the Hmong the family was nearly everything. Children in particular were cherished and enjoyed.

Like all peasant farmers, the Hmong recognized the economic benefit of children. An additional child eventually became an additional worker in the field. This was of special economic importance during the labor-intensive opium harvest. A child of seven could contribute much, and one of nine or ten could match the output of a woman carrying an infant. A large number of children also meant there would be someone to take care of you when you were too old to work.

But above all, children were a living testimony to the importance the Hmong have always placed on the family, clan, and race. It is these ties, extended through the generations, both living and dead, that gave life meaning for the Hmong and kept them going in the hardest times. The birth ceremonies reflected this.

Three days had to pass after the birth of an infant before it could officially become part of the human community. It was then that a soul was invited to join with the infant. If an infant died before the third day, no funeral rites were held on the assumption that since the infant had no soul, it was not a human being.

If available, a shaman presided over the ceremony during which sacrifices were made to invite a soul to become reincarnated in the infant's body. This was sometimes followed by the throwing of divination horns, or an examination of the tongue of a sacrificed chicken, to determine whether evil spirits were present. If this turned out to be the case, additional sacrifices might be made to placate them. The family asked its ancestors to unite with them to bless the event and offer the infant their protection. They gave the infant a silver necklace to prevent its new soul from wandering, because souls like pretty things. This belief prompted adults, for reasons other than vanity or ceremonial occasion, to wear jewelry.

Hmong children lived constantly in the presence of adults and did not lack supervision or moral education. Their socialization to Hmong culture began almost immediately. They absorbed the morality of their group much earlier than a child in Europe or America who, in comparison with the Hmong child, remains relatively isolated from the real world of adults until late puberty.

As soon as they were able, Hmong children joined in the work of the house and field. Older children were given the responsibility of watching out after the younger ones. At an early age girls became skilled in cooking and sewing, and boys learned how to hunt and trap. When there was free time, they played. Much of the time this consisted in imitations of adult activity, but they also made toys, modeled in clay, enjoyed games of hide-and-seek, or simply frolicked with the family dog.

Marriage

Hmong boys as young as fourteen participated in courting. For girls it began when they reached sixteen. Both boys and girls entered courtship with an adequate knowledge of the fundamentals of sex, for while Hmong parents might tell young children fairy tales when asked about sex, they gave straightforward answers to the older children.

The ultimate object of courting was marriage, and the strong incest taboo that operated in Hmong society dictated that courting occur only between members of different clans. If the families in a village all belonged to the same clan, a Hmong lad traveled to do his courting in another village where there were families from different clans. For this reason most Hmong preferred to live in large villages where several clans were represented. Courting had to be discreet. It was bad manners to court a girl in her own home. Her parents considered it a grave insult. However, a suitor could speak to his beloved on the road or in the field, and, if she agreed, arrange a meeting in the night. Often young men would gather outside a young woman's house and discretely coax her to come out and join one of them for a night of love.

Love songs abounded during courting. As one would expect, some were erotic, but many spoke of unrequited love. And some, like the following love song (sung by a girl), even addressed social issues, such as the inequality between the sexes:

> *My beloved, you have nursed at your mother's breast and also shared your father's bed, your face is as radiant as a blossom, as bright as the paper flowers sold by the Chinese.*
>
> *As for me, I have also sucked at my mother's breast, though I have not shared my father's bed; and my face is tired and creased as the soul of the feet of a Chinese grandfather.*
>
> *You have been able to lick your mother's spoon and to leave at will to go on long trips, you are the child who cares for the spirit of the center post.*
>
> *As for me, if I have eaten with my mother and sometimes leave on long trips, I am not able, as you, to protect the house. For that I am unhappy.*

Most courting occurred in late December during the New Year festival. It was a time of general merriment and leisure. Even more important for courting, it was a time when young people from different clans were brought together in large numbers. Eligible girls and bachelors dressed up in their best clothes. For the girls this might have included fine Hmong jewelry and delicately embroidered blouses and dresses.

Hmong women have long been famous for their fine embroidery which consists of detailed, symmetrical patterns produced by intricate cross-stitching and appliqué techniques. The traditional patterns of this ancient craft, which the Hmong call *pandau* (pronounced "pawn dew"), are created by combining five basic shapes: an eight point star, a snail shell, the outline of a ram's head, an elephant's footprint, and a heart. Because of the high quality of Hmong needlework, it fetched a handsome price in Chinese markets and was often given as tribute to the Peking Court. Hmong embroidery was thought so beautiful that representations of it found their way into Chinese art albums.

To facilitate courtship, ball games were held. The boys lined up on one side, the girls on the other. Pairing was by consent. And either the boy or the girl could initiate the invitation. While this posed no difficulties for the boys, a shy girl would sometimes employ a married woman as her intermediary to do the asking. Cloth balls, often made of brightly colored silk, were about the size of a softball. Two partners tossed a ball back and forth. If one of them missed a catch, a piece of clothing had to be discarded and handed over to the partner. The boys made few drops, the girls many, though modesty prevented the game from ever going too far. The boy returned the girl's discarded clothes that evening, when they met away from her house and out of sight of the villagers. Lovemaking may or may not have occurred during the first evening, but by the third meeting the girl was under considerable pressure to engage in sex, and could lose the attentions of her suitor if she did not. On the other hand, the girl was also free to change partners at will.

The high romance of all this courting was meant to make matches for marriages. Hmong bachelors who sewed their oats without regard to this social end were not only subject to moral reproach but often forced to pay heavy fines to the girl's family.

When a young man settled on a particular girl, he asked his father to begin marriage negotiations. If the father did not reject the choice outright, and his voice carried some weight since he paid the bride price, he chose two representatives from his clan to accompany the would-be groom and his best man to open negotiations with the girl's father. When they arrived at the girl's house, one of the negotiators offered the girl's father a gift, usually tobacco, and announced the business at hand. The girl's father then consulted with his relatives and the girl herself. She could reject the match, but unless she was absolutely adamant and threatened suicide, she could be overridden. If the girl's family agreed to the marriage, drinks of alcohol were prepared and the bride price discussed. If, on the other hand, the girl's family opposed the match, matters ended there.

Negotiations over the bride price sometimes involved more than the price of the bride. Old grievances against the groom's clan could be brought up and reparations demanded before the marriage contract could be finalized. The inclusion of such considerations in the negotiations enabled the institution of the bride price to serve the larger social end of inter-clan solidarity. Of course, this could sometimes have the reverse effect. Reparations could be refused and the negotiations broken off. In such cases, instead of drawing clans closer together, demands for reparations might drive them further apart. But if one is to judge by how negotiations proceed today, such untoward results were uncommon. With or without reparations, the bride price was invariably quite high, amounting to as much as several years' family savings which, given the high savings rate of the Hmong, was a large financial sacrifice.

It would be a mistake to construe the payment of a bride price as essentially a financial transaction. The bride was not literally bought by the groom's family. Rather, the bride price served to stress the importance of the marriage rather than portray the bride as a commodity to be bought and sold. The high price also helped to insure that marriages would last, since a divorce, which was rare, would require a refund.

Brides were sometimes abducted, especially when the couple were deeply in love and the girl's parents opposed the marriage. It was more an elopement disguised as an abduction. The girl was expected to put up a token resistance to save face with her family. Propriety also required that the parents of the groom had to notify the parents of the abducted bride and pay a bride price. On rare occasions, an unwilling girl was truly abducted against her will. In such cases, her furious parents might set an extremely high bride price to sanction the abductor and his family.

Bachelors from poor families who could not come up with a bride price sometimes still married by paying the bride price on an installment plan, or by agreeing to work for a period of time for the bride's family in lieu of a cash payment.

The actual marriage ceremony began at the groom's house where the family made sacrifice to the house spirits and the ancestors. After the bride price was delivered to the groom's go-betweens, the groom and his party proceeded to the bride's house where more sacrifices were made, the bride price paid, and the marriage feast begun. The next day, or several days later if the feast was lavish and there were many guests, the bride accompanied the groom to his house. After sacrificing a pig, they began another wedding party that continued late into the night. One final ceremony remained. The bride could not become an official member of her husband's family until she was introduced to the house spirits of her new home. Though this constituted formal acceptance into her husband's clan, she did not sever ties with her own clan, nor even change her name. She would still be known by her maiden name, including the surname of her own clan.

Though polygamy has long been condoned in Hmong communities, it has never been widespread, save during wartime when it was expected that a widow would be taken in by one of her husband's younger brothers, what anthropologist call levirate marriage. The high expense entailed by the bride price limited the practice of polygamy. Even for wealthier Hmong, the decision to become polygamous was colored by the realization that the polygamist was burdened with the obligation to share his affection equally with all his wives. For favoritism, when it occurred, was serious cause for complaint by an ignored wife or wives and could rightfully be aired before relatives or even the general community and, on occasion, be judged grounds for divorce.

Death

The death of a family member was announced by the firing of three shots in slow succession, each waiting for the echo of the last to fall away before taking its turn. The shots not only signaled the death and summoned all within listening distance to come and pay their respects but also frightened away evil spirits who might hinder the journey of the soul of the deceased to the home of its ancestors in the netherworld.

Family members, usually the dead person's sons, washed the deceased with warm water and placed new, brightly-colored clothes over the old. Stockings and slippers came next. Then they placed the body on a stretcher inside the home and covered the mouth of the corpse with a red veil. For several days while the body remained in the house amidst burning incense to mask the stench of putrefaction, mourners arrived to pay their respects to the family, tender gifts, and display their grief by moaning and crying, always directed to the mortal remains of the deceased, who was constantly fanned by women in attendance to keep flies away from the decaying flesh. All who came had to be fed, and if the deceased was a person of some importance, the number of guests might be quite large.

While the Hmong believed many souls inhabit a body, only two of these souls were of particular concern in death rites: the soul that would eventually be reincarnated, and the soul that would remain with the body in the grave. After the deceased had been washed and dressed, a shaman, or someone else who knew the rite, prepared the soul destined for reincarnation for its long journey into the spirit world. His first task was to make an offering of alcohol and use joss sticks or divining horns to determine if the offering had been accepted. If it had, he informed the soul that the body it inhabited was now dead and that it must prepare to leave it. He assured the soul that it was not alone and that it would be given direction for the journey to its spirit ancestors. He placed a sacrificed rooster, roasted without being plucked, next to the corpse. The rooster would be the soul's guide and helper on its journey into the netherworld. If the sun became too hot or if it rained during the journey, the soul could find shelter under the rooster's wings. The rooster also informed the soul when it had reached its destination. When the two approached a village the rooster would crow. If they had reached the village of the soul's ancestors, roosters in the village crowed back, informing the soul that its journey was over.

Then came the *qhuab ke* chant, which recounts the Hmong version of the creation of the world, the great flood, and the migration of the Hmong from Siberia into China. The chanter warned the soul of dangers on its journey into the netherworld, the deceiving genies who would attempt to sidetrack it, or monsters like carnivorous rocks and poisonous caterpillars. The chant told of lakes and oceans so treacherous they must not be crossed, and of water that was poisoned and must not be drunk. It described the guards stationed at the portals through which all souls must pass, and the answers that must be given before the guards would allow it to pass through.

The body remained in the house until work on the coffin was finished, which usually took several days. There might be other reasons for delaying the date of burial, such as the late arrival of relatives who lived far away or the temporary unavailability of an ox for the internment. The beast's soul would serve as a substitute for the one Ndu Nyong had devoured—the supposed real cause of death.

When all was in order, a male relative of the deceased sacrificed the ox, which was cooked and eaten. In the late afternoon, a funeral procession formed and clansmen, led by a piper, carried the body on a litter to the gravesite, which had been selected by the rules of geomancy, an arcane art borrowed from the Chinese. If the site was indeed a good one and the soul of the deceased fared well, it would have no need to make periodic visits to its living relatives to request sacrifices of chickens or pigs to sustain it. After the corpse was placed in the coffin, the master of the funeral ceremony burned spirit money, bogus slips of brightly colored paper that would be available to the soul in the spirit world so it would not enter there penniless. After the coffin was covered with earth, a stone cairn was constructed, the exact size and configuration determined by clan or sub-clan custom. For a few days following the burial, family members placed food beside the grave until it was certain that the soul had begun the journey to its ancestors.

After the burial, a separate ceremony, called the *xi plig*, was held for the soul that would remain in the grave with the corpse. It was greatly feared that this soul might wander from the grave and be transformed into an evil spirit. To placate this soul, it was invited to the house to partake in offerings of food and alcohol, and told it must return to the grave and remain there forever.

Among certain Hmong clans in the Kweichow province of China, care for the dead did not end with the burial ceremony. A year after the burial, relatives and friends were invited to the grave site where sacrifices were made to the deceased. The coffin was then opened and the bones carefully cleaned, wrapped in cloth and re-placed in the grave. This ceremony was repeated seven times at one- or two-year intervals. The practice stemmed from a belief that fail-ure to keep an ancestor's bones clean could make him or her angry enough to cause sickness or death in the family. Appropriately enough, the Chinese called these Hmong the "Wash-bone Aborigi-nes."

Strange as the practice may seem, it is not difficult to imagine how it might have originated. Repeated forced migrations meant leaving the graves of ancestors behind, and Hmong legend indi-cates that the conquering Chinese often desecrated Hmong grave-yards, a matter of critical concern for the Hmong since this would anger the ancestors and possibly bring illness, death, or misfortune to the family. For this reason many Hmong began to disguise their grave sites or fashion them in the Chinese way so that invading Chinese would not know they belonged to Hmong. Even today there are Hmong in southeast Asia whose grave sites ape those of the Chinese. Of course, one sure way to avoid desecration was to exhume the remains and transport them during a migration to a new grave site. The practice of exhuming and cleaning bones be-tween migrations might have been a way to symbolically affirm the community's concern with desecration and to put the souls of the departed at ease.

Whatever the exact origin of the practice, it did exist and Vietnamese reports in the 1860s that the Hmong of Quan Ba cleaned, wrapped, and stored the bones of their deceased make it almost certain that there were "Wash-bone" Hmong living in the area at that time.

NEW YEAR FESTIVAL

The most important communal event in Hmong society, the New Year festival, officially began on the first day of the waxing moon of the twelfth month of the year. More precisely, it began at the first cock's crowing of that day, about three in the morning. Unofficially, it commenced as close to that date as the demands of the harvest permitted.

The New Year festival was the only Hmong religious ceremony shared by the entire community. As often as not, it included members of neighboring communities. It was a time for eligible bachelors and young Hmong maidens, dressed in their finest clothes, to play the courting ball games. It was a time for feasting and visiting friends, and in the better-off communities, for bull fights.

The fights were not between man and beast but between bulls. The Hmong brought this sport with them from Kweichow where buffaloes rather than bulls are still used in ceremonial combats. The fights were not to the death. The match usually ended when one bull turned tail and ran. If one bull risked serious injury or death, referees jumped in with long poles to separate the two beasts. In Kweichow, buffalo raised for the sport were larger and stronger than those yoked to the plow. There the fights were also a matter of considerable ceremony. Before the contest, the combatants, draped in red cloth and with silver tips slipped onto their horns, were led around the arena. A shaman followed, beating a gong.

In addition to courting and bullfights, shamans performed ritual sacrifices to placate the spirits of the forest and field, to honor the house spirits, dead ancestors, and the souls of the living members of the family, as well as the souls of the family's livestock. Shamans burned the jaws of the pigs that were given in payment for their services during the year so that the souls of the sacrificed animals could be reincarnated. It was a time to honor all beings, living and dead, to show gratitude for whatever help they had given the family during the year, or if times had not been so good, to placate them in hopes that the new year would bring better fortune.

The festival lasted three days. And except for the time reserved for ritual sacrifices, during those three days Hmong, young and old, visited friends and relatives, ate and drank, and played games from dawn to dusk.

CHAPTER 7

The Hmong and the French · *Uneasy Allies*

*F*RENCH CATHOLIC MISSIONARIES, active in Vietnam by the early 1600s, gained converts slowly at first. But financial backing from the French business community in 1664 increased their success. The funds were funneled through the new French East India Company which had been created for the express purpose of expanding trade with Vietnam. As one might surmise, the East India Company's funding of missionary activity in Vietnam was not altogether an expression of altruism. A network of missionaries, fluent in Vietnamese and familiar with the country, was an invaluable asset in establishing trade relations with the Vietnamese; even more so when the missionaries did double duty and worked as bookkeepers and sales agents for the company in return for transportation to Vietnam.

Though Vietnamese rulers did not respond warmly to either French traders or French missionaries, gunboat diplomacy usually brought them around to the French view of what was in their best interests. In fact, the French often used Vietnamese resistance as an excuse for expanding their presence.

In 1859, under the pretext of retaliating for the persecution of French Catholic missionaries, Admiral Rigault de Genouilly guided his nine warships into Ganh Rai Bay and followed the river channels inland until he reached Saigon. Troops were sent ashore and the village easily captured. Only a sleepy fishing village at the time, Saigon held promise as an excellent deep water port, and as a beachhead for later operations in the Mekong delta region.

The French also had a larger plan. It was to use the Mekong River as a navigable route into southwest China where French goods could be marketed to millions of potential consumers, and China's natural resources such as timber, tin, coal, silver, and iron could be ferried downstream and shipped to European markets. Then, too, there were the opium fields of Yunnan. This cheap source of raw opium could place the French on a competitive footing with the British in the international drug market. To gain control of the Mekong required the colonization of Vietnam, Cambodia, and Laos. Cambodia was made a protectorate in 1863; all of Vietnam fell to the French in 1884, and Laos followed in 1893.

Though an 1886 expedition up the Mekong revealed that the river's upper reaches were so treacherous as to prove unnavigable, it was not until 1895, when invested capital from a Parisian syndicate failed to turn a profit from an upriver trading venture, that all thought of the Mekong's use as a back door to China was abandoned. By then the momentum of French colonialism had gathered such force that the issue of the navigability of the Mekong was rendered moot.

Because Vietnam offered greater potential for economic development than either Laos or Cambodia, most French investment in economic development went to Vietnam. The French borrowed enormous sums to construct roads, canals, and railroads. One of these projects, with a price tag in excess of $60 million, was the construction of a rail line from northern Vietnam across the Chinese border into Yunnan. The project was not only expensive but extremely hazardous for the Vietnamese rail gangs who hacked through jungle and carved railbeds out of the stone walls of mountain passes. One out of every three laborers who toiled on the project died before it was completed. But the French finally had their back door to China.

Ironically, the hoped-for profits never materialized. Trade with China was barely profitable, and the railroad itself turned out to be a commercial failure. On the other hand, an elaborate system of canals for the Mekong delta transformed the river basin into one of the most productive rice producing areas of the world. Unhappily for the peasants working the paddies, the increased productivity did not translate into a higher standard of living. The surplus rice was siphoned off for export to rice-hungry China, and the colonial administration pocketed the additional revenue. The French increased Vietnamese taxes to amortize the loans for these projects, and continued to increase them until they were the highest among the colonial powers in Southeast Asia and India. These taxes devastated the Vietnamese peasant class. Most were landless within fifty years.

Vietnamese tradition wisely forbade the confiscation of land for the payment of debts, but the French ignored this tradition. A peasant's land was treated like any other real asset that could be seized for the payment of debts. Fearing the confiscation of their land for non-payment of taxes, many peasants turned to wealthy Vietnamese for loans (at interest rates that often exceeded 100% per annum) to meet their tax obligation in a futile attempt to stall off the inevitable. Slowly but surely Vietnam was transformed into a land of huge estates on which approximately seventy percent of the population toiled as sharecroppers. French tax policy was exploitative and shortsighted. Within two generations it created the social and economic conditions for revolution.

This might have been remedied if the French had also encouraged Vietnamese commerce and industry, creating a source of alternative employment for an impoverished peasantry. They did quite the opposite, however, prohibiting industry and banking, and any other economic activity that might result in competition with imported French goods.

The Bank of Indochina, established in 1875 and controlled by the Bank of Paris, exercised virtual monopolistic control over all banking in Indochina and was an effective instrument in regulating the direction of economic development. French control over the flow of capital guaranteed that even ventures which did not threaten French imports would be owned and managed by Frenchmen and not Vietnamese. The bank provided the capital for French coal mines in Tonkin and in Khammouane province, Laos; it also floated the loans for the French rubber plantations in southern and central Vietnam and on the Blovens Plateau in southern Laos (on the eve of World War II, fifty percent of u.s. rubber was imported from French Indochina), and bankrolled French coffee plantations in central Vietnam and southern Laos.

Following the lead of the financiers, the colonial administration established government monopolies controlling the production and sale of opium, alcohol, and salt. Monopoly pricing naturally followed and provided the French with an additional, though hidden, tax on Vietnamese, Laotians, and Cambodians. On the other hand, French taxes did not hit Laotians and Cambodians as hard as they did the Vietnamese. Because neither country had much to exploit, as little as possible was spent to administer them.

In Laos, for example, the entire administrative bureaucracy at the turn of the century amounted to no more than seventy-two French officials. It was impossible for so few officials to directly oversee the administration of the country. French educated Vietnamese were therefore used to fill the middle levels of the bureaucracy. In turn, the Vietnamese employed Laotians as clerks and translators. This still left the French understaffed and forced them to rely on the traditional Laotian political system to carry out their edicts and collect taxes. One consequence of this arrangement was that tax evasion among the ethnic Lao was commonplace. As the French returned almost no benefits for taxes levied, Laotian politicians had little incentive to alienate large segments of the population by prosecuting tax evaders.

Non-Lao ethnic minorities were another matter. Viewed as barbarians and denied political representation, they were regularly exploited by Laotian officials. This was particularly true for the hill tribes. Because of their isolation and distance from centers of power, the hill tribes had no effective means to protest unjust treatment by local authorities. Their only recourse, once the level of exploitation became intolerable, was to rebel or migrate.

Because of their vulnerability, the hill tribes were often forced to bear the full burden of French taxes, though only a fraction of these revenues were passed on to the French. Tax collectors and local officials pocketed the rest, an additional reason why tax evasion by Laotian montagnards was treated more harshly than tax evasion by ethnic Lao. The Hmong objected to a double standard that punished tax evasion by montagnards and yet tolerated it among the ethnic Lao who enjoyed a higher standard of living and were better able to pay. They also resented the contemptuous way they were treated by the exploitative Laotian officials. The Hmong, in particular, were not permitted to stand in their company. If they approached an official, they had to literally crawl, head down, and wait patiently until he saw fit to recognize their presence.

The Hmong, however, did not want trouble, especially as the Laotians repeatedly reminded them of the military might of the French, whom the Hmong now called the Fabkis (pronounced "Fah Key"), a word derived from the Chinese expression "Fa Kouie"— French Devils.

In 1885 Ton That Thuyet, the advisor to the Vietnamese Emperor Ham Nghi, persuaded the young sovereign to rebel against the French. The rebellion failed, but Ton That Thuyet and Ham Nghi escaped and sought refuge in the highlands of Laos, where they organized a government in exile. Though the French replaced Ham Nghi with their own handpicked puppet, many Vietnamese remained loyal to him. It consequently became a matter of high priority for the French to locate the deposed emperor and eliminate him from the Vietnamese political scene. But forays into the Laotian mountains turned up absolutely nothing. Only after the Hmong consented to be their guides did the French capture Ham Nghi and defuse a potentially explosive situation.

Cooperation in the capture of Ham Nghi earned the Laotian Hmong praise and alerted the French to their strategic importance for future operations in the Laotian highlands. French officials began to bypass Laotian middlemen and deal directly with Hmong communities and their leaders. It marked the beginning of a special relationship between the French and the Laotian Hmong that would continue until France was forced to withdraw from Indochina. It was not all smooth sailing, however. French insensitivity to Hmong interests, and especially their failure to appreciate the devastating effect of tax increases on the already low Hmong standard of living, periodically incited large numbers of Laotian Hmong to armed rebellion.

TAX PROBLEMS

In 1896 the French raised taxes in Laos. The new taxes struck the Hmong as particularly unfair because they were applied almost exclusively to them. Opium cultivation in Laos was predominately a Hmong occupation. The French were fully aware of this. They were also eager to obtain a cheap source of raw opium for their opium monopoly and required the Hmong to pay a portion of the tax in opium, at an assessed value far below the market price.

The Hmong appealed to their kiatongs for help. It did not take much to urge them to action. They were already incensed over the fact that the French had failed to consult them about a tax which so adversely affected the Hmong community. Nor were tensions eased by the decision of the French Commissioner for Xieng Khouang to try to intimidate the Hmong by ordering a mixed contingent of Laotian and Vietnamese militiamen to conduct patrols in the Hmong highlands.

The governor of the province, Prince Kham Huang, was also unhappy. Descended from a long line of Xieng Khouang princes who ruled the province as an independent kingdom, Kham Huang chafed under French rule. His lack of cooperation earned him a demotion from prince to provincial governor. Seeing that the Hmong were in a rebellious mood, he advised their nominal leader, the Lo kiatong, to organize an armed resistance.

The Hmong first attacked the military post at Ban Khang Phanieng on the eastern edge of the Plain of Jars. Though they failed to take the post, they did give a good account of themselves. In their second more ambitious assault against the provincial headquarters at Xieng Khouang city, the Hmong were badly outnumbered and outgunned. Modern French rifles cut them down before they could get close enough to fire their flintlocks, which are only effective at short range. After suffering many casualties the Hmong withdrew into the mountains.

The defeat so damaged the prestige of the Lo kiatong that the leadership of the Laotian Hmong passed to Tong Ger Moua, the kiatong of the Moua clan. Tong Ger represented the Hmong in negotiations with the French at Ban Ban, a small town north of the provincial headquarters. It was the French who initiated the talks. Though they had defeated the Hmong, they had stirred up a hornet's nest that still buzzed and might yet sting. At Ban Ban, Tong Ger Moua proved to be an able diplomat. The French Commissioner agreed to lower Hmong taxes and pledged to consult Hmong leaders before implementing policies that might adversely affect Hmong interests.

While a climate of close cooperation between Hmong political leaders and French officials became the norm in Xieng Khouang province, Hmong communities elsewhere in Indochina complained bitterly about increasing exploitation. It was not the French who were doing the exploiting, but Tai, Laotian, and Vietnamese officials who claimed to enjoy the full backing of the colonial administration. Hmong living in the prime opium growing areas surrounding the high plateau of Dien Bien Phu in Vietnam perhaps had the most cause for complaint. Tai lords in the lowlands exacted such high opium taxes that entire communities were impoverished within a few years. The region was ripe for rebellion, though it would take nearly two decades of simmering before the pot finally boiled over. When it did, not only the Tai but also the French became the target of the rebellion.

BLACK FLAGS

This is not to say that it was all dark clouds. As late as 1914, many Hmong communities throughout Indochina welcomed French military protection against groups of marauding bandits known as the Black Flags.

In 1884 France and China signed the treaty of T'ien-Tsin, in which China acknowledged French sovereignty over all of Vietnam. Prior to the signing, China had maintained military garrisons along its common border with Vietnam, some inside Vietnamese territory. The French naturally expected the Chinese troops to be recalled. Instead of returning home, they pillaged and occupied various sectors of the frontier. Their generals became warlords. Each with his own army exercised absolute sovereignty over the native population. Since these renegades chose a black flag as their standard, the French fell into the habit of calling them, as well as all Chinese bandits in Indochina, the Black Flags.

The warlords were not without their supporters. Vietnamese emperors, as well as Tai tribesmen opposed to French colonial rule, occasionally allied themselves with the bandits and set them loose on the French. While the Black Flags seldom bested the French, they inflicted many casualties.

One encounter in particular transformed the name "Black Flag" into a rallying cry for French infantry. In 1874 Captain Henri Riviere led six hundred French troops against Black Flags who had gained control of Hanoi and the surrounding countryside. After driving the bandits out of Hanoi, Riviere pressed on northeast to the coal mining town of Hongay, which he meant to place under French control. A Black Flag ambush frustrated this aim and cost Riviere his life. After slaughtering the French troops, the Black Flags carried Riviere's head from village to village to celebrate their victory and to graphically thumb their noses at the French.

The French were not alone in wishing the Black Flags destroyed. Hmong communities were favorite targets of the bandits, for Hmong opium could be traded in China for supplies and munitions. This disposed the Hmong to cooperate with the French in any effort to crush the Black Flags.

In November 1914, Black Flags crossed the Vietnamese border and entered Sam Neua province in Laos, attacking the French garrison near Sam Neua city. After suffering heavy losses, the colonial troops abandoned the garrison and fled for their lives. Reinforcements were sent to retake the garrison, but were ambushed and driven off. It was only after more reinforcements were sent from Vietnam that the French were able to liberate Sam Neua city. The Black Flags retreated into Vietnam where they launched successful attacks on the French garrisons at Dien Bien Phu and Son La. These victories bolstered their confidence and they once again entered Laos, this time further north in Phong Saly province.

The Hmong in Phong Saly did not wait for the French to arrive and drive out the bandits. They established a position overlooking a Black Flag encampment inside a pass near the Vietnam border. Hmong cut down trees and constructed a triangular barricade, then rolled it down a trail on logs to engage the enemy below. The Black Flags raised their banners and attacked. Barrages of rifle fire chipped away at the barricade which moved relentlessly downward, closing the distance between the Hmong and the bandits. When the Hmong were nearly on top of the Chinese, they abandoned their protection and closed on the enemy.

Many Black Flags died in the skirmish, but they were only a small contingent of a much larger force encamped near the battle-field. When more Black Flags appeared in strength, the Hmong retreated. In the weeks that followed the Hmong mounted several ambushes against Black Flag outposts, but abandoned all hope of driving the bandits from the province. Nearly a year later, the French sent two full regiments from Hanoi to Phong Saly to engage the Black Flags. With nearly two thousand pack mules and several pieces of mountain artillery, the French were prepared for a long campaign. After rooting the Black Flags from their entrenched positions, French troops harried the bandits for over three months until they were driven out of Laos into China.

The success of the Laotian campaign encouraged the French to step up their lagging offensive against Black Flag strongholds in northern Vietnam. One Hmong, Yang Yilong, had already begun a campaign of his own against a group of Black Flags who for years had tyrannized the montagnards around Ha Giang, robbing them of food, livestock, and opium, and carrying off the most beautiful women of each village to serve as concubines for Black Flag notables.

Yang Yilong organized his Hmong volunteers into small guerrilla bands of two or three men. Their weapons were crude: knives, swords, and axes. They attacked isolated units of Black Flags and only when it was certain that all could be killed. The slain bandits were buried or thrown into deep grottos. Yang Yilong did not want reprisals. Missing soldiers tell no tales. The sudden and mysterious disappearance of a number of soldiers puzzled the Black Flag warlord until he learned from an informant that it was all the work of the Hmong. Yang Yilong was captured and imprisoned. On the day of the scheduled execution, he succeeded in generating an argument between the guards over which of them would get his clothes. A fight broke out and, in the confusion, Yang Yilong sneaked out of the prison compound to freedom.

Yang Yilong collected a number of his guerrillas and led them to the French garrison at Bao Lac, a small mountain village fifty miles east of Ha Giang. After listening to Yang Yilong's description of his guerrilla operations against the Black Flags, the post commander immediately donated sixty rifles to the cause. While Yang Yilong could have used twice that number, sixty rifles were sufficient to support more daring operations against the bandits. Three months of incessant harassment finally forced the Black Flags of Ha Giang to abandon their strongholds and return to China. Not all of them made it across the border. Yang Yilong's guerrillas always kept several days ahead of the fleeing Chinese, preparing rock slides to greet them when they passed by.

After Yang Yilong's victory over the Ha Giang Black Flags, the French began to recruit other Tonkin Hmong for the final push against the remaining Black Flags. Sometimes the Hmong served only as guides, but other times they fought alongside the French or coordinated their own independent operations with those of their French allies. One joint operation proved particularly costly for a group of Black Flags the French had driven from their mountain stronghold. Deprived of the sanctuary, they headed south toward the Red River delta. On their way they attacked a Hmong village situated north of Nghia Lo, where the French maintained a well-armed garrison. Hmong scouts had spotted the Black Flags earlier so the village was empty when they arrived. The bandits scoured the village in search of the opium which villagers had wisely carried away with them on their retreat into the forest. The Black Flags immediately set out after them.

Once they entered the dense forest, the Chinese were easy prey for Hmong ambushes. Poisoned arrows from Hmong crossbows thinned out their ranks. It was now the Black Flags's turn to retreat.

The Hmong kept close on their heels until the Chinese made the mistake of entering a deep grotto. They were outflanked by the Hmong and boxed in. More Black Flags felt the bite of Hmong arrows. When the bandits finally broke out they left behind so many dead that the grotto was later renamed the "Valley of the Dead Chinese."

The enraged survivors of this carnage pillaged and burned every Hmong village they came across. Another mistake. Hmong chiefs in the area swore a blood oath to destroy the bandits. They contacted the French garrison at Nghia Lo where plans for a joint operation were worked out. The Hmong would engage the Black Flags and drive them south, where the French would be in place to cut off their retreat.

The Hmong assembled their forces on the outskirts of a village occupied by Black Flags. They remained at the forest's edge, waiting for the signal to attack. A large cannon, made of wood and banded with iron, was already in position on a rise overlooking the rice paddies that ringed the village. The cannon was the handiwork of a Hmong blacksmith named Nao Ku Hlau. He had already loaded the cannon with powder and stuffed its wide mouth with old knives, axes, chains, and whatever else he had been able to retrieve from the scrap pile at his shop.

Nao Ku Hlau walked down the rise to a clearing where he began waving a white flag and taunting the Black Flags in the village. A detachment of bandits was sent to capture the impertinent Hmong. By the time they reached the last paddy, Nao Ku Hlau was already standing beside his cannon. He lit the fuse and ran for cover. The cannon roared and belched its junkyard at the advancing Chinese. While Nao Ku Hlau waited for the smoke to clear so that he could assess the effectiveness of his invention, his compatriots streamed out of the forest onto the paddies, stumbling over dead and dying bandits in their headlong rush for the village.

The Black Flags stood their ground until they were overrun. From then on they had to fight in retreat. The Hmong drove them south into the waiting arms of the French. Trapped, the Black Flags had no choice but to fight their way out. The French and Hmong dogged those who succeeded all the way to the Chinese border.

THE DECEIT OF BLIAYAO LO

While the experience of fighting a common enemy helped to improve relations between the French and Hmong, the momentum of other events soon strained them to the breaking point. When the French raised taxes in Laos in 1916, the taxes were not applied equally to all Laotians. Tribal minorities such as the Hmong were forced to shoulder a heavier burden than the ethnic Lao in the lowland valleys. In particular, the Hmong were now forced to pay several kinds of taxes: two annual per capita taxes, as well as a semi-annual tax. For the first time widows and adolescents were taxed. Also, adult males were obliged to provide two weeks of free labor on government work projects.

The burdensome taxes caused considerable grumbling. To insure they were paid, elements of the colonial militia made the rounds with the tax collectors. Hmong who could not pay were jailed until relatives paid the delinquent taxes. Accustomed to mountain living and habituated to a migratory lifestyle, the Hmong have always found imprisonment intolerable. It was this feature of the new tax policy, more than the taxes themselves, that led to a growing rebelliousness.

Then there were the new roads. Looking to the future, the French decided to develop an all-weather road system linking Laos to Vietnam. A network of new roads would make it easier to transport troops from Vietnam to Laos in case Thailand attempted to exercise its former hegemony over Laos. It would also facilitate communication between Laos and Vietnam and prepare the way for linkages between the two economies. The hope was that the investment in the Vietnamese economy would, through a process of economic osmosis, pay off for Laos as well.

The French were still unwilling to spend much on Laos, so the local population had to pay the taxes to raise the necessary revenue

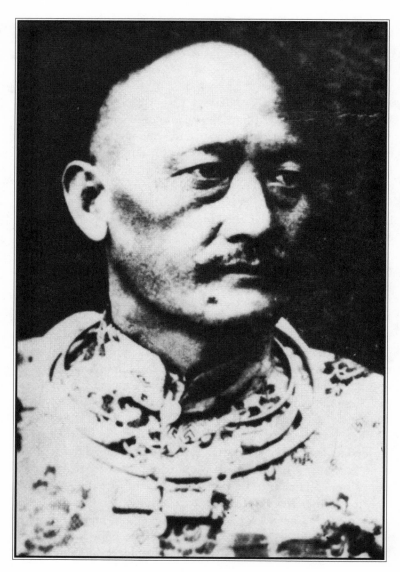

for the project and supply the labor for construction of the new roads. Since major roads running all the way to the Vietnam border were planned for Xieng Khouang and Phong Saly, Hmong in these provinces supplied most of the manpower for the work crews. As it was mountain construction, the work was particularly arduous and the available pool of labor small. It meant that the Hmong had to work hard, and for weeks at a time, which resulted in neglected crops, poor harvests and, consequently, less income to pay taxes. In parts of Phong Saly province, the burden on some Hmong communities was so great that entire villages pulled up stakes and moved away. Many did not return until work on the roads was completed in 1924. While few Xieng Khouang Hmong opted for this solution, they nevertheless complained bitterly about their plight.

The French ignored the grumbling. After all, the workers were compensated, even if it didn't amount to much and applied only after workers donated fourteen days of unpaid labor. Moreover, Hmong leaders had been consulted before the plan was put into effect and they had endorsed the work gangs; as far as the French were concerned, they were keeping to their earlier promise to undertake nothing affecting Hmong interests without prior consultation with Hmong notables.

Sometime in late 1917 or early 1918, a number of village chiefs in Xieng Khouang province appealed to the Lo kiatong, Bliayao Lo, for relief. Selected as the kiatong of the Lo clan in 1910 and appointed that same year as the aging Moua kiatong's assistant, Bliayao Lo took over as the leader of the Xieng Khouang Hmong when Tong Ger Moua retired from all official duties in early 1917. The Xieng Khouang Hmong had tolerated the *corvée* system because the French had relied on Bliayao Lo to organize the work crews and pay them their wages, which up to that time amounted to two Laotian kip per day. Even so, it had become painfully clear that the wages were too low. Since the average yearly tax load per Hmong family had risen to around thirteen kip, three weeks of work on the road crews (two unpaid, one paid) left a worker with just enough wages to cover his tax liability. It also cost him nearly a month's work on his own fields.

Though Bliayao Lo eventually demanded and received higher wages for the road crews, very little of it reached the workers. In place of two kip per day, workers were to be paid three. But instead of passing on this extra pay to the Hmong, Bliayao Lo set it aside for himself. There were two exceptions, however: his nephew, Song Zeu Lo, and his son-in-law, Foung Ly. They were his top aids for the *corvée* project and received the full three kip per day for organizing the labor gangs and distributing the short wages.

Whether it was because they weren't allowed to share in the graft or because they couldn't stomach such calloused behavior toward fellow Hmong, the two assistants became increasingly disenchanted with their boss as they watched him become the richest Hmong in Laos. While the experience radicalized Song Zeu Lo and set him on the path of rebellion, Foung Ly's plan for revenge was more long range: to work patiently to advance the political careers of his sons and eventually take over the leadership of the Xieng Khouang Hmong.

Bliayao Lo's deceit did not remain undetected. Whether, as one Hmong recounts, he arrogantly (and foolishly) told the Hmong to ask the French why they were not receiving higher wages, or whether his aids quietly let it be known that Hmong on the road crews were being shortchanged, the truth of the matter became common knowledge and resulted in a general strike.

When Hmong selected for work crews did not show up, Bliayao Lo persuaded the French to use colonial militiamen to intimidate strikers and force them back to work. This did not put out the fire; it fanned the flames. The time was ripe for a general Hmong uprising in northeastern Laos. Indeed, in Vietnam Pa Chay had already begun one.

PA CHAY

Born in a small village in southern China just a few miles from the Burmese border, Pa Chay was orphaned at a young age. He left China in his teens and migrated to northern Vietnam, where he

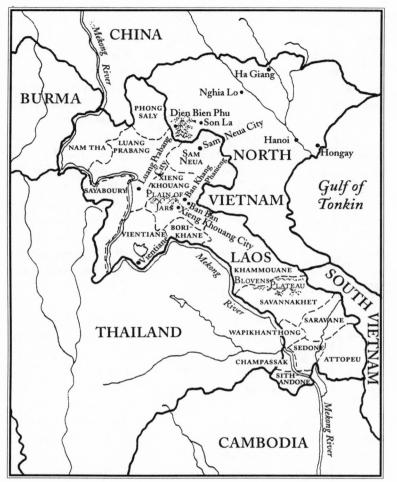

was taken in by Song Tou, a member of the Vue clan who lived in a village near Dien Bien Phu. According to legend, Pa Chay was able to speak and write not only Chinese but also Vietnamese and Laotian all without ever attending school. This was what one would expect from a Hmong messiah, although Pa Chay never claimed to be anything more than a Hmong "John the Baptist," a messenger whose mission was to prepare the way for the long-awaited savior.

Pa Chay received the revelation sometime in 1917; he must assume leadership of the Dien Bien Phu Hmong and lead them in a holy war against their Tai oppressors whose abusive treatment and excessive taxes had reduced the Dien Bien Phu Hmong to near slavery and abject poverty. Song Tou Vue presumed Pa Chay had gone mad and tried to dissuade him from taking up arms. Fearful that the argument might turn violent, Song Tou Vue's wife tried to intercede and calm things down. It was too late, Pa Chay had already picked up a spear. Meant for her husband, it caught her in the chest. When Pa Chay came to his senses, he fled to the safety of the mountains.

Song Tou Vue rushed to the authorities to report the incident and to beg for protection from Pa Chay. The officials were not sympathetic. They accused Song Tou Vue of being in league with his adopted son and imprisoned him at Lai Chau (north of Dien Bien Phu) along with his four sons. During the incarceration, Song Tou Vue committed suicide by taking an overdose of opium.

Meanwhile, Pa Chay was busy organizing a rebellion. It was reported by some of his early followers that he used magic to gather a following and to authenticate his claim that he was sent by the messiah to liberate the Hmong from their Tai oppressors. On one occasion, it is said, he fell into a deep trance while a number of Hmong sat around him in a villager's home. To their astonishment he suddenly leaped from the floor right up through the roof of the house. When he descended through the roof a few moments later, Pa Chay held several eggs which he placed in a rice grinder. After working the handle of the grinder, he retrieved the eggs. Not one of them was broken. Another time, during a village celebration, Pa Chay was supposed to have wadded up a piece of cotton and thrown it into the air where it miraculously exploded.

Pa Chay's first act of rebellion was to convince many of the Hmong around Dien Bien Phu to refuse to pay their taxes. The French responded by sending troops to the area, though they were unable to capture Pa Chay and were repeatedly ambushed by his guerrillas. According to one Laotian Hmong, Shue Long Vue, every effort to capture Pa Chay failed. First, the French sent four soldiers to capture him. Pa Chay's men killed two and spared two, whom they released so the French would learn of Pa Chay's power. Unimpressed, the French sent twelve more soldiers. Ten were killed and two released. More soldiers were sent and more killed. Pa Chay sent no more than a few Hmong on these ambushes. And he was careful, for reasons only he understood, that the number sent was never odd. Pa Chay's followers were amazed by his ability to know when soldiers had been sent by the French and just the route they would take, which made ambushes easy.

The legend also tells how Pa Chay continued to use magic to insure the success of his rebellion. He performed the egg ceremony before sending his men out on a mission. Now, however, the eggs were distributed to the soldiers. Each wrote his name on his egg and placed it in the rice grinder with the others. Those whose eggs broke were exempted from the mission on the understanding that this was a message from heaven foretelling their injury or death. Those with unbroken eggs were guaranteed complete safety. Pa Chay also distributed sacred water to his men which was supposed to make them invulnerable to injury once they drank it.

As the rebellion progressed, Pa Chay introduced other ceremonies. He made a flag which he claimed was magical. It was placed in a special area. Before engaging the enemy he ordered his soldiers to throw spears at the flag. If any spear pierced the flag, Pa Chay took this as a bad omen, a sign that the time was not yet ripe for an attack. Pa Chay entrusted another magical flag, this one white, to a Hmong virgin, the seventeen-year-old Ngao Nzoua. Pa Chay told her that by waving the flag she could deflect bullets aimed at his soldiers. Ngao Nzoua led Pa Chay's soldiers into several battles against the French, each time protecting the Hmong with her white flag. If we are to believe the French officers who witnessed the events, she was never once struck by a French bullet.

In December of 1917, Pa Chay stepped up his campaign and ordered attacks on several Tai military posts around Dien Bien Phu. Pa Chay himself led eighty Hmong against one of them. After a brief struggle, the Tai surrendered. According to legend, he spared their lives on the condition that they treat the Hmong fairly in the future.

Alarmed by Pa Chay's successes, the French sent the best of their troops stationed at Son La against him. The detachment was ambushed and badly mauled. More troops were sent with similar results. For nearly a year Pa Chay bested the French in one engagement after another. Then the tide turned. By early 1919 Pa Chay had suffered numerous defeats and was forced to retreat across the Vietnamese border into Laos where he eventually sought refuge in Xieng Khouang province. There he encouraged the Xieng Khouang Hmong to join his rebellion, drive out the French, and establish an independent Hmong kingdom with Dien Bien Phu as its capital.

Many Hmong responded to his call, among them the Lo kiatong's nephew, Son Zeu Lo, who assumed leadership of one contingent of the Xieng Khouang rebels. With the support of Pa Chay's guerrillas, the new rebels gained control of the province's highlands. From there they conducted successful attacks against major Tai, Lao, and French installations in the region. During one of these attacks, Son Zeu Lo led the Hmong under his command on a detour to Bliayao Lo's house with the intention of settling an old score. After his men surrounded the house, Son Zeu Lo called Bliayao Lo out. The kiatong emerged from his home and stood defiantly before his nephew. Son Zeu Lo ordered his men to open fire, but none wished to take responsibility for killing a kiatong, and Bliayao Lo escaped.

The local French garrisons, manned mostly by Vietnamese and Laotians under the command of French officers, were no match for the Hmong. Each time they ventured into the mountains to crush the rebels, the Hmong employed rock slides and homemade artillery to drive the colonial troops back to the safety of their garrisons.

It was Hmong artillery more than the rock slides that demoralized the colonial militiamen. The rebels constructed each piece from a hollowed-out tree trunk, about six inches in diameter and ten feet long. After loading the gun with powder and topping it with shot, they cradled the mini-cannon in a forked stick, braced its butt against the ground, and lit the wick running from the powder to the cannon's mouth. The cannons were light, mobile, and could be fired relatively quickly, ideal for mountain fighting.

Besides considerable killing power, the cannons had a marked psychological effect on the enemy. The spray of shot nearly always struck one of the militiamen. This led to the belief that the rebels were incredible marksmen. Each time they fired their guns a militiaman fell. The Vietnamese and Laotians began to talk of the Hmong possessing magical powers. The resulting loss in morale brought the campaign against the Hmong rebels to a standstill. The tide would eventually turn, however.

One Laotian Hmong, eighty-year-old Tong Leng Vue, recalls that the event which precipitated this change was Bliayao Lo's eagerness to help the French suppress the rebellion. The kiatong explained the workings of the rebels' artillery, and revealed their weakness: their wicks could not be lit in the rain. He told the French to remain in their garrisons until the rainy season and then launch an all-out campaign against the rebels.

The story is likely apocryphal. Realizing the local garrisons were no match for the Hmong, the French brought in two companies of regular infantry from Vietnam to beef up the operation. These regular forces spearheaded a vigorous pacification program aimed at depriving the rebels of their local support. Similar in aim, and more successful in outcome, to the United States' "Strategic Hamlet" program in South Vietnam in the early 1960s, the French pacification effort continued for nearly a year. Entire villages were singled out for relocation. First their crops were burned so that they would be of no use to the rebels, then the villagers were moved to protected areas.

By the beginning of 1921, the effects of the pacification program began to show on Pa Chay's forces. Food and ammunition were in short supply, casualties began to mount, and many rebels were captured. This included Son Zeu Lo, who offered his uncle bribes for his freedom and was eventually poisoned by one of his jailers. Morale was understandably low. Pa Chay saw many of his original converts leave the movement and return home to Vietnam. Soon the Xieng Khouang rebels were also returning to their villages. The revolt was all but over.

Pa Chay finally conceded defeat and vowed that he would never fight again. Accompanied by a few of his most loyal followers, he left Xieng Khouang province and settled in northern Laos where he lived in a small hut in the heart of the forest. On November 17, 1922, he was tracked down and assassinated.

To Pa Chay's followers the collapse of the great rebellion, later known as the "Mad Man's War," was due not to superior French forces or even to the treachery of Bliayao Lo. Pa Chay simply lost his magic. According to one legend, when Pa Chay suffered his first defeat against the French, he tried to raise the spirits of his followers by announcing that heaven would soon send him something that would guarantee their victory. On the same day a large wooden box magically appeared in the village. There was a note attached that warned the box was not to be opened for three years. Several months later a curious Hmong opened the box and found it was full of grasshoppers. As Pa Chay later explained, if the box had remained closed for three years, the insects would have been transformed magically into men and formed the nucleus of his future army. Now that they were gone, he admitted the Hmong had no hope of winning the war against the French.

Another story tells how Ngao Nzoua, the Hmong virgin entrusted with the magic flag, was violated by some of Pa Chay's soldiers and as a result lost her power to protect the rebel troops. A related account indicates that it was not Ngao Nzoua but a French woman who was violated. Pa Chay had ordered his men to take a town in which there were French civilians. Before they left for the mission, he expressly warned them against committing any wicked acts against French civilians, for to do so would lose them the support of heaven. Not heeding the warning, his men raped and murdered a French woman. Pa Chay knew of the event the minute it occurred. When the soldiers returned, he informed them that their crime would cost them the war. A sign confirming this prediction supposedly occurred a short time later when Pa Chay performed the egg ceremony before leading his troops into battle. For the first time all of the eggs broke.

Like the explanation of his defeat, the account of Pa Chay's death blends fact with legend. Part of this legend is that Pa Chay predicted his own death. The night before he was assassinated, he heard a tiger roar and a deer pawing the ground. He told his few remaining followers that this meant he would die the next day. He asked them to bury him in the forest on the spot where the deer had turned the earth to guarantee he would return in fifty years to lead the Hmong once again in their struggle for independence.

The identity of Pa Chay's assassins remains uncertain. By one account they were Kha tribesmen, bounty hunters eager to collect the price the French had placed on Pa Chay's head, which they delivered to the French as proof of his death. In another account, the assassins were former Hmong rebels who had served under Pa Chay and to whom the French had promised 150 silver piasters if they could deliver Pa Chay to the French authorities at Luang Prabang. If they could not take him alive, then they were to bring his head. They were also to deliver his rifle, a one-of-a-kind Hmong flintlock with a copper stalk. The French knew that a Hmong and his rifle are inseparable; he will part with it only in death. Since no Frenchman knew for sure what Pa Chay looked like, his rifle would constitute good evidence that the rebel leader had indeed been killed.

The two Hmong knew just where to find Pa Chay. When they found him he did not put up a fight, but sat quietly in front of his hut, consigned to the fate which he himself had prophesied. After they shot him, they cut off his head, fetched his rifle, and set off for Luang Prabang and their reward.

As the story goes, the trip back was uneventful until they approached the Nam Ou River. It began to rain. They had crossed the Nam Ou in a makeshift raft a few days earlier. Since it was the beginning of the dry season, the river had been shallow and the crossing easy. By the time they located their raft, the river was up several feet, the current rapid, and the water churning. They debated whether to cross now or wait out the storm. The lure of the reward clouded their judgment. Once in the river, the raft bobbed and pitched uncontrollably and then capsized. The two Hmong held onto the raft until it came to shore downstream. They still had Pa Chay's gun, but his head had been carried away by the current. Then, as suddenly as it had started, the rain stopped.

The two assassins spent a day and a half walking the river bank, looking for Pa Chay's head. They found a head lodged in the branches of a half-submerged tree. But it wasn't Pa Chay's. It was the head of one of the two assassins, Yang Koua, or at least a double since Yang Koua's head was still firmly attached to his shoulders.

The two were more than a little puzzled; they were frightened. Even so, they had the 150 silver piasters to consider. Despite their misgivings, they continued on to Luang Prabang with the strange head and delivered it, along with Pa Chay's rifle, to the French. Reportedly, a few months later a new species of flower bloomed in the mountains of Laos. The flower is real, even if its origin is questionable. Its delicate blue blossoms dot the mountain slopes in the late fall. To the Laotian Hmong it is a living memorial to Pa Chay, and to this day they call it Pa Chay's Wheat.

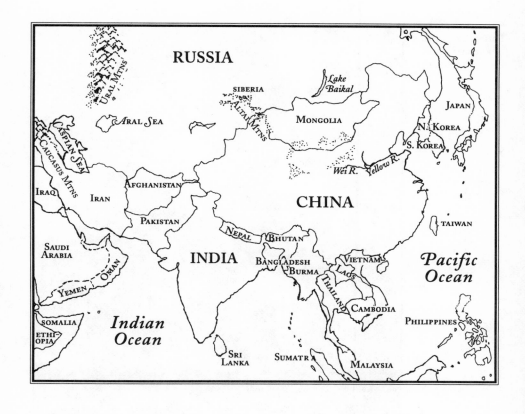

RUSSIA

URAL MTNS

ARAL SEA

SIBERIA

ALTAI MTNS

Lake Baikal

MONGOLIA

JAPAN

N. KOREA

S. KOREA

CASPIAN SEA

CAUCASUS MTNS

IRAQ

IRAN

AFGHANISTAN

CHINA

Wei R.   Yellow R.

TAIWAN

PAKISTAN

NEPAL   BHUTAN

SAUDI ARABIA

INDIA

BANGLADESH

BURMA

VIETNAM

LAOS

Pacific Ocean

YEMEN   OMAN

THAILAND

SOMALIA

ETHI-
OPIA

Indian Ocean

SRI LANKA

SUMATRA

CAMBODIA

PHILIPPINES

MALAYSIA

CHAPTER 8

Touby

*W*HEN PA CHAY was assassinated in 1922, the Hmong rebellion he inspired officially ended. But an earlier and even bloodier uprising in China, the Great Panthay Rebellion, set in motion events that would culminate in the rise of Touby Lyfoung, a Hmong leader whose renown would rival Pa Chay's. Though thousands of Hmong in Yunnan and Szechwan sided with the Haw in their struggle for an independent state, some Hmong tried to remain on the sidelines. The Chinese generals charged with pacifying the region slaughtered them anyway. Among the neutralists who survived were Ly clansmen who fled to Laos from Szechwan. They harbored ill feelings toward the Yunnanese Hmong who, by openly allying themselves with the Muslims, caused the deaths of innocent Hmong and forced many Ly to abandon their homes and fields for a strange land.

One of these hated Hmong, traveling with a Haw, arrived in Laos in 1865 and settled near Nong Het where other Ly immigrants resided. His fellow clansmen ostracized him. The chilly reception caused him to move to a small village on the outskirts of Nong Het, where he married and raised three sons. One of them, Foung, was unusually bright, having mastered at an early age not only Chinese but also Vietnamese and French. Quite early Foung set his mind to removing the taint on his family name by marrying into one of the most prominent of the Laotian Hmong families, that of the Lo kiatong, Bliayao Lo.

Foung's marriage to Bliayao Lo's daughter, May, took place in 1918. The marriage was reportedly by abduction, though it is inconceivable that Foung would have attempted anything so bold without first having made certain that Bliayao Lo considered him an acceptable son-in-law, hampered only by the inability to pay a large bride price. Foung found immediate employment as the kiatong's personal secretary, and the fortunes of the once outcast Yunnanese Ly family improved both economically and socially. Foung's new employment pulled him out of poverty, and his close association with the Lo kiatong insured that he was at last accepted by the Szechwan Ly as a clansman in good standing.

RIFT BETWEEN THE LO AND LY

Foung and May had a son and a daughter, Touby and Mousong. While May must have taken considerable pride in the fact that little Touby was every bit as precocious as his father, her marriage turned sour when Foung took a second wife whom he favored over her. While such favoritism was contrary to the spirit of Hmong polygamy, there was little May could do but complain, for which she reportedly received numerous beatings, something that was also contrary to the spirit of Hmong marriage, polygamous or not. No doubt relatives on both sides tried to bring Foung to his senses, but before anything was resolved, May committed suicide by taking an overdose of opium.

Not only did May's suicide cause a serious rift between Foung and Bliayao Lo, it also strained relations between the Lo and Ly clans. In 1922 Foung was dismissed from his position as Bliayao Lo's personal secretary. Sensing that tensions between the two clans might lead to armed conflict, Hmong elders approached the French and recommended that authority over the district of Nong Het be divided between Lo and Ly. With the memory of the Pa Chay rebellion still quite fresh, the French were eager to do anything to smooth rough waters. They gave the Ly clan authority over the Nong Het subdistrict of Keng Khoai, and allowed the Lo to administer the subdistrict of Phac Boun. For over a decade, until Bliayao Lo's death in 1935, an uneasy peace was maintained by means of this compromise.

It was during this period that the first Hmong attended the French elementary school (Groupe Scholare) in Xieng Khouang city. Nao Tou Moua, the head of the Moua clan in Xieng Khouang province, was the first to send his children to the school; in addition to his two sons, Yang and Chu Chao, he financed the education of three nephews, Ya Tong, Chue No, and Nao Pao. In due course, Foung' sons, Touby and Tou Zeu, began their lessons. Of the handful of Hmong children who entered school at this time, only the two Ly boys completed their education at the lycée and received baccalaureate degrees. Tou Zeu was one of the first Hmong to graduate from college, and Touby went on to attend college at the School of Law and Administration at Vientiane.

The value of a French education for future Hmong politicians was not lost on Bliayao Lo who packed up three of his younger sons, Faydang, Nghia Vue, and Fong, and enrolled them in the French school. The kiatong's eldest son, Song Tou, was too old to attend school and was appointed tasseng (administrative head) of the Keng Khoai subdistrict of Nong Het. The aging kiatong pinned his hopes on Song Tou to take over after his death and outwit the Ly clan in what had become a struggle for political leadership of all the Hmong of Xieng Khouang province. Bliayao Lo was certain that before his body was cold Foung Ly would begin to jockey for power and, if successful, pass it on to his talented son, Touby. The kiatong must have expected the worst. From his deathbed he left instructions that should the Ly begin to gain the upper hand, his family must immediately sacrifice several oxen as a sign to his spirit to return to Nong Het and help Song Tou struggle against the Ly.

Song Tou was certainly in need of any help he could get. Bliayao Lo died in 1935, and in the years that followed, Song Tou's political incompetence became a matter of record. Instead of discharging his duties as tasseng, he spent his days hunting and gambling. This got him into trouble with the French. While the colonial administration might look the other way when native administrators abused citizens, they considered tax collection a sacred trust. Not only did Song Tou fail to regularly collect taxes, he also sometimes used tax revenues to pay off gambling debts.

When Foung offered to make up for the lost tax revenue out of his own pocket, the French displayed their gratitude by dismissing

Song Tou and giving Foung his post. Foung immediately appointed Touby tasseng over Phac Boun, expanding the Ly power base which now encompassed nearly all of Nong Het district.

Song Tou and the Lo clan were disgraced. Song Tou appears to have been less affected by his fall from power than his younger brother Faydang who traveled all the way to the Royal Palace at Luang Prabang to lodge a complaint. Prince Phetsarath granted him an audience as well as a concession. While the decision of the French could not be reversed, Phetsarath promised that on Foung's death, authority over Keng Khoai would revert to the Lo clan and Faydang himself would be made tasseng of the subdistrict. It was an attractive compromise since Foung was already quite old and not in the best of health. In fact, he died just nine months later, in September of 1939.

The French chose not to honor Phetsarath's promise to Faydang. The tasseng position was given to Touby instead. One reason for the bad faith was the perception that Faydang had obstinately defied French authority by going over the heads of local colonial administrators and directly appealing to the royal court at Luang Prabang for a redress of grievances. Put simply, the man was not to be trusted. Of equal importance, however, was Touby himself who not only spoke fluent French and was something of a Francophile but whose training in French law and administration, as well as his talents as a bureaucrat, made him an ideal choice. In fact, the French were as eager as Touby to see his political star rise.

Touby's ambitions were larger than even the French imagined. Once he had won French confidence and support for a Hmong power base, he planned to use it as a lever to gain concessions for Hmong schools and government positions. Eventually he would demand the integration of the Hmong into Laotian national politics.

At the time, most Laotian Hmong would have viewed Touby's aspirations as hopelessly utopian. They had always been treated as second-class citizens by the ethnic Lao and exploited by Laotian officials. It was particularly humiliating to the proud Hmong to have to literally grovel before Laotian bureaucrats. Head down, crawling on hands and knees up the steps of the official's office to his desk, they had to kneel patiently until the Laotian recognized their presence. Trade with the Laotians was a constant reminder to the Hmong of their inferior status. They were charged several times more than Laotians for goods, and when they sought employment in lowland towns, their wages were invariably half of what a native Lao received. Few Hmong expected this to change. The general perception was that the most that could be hoped for was an increase in village autonomy so that the Hmong might get by with as little contact with Laotian officials as possible.

The principal strategy behind Touby's plan to raise both the social status and political clout of the Hmong was at once simple and persuasive. It was to make the French dependent on the Hmong. Should such a dependency come to pass, the Hmong could pressure the French to exert their considerable influence over Laotian political elites to concede political power to the Hmong.

Whether Touby had, at this early date, worked out in his mind the details of what this concession should include, a reading of his later actions suggests that quite early on he considered it imperative for the Hmong to find representation in the councils of the national government and to be granted political autonomy at the local level. These were actually two sides of the same coin. Local political autonomy would bring an end to the exploitation of the Hmong by local authorities who would now be Hmong rather than ethnic Lao. And with more Hmong occupying positions of power in provincial bureaucracies, Hmong would naturally achieve political maturity and their chances of becoming a permanent political force would improve.

This was not just wishful thinking. Laotian demographics dictated it as the natural course of Laotian politics. While ethnic minorities make up a large proportion of the populations of every nation in Southeast Asia, only Laos can justifiably be called a nation of minorities. Fewer than fifty percent of Laotians are ethnic Lao; the rest are Kha (*Khmu*), highland Tai, Akha, Lolo, Lisu, Lahu, Yao, Vietnamese, and Hmong. The ethnic Lao monopolized power only because the other ethnic minorities remained politically backward. Touby meant to turn things around, at least as far as the Hmong were concerned. With French patronage, the Hmong would have representation in the national government and establish a provincial political base of sufficient size and strength to give their representatives bargaining power with the Lao elite. In time this would translate into new schools for Hmong children who would, at last, be able to compete on an equal footing with the ethnic Lao. There would also be new hospitals, and new roads would be constructed to integrate Hmong communities into regional markets, permitting the diversification and growth of the Hmong economy.

Before all this could come about, the Hmong would have to become indispensable to the French. In this endeavor, Hmong opium would play a key role, as would Hmong proficiency in mountain warfare, demonstrated to the French in the last days of the Japanese occupation of Indochina and during the post-war campaign to reestablish colonial rule in Laos.

SUPPORTING THE MAQUIS

When France fell to Germany in 1940, it was relatively easy for the Japanese to obtain the concession from the colonial administration for the free movement of Japanese troops in French Indochina. Isolated from the home government in France, the French colonial administration, headed by Admiral Decoux, adopted a policy of business as usual. No military action was mounted against Japanese troops, and every effort was made to avoid confrontations that might antagonize the Japanese and lead to reprisals. For their part, the Japanese were perfectly content to permit the French to administer Indochina so long as it did not hamper the Japanese occupation or hinder efforts to monopolize exports of rice and certain minerals such as tin, tungsten, and manganese needed by Japanese arms and munitions factories to meet the growing demands of the Japanese war machine in the Pacific.

With the liberation of Paris in August 1944, all this soon changed. De Gaulle quickly set about planning a resistance movement in Indochina. French commandos (maquis) were parachuted onto the Plain of Jars in November with orders to establish guerrilla bases. When Japanese intelligence learned of the event, it was misinterpreted as a preparation for an allied invasion of Indochina, a view that was reinforced several months later by u.s. air raids on Japanese ships in Vietnamese harbors and rail yards in the Red River delta region of northern Vietnam. In March 1945 the Japanese moved quickly to disarm and imprison thirteen thousand French soldiers. Some French garrisons, like the those in Hue and Tonkin, put up a fierce resistance, inflicting heavy casualties on the Japanese before surrendering.

In Laos, new life was breathed into the French resistance when more French commandos were parachuted in from India. The commandos received much needed logistical support from a handful of colonial army officers and noncommisioned officers who, with the help of Touby and his Hmong partisans, had managed to elude the Japanese dragnet. When the Japanese caught wind of Hmong involvement in the operation, they arrested Touby. He might very well have been executed had it not been for the intercession of Monsignor Mazoyer, the Catholic bishop of Vientiane, who advised the Japanese that mistreatment of a Hmong leader could easily invite a Hmong uprising. Touby was released, wiser but hardly repentant. In short order he presented himself to Captain Bichelot, who commanded the French maquis at Phoun San on the eastern edge of the Plain of Jars, and pledged Hmong support to the beleaguered commandos. Since the Hmong did not have modern weapons and were no match for Japanese units equipped with machine guns, they played chiefly a support role for the maquis, serving as guides and interpreters and hiding French officers from the Japanese in Hmong villages.

Hmong support was not without its costs. In an attempt to intimidate the Hmong and coerce them into abandoning the maquis, the Japanese repeatedly attacked defenseless Hmong villages which were suspected of helping the French. It was testimony to Touby's rising popularity that despite the attacks the Hmong rallied solidly behind him. The French were appreciative, too, promising Touby that, at the close of the war, the Hmong would be guaranteed positions in the colonial administration and especially in the ministry of education to insure that there would be schools for their children.

Not all the Hmong supported the French. Faydang, still seething over the French refusal to honor Prince Phetsarath's promise to grant him the tasseng position at Keng Khoai, actively collaborated with the Japanese in hunting down French commandos. His guiding principle, which he would publicly avow a year later, was simple: "Whatever Touby and his men do, I and my men will do the opposite."

REOCCUPATION

When the war was over, the French lost no time attempting to regain control of Indochina. They reoccupied the southern delta region of Vietnam with relative ease, though to France's discredit this was accomplished with gratuitous savagery. The reoccupation of northern Vietnam was another matter.

There were nearly two hundred thousand Chinese troops in northern Vietnam when the Japanese surrendered. The French paid a high price to get them to leave. In February 1946, France signed the Chungking agreement in which China promised to pull all troops out of northern Vietnam for France's promise to relinquish its concessions in Shanghai, Tientsin, Hankow, and Canton.

The next item on the agenda was the Vietminh. Supported by the u.s., Ho Chi Minh had organized the Vietnamese military resistance against the Japanese. The Vietminh army, led by Vo Nguyen Giap, had grown to dangerous proportions, which became all the more ominous when the Japanese, preferring to surrender to Asians rather than westerners, handed over their weapons to the Vietminh. On the political side, the Vietminh had spearheaded an independence movement, conducted elections, and installed Ho as the president of an independent Vietnam. While the French refused to formally acknowledge the legitimacy of the new government, they nevertheless invited Ho to Paris in the hope that he might be persuaded to accept the status quo with only minor modifications. To strengthen their position, the French installed a puppet regime in the south which claimed to represent the entire nation. Once in Paris, Ho realized the hopelessness of his position and was forced to accept a loose agreement that included a national referendum on the independence issue that was to be followed with a resumption of negotiations on full Vietnamese independence sometime in 1947.

An uneasy peace between the Vietminh and the French forces, who had reoccupied the Red River delta region, was shattered in late November of 1946 when a dispute between Vietminh and French custom officers over tax authority in Haiphong harbor led to an exchange of gunfire. The French shelled the city of Haiphong, killing six thousand Vietnamese citizens. Within a month the Vietminh responded with coordinated attacks against French military and civilians in Hanoi and guerrilla raids on French installations throughout Vietnam before retreating into the northern Vietnamese highlands and settling in for a long war.

Compared to the troubles the French encountered in northern Vietnam, the reoccupation of Laos was relatively uncomplicated. True, troops had to be held back from northwestern Laos until China's 93rd Infantry Division pulled out. The 93rd had remained in Laos beyond the agreed-upon withdrawal date so they could confiscate all the Hmong opium they could carry home. For the French the delay was an inconvenience, nothing more.

Of greater concern was the Laotian independence movement led by Prince Phetsarath. The movement had earlier received an unexpected shot in the arm when, in March 1945, the Japanese occupation force imprisoned all French colonial administrators and demanded that king Sisavang Vong proclaim Laos an independent state and formally sever all political ties with France. Phetsarath quickly persuaded the Japanese to fill the Laotian civil service with pro-independence Laotians. By October of that same year he succeeded in organizing a new government, the Lao Isalla or Free Laos, in Vientiane. A constitution was drawn up and members of a provisional people's assembly selected.

Elements of the French commandos who had been parachuted onto the Plain of Jars in northeastern Laos several months earlier occupied the royal palace at Luang Prabang and forced the aging king to renounce independence and strip Phetsarath of all power. Though Phetsarath felt obliged to obey the edict of his king, other members of the Lao Isalla turned to the Vietminh for support, granting Vietminh military units complete freedom of operation in Laos. Vietminh agents hurried to Laotian towns with large Vietnamese populations and encouraged residents to whip up support among the ethnic Lao for the Vietnamese communists.

The Vietminh flag waved in many of these communities. In Xieng Khouang province, however, the Vietnamese community at Khang Khay did more than just wave flags; they armed themselves with weapons stolen from the Japanese and declared Xieng Khouang a prefecture of Vietnam. With the arrival of Vietminh troops from Hanoi, joined later by units of the Lao Isalla dispatched from Vientiane, the Vietnamese dug in and prepared to defend the newly claimed territory from being reoccupied by the French.

SETTLING OLD SCORES

By this time Touby's forces had received modern weapons and he was eager for every opportunity to prove the worth of his Hmong guerrillas to the French. In November 1945, in a joint action with French commandos, Touby and his Hmong routed the Vietminh forces and drove them out of Xieng Khouang. By January, when French reinforcements arrived in the province, the Lao Isalla partisans had already departed, retreating across the Plain of Jars to safety. Fearing French and perhaps even Hmong reprisals, thousands of Vietnamese living in Xieng Khouang packed up and left for Vietnam. The French allowed Hmong to claim the abandoned villages, many containing the best farmland in the region.

With the province firmly under French control, Touby turned his attention to the matter of settling old scores. Faydang was in the area, still carrying on his war against the French, his most recent triumph being an ambush against sixty troops commanded by two

French officers. Armed only with traditional crossbows, Faydang's guerrillas killed eight of the soldiers and sent the rest packing for the safety of their garrison.

Touby itched to get his hands on the rebel. When he learned from two of his partisans that Faydang's brother, Nghia Vue Lo, was in Nong Het visiting his father-in-law, Nao Tou Moua, he sent thirty of his soldiers to capture him.

Nghia Vue had an ulterior motive for visiting his father-in-law. A direct descendant of the Moua kiatongs and leader of his clan, Nao Tou Moua was much respected by the heads of the other clans. When Touby's work for the French maquis took him to Nong Het, he often stayed at Nao Tou Moua's home. Nghia Vue believed that if anyone could help mend the rift between the Lo and Ly clans it was Nao Tou Moua. When he broached the issue, the old man immediately agreed to act as an intermediary and suggested that if Faydang was sincere about returning to the fold, a simple monetary penalty might be sufficient to settle matters. He even offered to help raise the needed funds.

Nghia Vue went to sleep that night with high hopes that an end to the clan feud was near at hand. They were shattered when he was dragged out of bed by Touby's partisans in the middle of the night. Nao Tou Moua was furious that Touby had so little respect for their friendship and his own standing in the Hmong community that he would sanction the raid. He ordered the soldiers out of his house. They ignored the command and proceeded to beat Nghia Vue, breaking his ribs and knocking him unconscious.

By this time other villagers had gathered around the home, most of them Moua clansmen. One of them, Chia Xa, confronted the soldiers and asked why they did not show Nao Tou Moua the respect he deserved. When they threatened to lay hands on him, he called his fellow clansmen to arms. In short order a small army of Moua riflemen were gathered in front of the house. The soldiers were in over their heads. Touby would not be pleased if they started a feud with the Moua clan. No doubt they were relieved when Nao Tou Moua ordered them to take their prisoner and leave the village. He did not like turning Nghia Vue over to them, but it meant the soldiers could leave and still save face. The soldiers hastily carted Nghia Vue out of the house and left for the village of Phou Do where Touby was headquartered at the time.

After Nghia Vue recovered from his beating, Touby had him taken to Xieng Khouang city, perhaps with the intention of handing him over to the French. On the way Nghia Vue escaped into the forest and made his way back to his brother's village near Nong Het. Touby quickly organized an attack on Faydang before he had a chance to retaliate for his brother's mistreatment, but when he arrived at the village with sixty of his men, he found it deserted. Faydang had been warned of the attack and moved his forces across the Vietnamese border to the village of Muong Sen.

Touby opened a brief, but inconclusive, round of negotiations with Faydang by mail. Bargaining from strength, Touby expected Faydang to be conciliatory. Though Faydang desired peace between the two clans, he was unwilling to admit guilt when he believed it was all on the other side. It was Touby and the French who had wronged him and not the other way around. Touby stopped writing letters and led troops across the border to attack Mouong Sen and kill Faydang. Only a few Lo clansmen were killed during the assault. Faydang and the rest of his men (about two hundred in all) escaped and fled deeper into Vietnam.

Shortly after the failed assault, Faydang made contact with the Vietminh who promised to support him in his struggle against Touby. Two months later he was guiding a Vietminh column into Laos. The die was cast. The French branded him a diehard communist, which was confirmed in the summer of 1950 by Faydang's participation (as a minister without portfolio) in the Pathet Lao's First Resistance Congress. Branded a communist and outlaw by the French, it was impossible for Faydang to ever again live freely among the Laotian Hmong unless the French were driven out of Laos. When the Americans replaced the French, it meant he would never be free unless the Vietnamese-backed Pathet Lao (Laotian Communists) succeeded in their efforts to transform Laos into a communist state.

TOUBY AND OPIUM

As Touby had hoped, Hmong support for the French maquis against the Japanese and Vietminh fortified the ties between the French and Hmong. There would be many other occasions when the Hmong would demonstrate their military value, not only to the French but also to the Americans who became increasingly involved in Laotian politics and military affairs following the 1954 Geneva Conference that gave Laos its independence. But Touby had not relied on Hmong military prowess alone to ingratiate his people to the French.

When shipping to Indochina was interrupted during the Second World War, the French were no longer able to rely on imported opium to supply the needs of the colonial opium monopoly. They turned to domestic sources to fill the gap. Touby realized that since the Hmong were the principal producers of raw opium in Laos, they were in a good bargaining position to gain French support for greater Hmong political and economic equality in Laos.

Before this could come to pass, however, the Hmong had to dramatically increase the size of their opium harvests. Touby used his influence with the French to land a position on the Opium Purchasing Board, the first Hmong to ever do so. He sat on the board for eight years, long enough for the traditional Hmong economy in Laos to change from subsistence to cash crop farming, and the annual opium harvest yield to expand from fifteen to forty tons. The key to this transformation was new taxes. With Touby's blessing, the existing per capita tax was doubled. Given the meager incomes of Hmong farmers, the tax asked the impossible. Many Hmong did not earn that much in a year. Touby knew this, but then the object of the tax was not to directly increase tax revenues but to indirectly increase opium production. To serve this end, the new tax had a loophole. It could be paid in kind rather than in specie. The specific amount was two kilograms of raw opium, nearly twice what the average Hmong farmer harvested prior to the new tax scheme which went into effect in 1943.

Few Hmong welcomed the new tax; even fewer understood Touby's reasons for backing it. Certainly he did not make the rounds of Hmong Villages advertising the tax as a way to expand opium production and increase French dependency on the Hmong. It is doubtful many would have found the scheme plausible anyway. The coercive nature of the new plan was sufficient to make it unacceptable.

To thwart tax evasion, Touby made Hmong chieftains responsible for collecting the tax. The minimum aggregate tax was determined by a census. Village chiefs informed subdistrict heads of the number of adult males in their village. This information was passed on to the Hmong tasseng who counted up the total and delivered the figure to the French. On the assumption that the lion's share of the tax would be paid in opium, the census provided the opium board with an estimate of the amount of Hmong opium available to the French opium monopoly. However, the estimate was only reliable so long as the Hmong paid the tax in opium instead of selling it on the black market and paying the tax out of the proceeds.

The in-kind provision of the tax fixed the price of a kilogram of raw opium at a little over two piasters, far below the black market price. To prevent Hmong from selling on the black market, the French prohibited private agents, mostly Chinese Haw, from purchasing Hmong opium in the prime opium-growing provinces of Xieng Khouang and Sam Neua. As an additional safeguard, Touby persuaded the French to give kickbacks to Hmong tax collectors for opium collected in excess of census estimates, creating an incentive for them to police illegal sales to black marketers. Judging by the fortunes made by some tax collectors, amounting in certain cases to hundreds of bars of silver, the program was a remarkable success.

The only drawback was that the reduction in black market sales reduced the potential income of Hmong farmers and created hard feelings between them and their leaders. Even so, Touby's prestige remained high. Not only did the French increase Hmong autonomy at the local level, they became less tolerant of Lao abuses of the Hmong. For the first time a marked, albeit grudging, deference was being shown by native Lao in Xieng Khouang province toward their Hmong neighbors. For Touby, this was just one of many changes he was certain would inevitably follow increasing French dependence on Hmong opium.

By 1946, however, events forced Touby to ponder whether it was feasible in the long run to rely on Hmong opium to gain political leverage with the French, for in that year France at last gave in to international public opinion, officially dismantled the opium monopoly, and launched a five-year program to cure opium addiction in Indochina.

If the colonial administration had been sincere, the program might have succeeded because the post-war surge in imported opium declined precipitously in the early 1950s before coming to an abrupt halt. This was the result of two events: the 1949 communist takeover of China and the 1953 United Nations protocol on international opium trade.

Under Mao, China finally eradicated opium production on Chinese soil. The move was not entirely humanitarian. Yunnan was the principal opium-producing province in the country, and much of the opium smuggled out of the province into Burma was controlled by the remnants of Chiang Kai-shek's Nationalist Army. Revenue from these operations kept both the army and Chiang's dreams of a counterrevolution alive. Every poppy field eliminated in the province reduced that revenue which, by the mid-1950s, declined to almost zero. Not only did this affect the fortunes of Chiang Kai-shek, it also cut off Indochina from this once lucrative source of raw opium and increased its dependency on imports from the Middle East, in particular from Iran which had become the major exporter of raw opium in the area.

Iran, however, was unable to make up the difference. It could not even maintain its customarily high level of exports, for as one of the signatories to the 1953 United Nations protocol, Iran was obliged to reduce its opium production. By 1955 this obligation was nearly met. The opium harvest yielded only 4.1 tons of raw opium, approximately sixteen percent of the harvest five years earlier.

If this dramatic reduction in imports had been coupled with a zealous program of opium crop reduction in Indochina, the French could have significantly diminished the size of the narcotics market in southeast Asia. This did not occur. Instead, Southeast Asian opium production was dramatically increased, and continued to increase for another fifteen years until 1970 when southeast Asia produced enough opium to supply not only its own markets but also the illicit international narcotics market.

A principal cause of the French failure to reduce opium production in Indochina was that, whatever the official declaration, they did everything to expand it. The opium monopoly did not actually disappear; it went underground. And for good reason. The financially strapped colonial administration was in desperate need of funds for the war against the Vietminh. Correspondingly, Hmong opium increased in importance. It was a crucial source of revenue, and purchasing Hmong opium was perceived as an important way to retain their loyalty at a time when they played and ever more active role in the war.

This was the situation in the early 1950s. In 1946, however, when the French officially dismantled the opium monopoly and the war with the Vietminh was just heating up, the incentive to increase opium production had not been so high. It is possible that Touby sensed that the Hmong were at a crossroads. For the short term the French would continue to purchase Hmong opium. A 1948 edict issued by the High Commissioner for Indochina granted the Hmong a virtual monopoly in opium farming in Laos. Touby knew full well at that time that one of the reasons the French were purchasing nearly every kilo of Hmong opium was to keep it out of the hands of the Vietminh who could exchange opium for arms on the Chinese border and outfit a full division with the harvest from one province. If the Vietminh were to lay their hands on the majority of Hmong opium in Laos and northern Vietnam, they could easily outfit an entire army. In 1947 alone the estimated value of the opium harvest was 400 million piasters, nearly equal to the revenues for rice exports for all of Indochina that year. But purchasing Hmong opium just to keep it from the Vietminh was not the sort of relationship Touby wanted between the Hmong and French. It made the Hmong and their opium a nuisance—hardly the kind of situation that increased French dependency on the Hmong.

Fortunately, the French High Command was already considering an expansion of a montagnard-supported maquis, modeled after the joint operations that had functioned so well during the Japanese occupation, into a major guerrilla force that would employ the same hit-and-run tactics against the Vietminh that the communists used with devastating consequences against the French Expeditionary Corps. Because of their previous support, the Hmong occupied a pivotal place in these ruminations. In 1948 Touby was flown to Saigon to discuss the possibility of launching an expanded Hmong maquis. While it would take nearly two more years for the French to fully commit to the plan, Touby realized that regardless of the fate of Hmong opium, the chances were good that the French would continue to depend heavily on his people, this time not as opium farmers but as guerrillas.

Thus, by 1950, Touby was pleased to acknowledge that all of his earlier fears about the declining utility of the Hmong for the French had been entirely unfounded. Now not only did the French need the Hmong for their war, it was clear that they meant to finance many of their operations from opium revenues.

Beginning in 1951, and continuing until 1954 with the full knowledge and support from the High Command of the French Expeditionary Corps, a secret project dubbed Operation X supplied much needed revenue for clandestine military operations in Indochina. Its purpose was to airlift Hmong opium from northeastern Laos to Saigon, where it was sold to representatives of international narcotics syndicates and the revenues set aside for the provisioning and training of French-sponsored guerrillas. The first major shipment was actually stored in a military warehouse and accidentally discovered by a French customs inspector, causing a considerable scandal. More circumspect methods were employed after this incident.

Touby's role in Operation X was to collect the shipments from Hmong farmers. Whenever he had gathered close to a ton, he was flown to Saigon where Le Van Vien, former head of a South Vietnamese criminal syndicate and then Chief of the Saigon police, received the illicit goods and tendered payment. Out of this sum Touby set aside five thousand silver piasters that were earmarked for training and equipping his Hmong maquis. The rest was distributed as payment to the farmers who had supplied the opium for the transaction. During this brief period nearly $4 million was collected for the support of Hmong guerrillas under French command. With the French dependent on Hmong guerrillas, and the revenue from Hmong opium set aside to support them, Touby had every reason to be optimistic about future relations between the French and his people. That relationship had already begun to pay large dividends. In 1946 the French granted autonomous status to Laos as a free state in the French Union and helped organize elections for a national assembly. In Xieng Khouang province, a Hmong stood for one of the seats. He was Toulia Lyfoung, Touby's older brother. Toulia won the election and pressed hard in the national assembly for greater recognition of the rights of ethnic minorities at both the national and provincial levels of government. Though the other deputies to the assembly refused to deal with the issue, it was settled for them by a new constitution which, due partially to pressures from the French, contained provisions that guaranteed equal citizenship rights to all Laotians regardless of ethnic origin, and provided for proportional representation of ethnic minorities on the provincial councils. This resulted in the creation of two new Hmong subdistricts, cantons, in Xieng Khouang province, and Touby's appointment as a deputy to the provincial governor, and former schoolmate, Chao Say Kham. The position offered Touby greater power than a seat in the national assembly, for it gave him the opportunity to consolidate Hmong political power in the province and work for an expansion of the number of Hmong cantons, which eventually numbered twenty-four, a seven-canton increase since the end of the Second World War. Even greater political victories were to come. Touby could not foresee at the time that the French were near the end of their rule in Indochina, and the Hmong would eventually be forced to look elsewhere for sponsors.

When the Americans took over from the French, they became

the likely candidate, but by that time Touby's very success with the French damaged his cause with the Americans who considered the French bunglers for having lost Indochina. However, another Laotian Hmong, a professional soldier by training and temperament, would rise to take Touby's place as the representative of his people before a foreign power. The Americans would lavish more on the Hmong than the French ever could have afforded, had they the will to attempt it. Yet, in the end, the Americans would also demonstrate that they were no more adept at governing Indochina than the French.

CHAPTER 9

The Fall of Tonkin

*W*HILE TOUBY WAS BUSY collecting opium and organizing Hmong guerrilla units to counter incursions of Vietminh in northern Laos, the French had their hands full with the Vietminh in northern Vietnam. In January 1950, fifteen Vietminh battalions overwhelmed a small French outpost in the Black River valley, due east of Dien Bien Phu. Another offensive, larger and further north toward the Chinese border, took several towns and badly mauled French forces.

A few months later, in May, four Vietminh battalions, newly trained and supplied by the Communist Chinese, engaged and routed three companies of French infantry who were defending the border town of Dong Khe. Colonial Road 4, a single lane dirt road that ran from Cao Bang in the north all the way to the Gulf of Tonkin, ran along the edge of the town. Since the road was the only link the French had with the north, they quickly organized an airborne strike force to retake Dong Khe and eliminate the enemy's foothold on Colonial 4. The French recaptured the town, but only after suffering heavy casualties.

The French High Command made an urgent request to politicians in Paris to allow for more reinforcements to keep the road open. The politicians not only denied the request, they ordered a force reduction of nine thousand men. It could not have come at a worse time, for Dong Khe was attacked again in September, leaving Cao Bang isolated in the north. Since the mandated troop reduction ruled out a major offensive to regain control of the north, the French decided to withdraw existing troops to the security of the Red River delta. The commander of the garrison at Cao Bang was ordered to immediately evacuate all of the garrison's troops, as well as all Cao Bang civilians, after blowing up the garrison's heavy equipment, including trucks and jeeps. He was then to lead the evacuees south to Dong Khe. A task force of nearly four thousand was already rushing to Dong Khe up Colonial Road 4. Its mission was to retake the captured town a second time and hold it long enough to keep the road open for the Cao Bang refugees.

The majority of the refugees never made the link-up. The commander at Cao Bang did not blow up the equipment as ordered and was forced to stay on the main road with his trucks and heavy artillery. Only after repeated ambushes did he finally realize the wisdom of the original order and, at last, destroy the trucks and artillery. By then precious time had been lost. There were more ambushes on the eighty-five mile march, mostly over mountain trails, to Dong Khe. After four days the few survivors of the march joined what was left of their badly outnumbered rescuers who had retreated to the hills outside of Dong Khe to make their last stand. It was there that the two groups finally linked up and held out against repeated assaults long enough for three battalions of paratroopers to join them and share their deaths.

By the end of the year, the French had lost almost all of the northern border region of Tonkin to the Vietminh. Communist Chinese support had turned the tide. By providing sanctuary, arms, and training camps, the Chinese communists gave the Vietminh what they sorely needed to mount a major offensive against the French. Chinese aid was also a primary reason why the Vietminh concentrated their operations in northern Tonkin, and especially against French garrisons near the Chinese border. The object was to maximize the effectiveness of Chinese aid. Despite China's eagerness to provide supplies to the Vietminh, they could only be delivered to military units by coolies traveling at a snail's pace over mountain passes and through dense jungle. This was not only time consuming but also labor intensive. Forty thousand coolies were required to maintain a supply line to an infantry division in the field. The long term prospects of the Vietminh depended upon driving the French from their border enclaves and beginning road construction so supplies could be delivered by trucks instead of coolies.

For the French, the Vietminh offensive was a military disaster. Six thousand French troops were killed in action, equal to fifteen percent of all French losses in the war since 1946. Even more alarming was the fact that supply routes from China stood wide open. Once motor vehicles replaced coolies, the war would be as good as lost. This was not merely Vietminh wishful thinking, even members of the French High Command accepted this assessment.

The one unforeseen bright spot for the French was that the Vietminh offensive had coincided with the outbreak of the Korean war. Rhetoric about a communist takeover of Southeast Asia now had a ring of reality. President Truman was at last persuaded by the hawks in his cabinet to increase military aid to the French. In the next four years the French would receive three billion dollars from America to continue the war. Yet even with the prospect of increased American aid, the French could not defeat the Vietminh by adhering to traditional tactics alone. If the war was to be won, it was imperative to harass and wear down the Vietminh in their own sanctuaries, to cut their supply lines and, if possible, to regain control of border territory. For this guerrillas were needed.

The original idea was to style them after the American and British jungle fighters, Frank Merrill's Marauders and Orde Wingate's Chindits, who kept the Japanese from interdicting supplies sent over the Burma Road to Chiang Kai-shek's forces in China between 1943 and 1944. The problem was that the success of these operations hinged on the ability of the guerrillas to secure bases behind allied lines where they could rest, regroup, and be resupplied after each mission. French guerrillas could not count on this luxury. They would have to work more or less permanently behind enemy lines. Only montagnards like the Hmong, able to live off the land and to count on support and supplies from their own people, could be expected to carry off this kind of operation.

THE GCMA

In early 1950, Colonel Grall was placed in charge of the newly formed Groupement de Commandos Mixtes Aeroportes (GCMA) and given twenty French officers to recruit, train, and equip the new guerrillas. It was a clandestine operation. Although nominally under the authority of the French Expeditionary Corps, the GCMA was actually run by the Service de Documentation Extérieure et du Contre-Espionnage (SDEC), the French equivalent of the American CIA.

There was good reason for all the secrecy. The scope of GCMA operations involved the organization of a montagnard maquis and close cooperation with Saigon criminal syndicates in monitoring and interdicting the activities of communists and pro-communist Vietnamese in the Mekong delta. Then there was the collection and sale of opium to finance GCMA projects, an activity that contradicted official French policy and would embarrass the French if it became public knowledge.

The first maquis recruits to arrive at the training school at Cap St. Jacques (present day Vung Tau), a seaside resort forty miles southeast of Saigon, were not Hmong but montagnards from the High Plateau in southern Vietnam. The High Plateau region was just one of the four areas where guerrillas were to be organized. The other three were Laos, northern Vietnam, and southern Vietnam. Northern Vietnam and Laos, especially Phong Saly, Sam Neua, and Xieng Khouang provinces, had top priority, however.

Grall brought in Colonel Roger Trinquier to take charge of the organization of the maquis in the two most important areas. By the beginning of 1951, Trinquier had recruited Touby into the new guerrilla force. After receiving training at Cap St. Jacques, Touby and a handful of his Laotian Hmong returned to Laos to organize a network of Hmong maquis in Phong Saly, Xieng Khouang, and Sam Neua.

THE TERRESTRIAL DRAGON

Guerrilla operations in northeastern Laos were crucial for denying the Vietminh sanctuary after conducting operations west of the Black River in the troublesome ethnic Thai region of Sip Song Chau Thai (The Land of the Dozen Thai Fiefs) near the Laos-Vietnam border. Even more important was an effective guerrilla force in northern Tonkin where, up to now, the Vietminh had operated with complete impunity. Trinquier had someone in mind for heading up the operation—Chao Quang Lo, a Hmong chieftain from Lao Cai, a town located where the Red River flows across the Chinese-Vietnam border. Chao Quang Lo's birthplace, Lao Pa Chay, was named in honor of the famous Hmong rebel Pa Chay. Given the course of events after the French evacuated the region, this fact seems almost prophetic.

An imposing figure, Chao Quang Lo was extremely tall and slightly stoop-shouldered. His appetite matched his strength which was twice the ordinary man's. Despite his size, he was blessed with the remarkable endurance that is so common to his race. More than once when pursued by superior forces, he led his guerrillas on forced marches covering as much as two hundred kilometers over difficult mountain trails, stopping only occasionally to permit his soldiers to eat.

When he was a boy, a flintlock exploded in his face and blinded him in one eye. The accident did not affect his aim. Chao Quang Lo's reputation as a marksman spread from Vietnam across the border into China. From time to time a Chinese wanting to test his mettle against this renowned Hmong rifleman traveled to Lao Cai for a contest. The stakes were high, a fine rifle or even a horse. The men fired shots nearly seven hundred feet to the target, a small bronze coin imbedded in a tree trunk. Chao Quang Lo seldom missed, a fact evidenced by his ever growing collection of horses and rifles.

Chao Quang Lo's personality was as imposing as his person. He had an aversion for lying that bordered on the obsessive. Any officer under his command who lied to him was summarily shot. Nor did he have much sympathy for cowardice. Few who served under him contemplated retreat or desertion; it was as good as a death sentence. And though Chao Quang Lo appreciated the economic necessity of growing opium as an export commodity, he detested opium smoking and would not tolerate it among his troops. Nor would he trust a civilian who smoked the drug, not even his rich uncle whose social prestige perhaps merited confidence but whose habit made the old man untrustworthy in his nephew's eyes. Convinced his uncle would sell him out for a pipe of the drug, Chao Quang Lo told him nothing at all about his activities, which was wise because the Vietminh would later periodically interrogate the old man who was always able with complete honesty to plead total ignorance of his nephew's whereabouts.

Chao Quang Lo was a natural leader and a superb guerrilla commander. Just the sort of man Trinquier needed to command a montagnard maquis in northern Tonkin. Equally important, he had supported the French in the past and was an avowed enemy of the Vietminh who had more than once tried to confiscate Hmong opium crops near Lo Cai.

Trinquier would have recruited him for the job except that the Hmong guerrilla was presumed dead. When Lao Cai was evacuated along with Cao Bang after the Vietminh captured Dong Khe, Chao Quang Lo refused to abandon the area and remained hidden in the forest with a portable radio to keep the French informed of Vietminh troop movements. Within a month, however, his messages ceased. The logical conclusion was that he had been killed or captured by the enemy. To Trinquier's surprise and delight, he later learned from two Hmong refugees in Hanoi that Chao Quang Lo was still alive.

The cause of the communication break was a Chinese battalion that had crossed the border into Vietnam to sweep the area around Lao Cai for French partisans, and in particular for the one-eyed maquisard, whom the Chinese would later nickname the "Terrestrial Dragon." The Chinese were called in because the Vietminh had mistakenly presumed that with the French gone the Hmong would offer no resistance. To their surprise, when they sent their commissars to Lao Pa Chay to confiscate weapons, Chao Quang Lo politely, but firmly, refused to hand them over. The commissars paid another visit to the village later on, but this time in the company of Vietminh troops. Chao Quang Lo again refused to relinquish the arms, and in language that turned the commissar's face red with rage. "You want our weapons but we very much regret that it is not in our power to grant this wish. On the other hand, if you need bullets, we are able to supply them. More, I trust, than you want." Chao Quang Lo escorted the commissars to the edge of the village and bid them adieu.

The Vietminh attacked that same night, were repulsed and repeatedly ambushed as they vainly tried to retreat to safety. More skirmishes followed until, toward the end of 1951, Chao Quang Lo completely routed the 148th Vietminh regiment stationed at Lo Cai. It was after this humiliating defeat that the Vietminh appealed to the Chinese communists for help.

The Chinese launched a surprise attack against Chao Quang Lo's village. The guerrilla chief put up a fierce resistance, but after a day and a half of constant artillery bombardment, he was forced to retreat into the forest and regroup. The morale of his partisans was low. They were not eager to engage the Chinese a second time. But that is just what Chao Quang Lo ordered. The attack was to take place that very night, for Chao Quang Lo was certain the Chinese would be celebrating their victory and never expect the defeated Hmong to launch a counterattack. He placed his own father in charge of one contingent, an uncle in charge of another. They were to retake Lao Pa Chay from the east and west, while he assailed it from the south. Most of his partisans no doubt imagined that they were being sent on a suicide mission. What they did not know was that Chao Quang Lo had held back a store of machine guns and mortars for just such an occasion, which accounts for his confident remark to one of his men that "tomorrow we shall have lunch together in my home village. There will still be Chinese there, but they will all be dead."

The operation unfolded just as Chao Quang Lo had planned. The Hmong surprised the Chinese, who predictably responded by withdrawing into the center of the town where they were easy prey for the Terrestrial Dragon's mortars and machine guns. By first light the battle was over. The only Chinese who survived were those who had fled during the night. Chao Quang Lo had lunch in the village that afternoon.

The French knew almost nothing about these exploits at the time and were eager to contact the Hmong chief and organize a maquis, later code-named "Chocolate." In February 1952, two Hmong refugees boarded a plane in Hanoi and took off for Phalong, just north of Lao Cai, where they parachuted down with a message to Chao Quang Lo from his cousin in Hanoi, Lo Wen Teu. The essence of the message was simple: prevent the Vietminh from taking over the area at all costs. Of course, the task was already well underway. What Chao Quang Lo needed was not inspiration but arms and munitions to equip his rapidly expanding partisan following.

ARMS AND MUNITIONS

Once the French were apprised of the situation, arms and ammunition were airlifted from Hanoi to Chao Quang Lo's forces. At first only 100 rifles were parachuted in, then 400 more dropped from the sky a week later. By April 1952 Chao Quang Lo had received 2,500 rifles from the GCMA and was well on his way to establishing complete control over the sixty-mile stretch of mountainous terrain between Lao Cai and Hoang Su Phi.

Trinquier was so pleased he awarded Chao Quang Lo the *Croix de Chevalier* and integrated him into the regular army, advancing him to the rank of lieutenant. Though Chao Quang Lo would never serve with the French Expeditionary Corps, the gesture was properly interpreted as a great honor. Trinquier very much wanted to personally award the medal to the Hmong chieftain, but Chao Quang Lo still operated in complete isolation from the French behind enemy lines and the rough terrain made it impossible to clear even a landing field large enough for a Cricket, the nickname for the Expeditionary Corps's all purpose reconnaissance plane, the Morrane-500. While a helicopter could certainly have negotiated a landing, the GCMA did not have any at that time. Under such conditions the best Trinquier could do was fly over the Hmong lieutenant's field headquarters and drop the medal to him.

Chao Quang Lo assembled five hundred of his partisans at the old French post at Phalong for the occasion, all standing at attention as Trinquier flew by in a Dakota. As the colonel passed over the makeshift parade ground, he gave a quick salute and dropped the medal which floated down to the assembly dangling from a small parachute. As the Dakota veered away and began to climb, Vietminh antiaircraft guns opened up. Fortunately, Trinquier had worn a flack jacket. The jacket stopped several large pieces of shrapnel that would have ripped open Trinquier's chest and made his brief fly-over not only his shortest, but also his last, official ceremony as a French officer.

CHINESE REINFORCEMENTS

By April 1952 the survivors of the Chinese battalion charged with defeating Chao Quang Lo fled across the border into China. Chao Quang Lo knew they would be replaced. The Vietminh could not allow the region to slip from their control. It would hamper their supply lines and leave them constantly open to debilitating ambushes. Moreover, as documents captured from the 412th Vietminh reconnaissance battalion revealed, the Vietminh were not in a position to assemble the forces necessary to defeat what Vietminh intelligence estimated to be a rebel force of two thousand men.

To prepare for returning Chinese, Chao Quang Lo radioed Hanoi for a thousand land mines. He placed the mines along a mountain corridor that encompassed an area of nearly sixty square miles. It was a massive undertaking. Rather than divert all his troops to the task, Chao Quang Lo recruited Hmong from the surrounding villages, who were trained for the task by instructors parachuted in from Hanoi. After receiving their instruction, each man carried four land mines and placed them on mountain paths that might be used by Chinese attempting to infiltrate the region. Chao Quang Lao mapped the location of the mines so he could later draw enemy fire and lead the unsuspecting Chinese over the mine fields or, if they were routed, herd them toward the mines.

On June 18, 1952, three regiments of the 302nd Chinese infantry division crossed the border into Vietnam. Within eight hours after they were first spotted, Chao Quang Lo had mobilized all his forces. They engaged the leading regiment high in the mountains, assaulting it in waves. The battle lasted for days until the Chinese finally retreated, goaded on by the Hmong who, like sheep dogs herding a flock to the slaughter, maneuvered the Chinese regiment onto heavily mined trails. Land mines exploded every few minutes. The Chinese soldiers panicked and ran, which discharged more mines. White handkerchiefs appeared everywhere. Hundreds surrendered and were marched down the mountain to Hmong villages below. Within a few days another six hundred laid down their arms and were taken prisoner.

After gathering the captured weapons, Chao Quang Lo had the prisoners divided into groups of ten and each group taken to a separate village with orders that they were to be accorded good treatment. The intent of this was to convince the prisoners that the Hmong really had no quarrel with the Chinese. A number of their officers were persuaded to write letters to that effect and to emphasize that there were no French among Chao Quang Lo's guerrillas, that it was a popular uprising and no threat to the Chinese. Mention was also made of the devastating defeat they suffered at the hands of Chao Quang Lo's Hmong. These letters were then delivered to the commander of the Chinese People's Army headquartered in southern Yunnan.

There were still two other regiments of the 302nd division to contend with. Exploding land mines announced their approach late that evening. Everywhere the advancing division went, each trail, every path, had mines. The explosions continued into the next morning, when members of the Chocolate maquis worked their way up the mountains until they were above the advancing enemy. Dead and dying Chinese were everywhere, yet they continued to advance under the prodding of their commander who used his men as human mine sweepers. Though hundreds had been killed, there were hundreds still left and soon the mines would all be exploded. Chao Quang Lo called a war council. His few hundred guerrillas were no match for a division of Chinese regulars equipped with machine guns and artillery. Their only chance was to split up into small groups. Chao Quang Lo ordered the majority of his maquis to retreat north across the border into China and wait for his instructions. He led the rest south along the Clear River to Song Chay.

Shortly after his departure two more Chinese divisions (104th artillery and 103rd infantry) advanced on the area. One village after another was attacked. Though Chinese machine guns riddled Hmong huts, there were few casualties since most of the Hmong had already left their homes and moved higher up into the mountains. They remained safe until the Chinese opened up with heavy artillery. Many villagers panicked and rushed down the mountain slopes to the valleys below where they were easy prey for the Chinese troops.

Chao Quang Lo was having a hard time also. Besides the constant harassment of the Chinese, the lowland climate took its toll. Chao Quang Lo lost more men to tropical diseases at Song Chay than he had to enemy bullets during all his previous campaigns. He had no choice but to return to mountains and flee through enemy lines into China.

When in late 1952 the French again made contact with elements of the Chocolate maquis still operating near Lao Cai, they found it reduced to a few dispirited partisans hiding in the forest, waiting for their leader to return from China. Hundreds of rifles were dropped from Dakotas in hopes of reviving the Hmong guerrilla organization. The gesture raised the spirits of many who had given up hope and abandoned the fight. Soon hundreds of former maquis were back in harness, collecting new recruits and planning missions.

THE DEATH OF CHAO QUANG LO

When Chao Quang Lo got wind of the revival, he immediately marched south with three hundred men to join his former comrades. He requested machine guns and mortars from Hanoi. Within a few days, thousands of Hmong had joined the refurbished Chocolate maquis. One after another, captured villages were liberated from the Vietminh and Chinese. Everywhere, the enemy was in retreat.

In August 1953, the 103rd artillery and 104th infantry divisions, revitalized with fresh troops, began a new offensive against the Terrestrial Dragon. They attacked from the east. They were joined by the Vietminh 118th division from Lao Cai which attacked from the west. The Chinese set up antiaircraft guns to prevent the French from dropping more arms and ammunition.

It was an effective ploy. Fighting nearly day and night on two separate fronts resulted in high casualties for Chao Quang Lo's men, who were running out of ammunition. By late August, many of Chao Quang Lo's maquisards were near starvation, and he was forced to lead what was left of his guerrilla force up into the mountains where they hid in a deep grotto. Completely encircled by two Chinese divisions, their only hope was that the enemy would not find them. But the Chinese captured Chao Quang Lo's adopted son and tortured the truth out of him.

The Chinese struck in the night. They wanted Chao Quang Lo alive and expected him to surrender once he realized he was surrounded. It was not to be. With a revolver in one hand and a machine gun in the other and a carbine slung over his shoulder, he rushed the enemy. Before he emptied the machine gun he had cut down the first line of Chinese. When he breached the second line his carbine was empty. Armed only with his revolver he continued the charge until he was brought down by a barrage of AK-47s.

The Chinese carried his body from one village to another, putting the corpse on display so the Hmong would know that they no longer had a leader. They then transported the body to China to bolster the spirits of Chinese infantrymen and as material proof that the Terrestrial Dragon was not invincible. Chao Quang Lo's valiant death did not go unacknowledged by the French. Colonel Trinquier awarded him, posthumously, the *Légion d'Honneur*.

THE INVASION OF LAOS

With northern Tonkin under control, the Vietminh concentrated its efforts in the southwest, sending three divisions against French posts located in the Thai tribal territory near the Laotian border. Long allied with the French, the Thai around Dien Bien Phu accepted responsibility for blocking Vietminh incursions into northeastern Laos. However, they were no match for the Vietminh and the communists broke through, leading the French to fear that the

Vietminh would do to northeastern Laos what they had accomplished in northern Tonkin: use it for supply depots and a sanctuary to which they could retreat from the forces of the Expeditionary Corps. The French High Command also worried that if the Vietminh launched a major invasion of Laos, it would so shock French public opinion at home that politicians would demand a withdrawal from Vietnam.

To prepare for this eventuality, the French established a training camp for Laotian Hmong guerrillas on the Plain of Jars and sent five hundred Hmong to Cap St. Jacques for special instruction in the use of field radios. Following the training, Hmong units infiltrated the border areas to observe and report on enemy troop movements. An air field was hastily constructed on the Plain of Jars so that regular troops and armor could be flown in. In early April 1953 the Vietminh and Pathet Lao initiated a combined offensive in Sam Neua province.

Giap, the Commander in Chief of the Vietminh armed forces, was convinced a successful invasion of Laos would turn public opinion in France against the war. He also saw an invasion as an opportunity to draw the French across the border and stretch their supply lines thin. Should they foolishly decide to fight under these conditions, the results might prove catastrophic, as the fall of Dien Bien Phu would later attest.

The Vietminh and Pathet Lao conducted a two-pronged attack. Fifteen battalions drawn from the 308th, 312th, and 316th Vietminh divisions marched south through Sam Neua and attempted to occupy the Plain of Jars. Five more battalions drove due west toward Luang Prabang.

Faydang, Touby's old foe and chief of Laotian Hmong who had cast their lot with the communists, was also on the scene. Commanding his own Hmong unit, he joined in the first prong of the offensive, no doubt hoping for an opportunity to settle old debts after the Vietminh battalions stormed into Xieng Khouang province.

Because of the excellent information supplied by Touby's Hmong, the French were ready for the Vietminh when they reached the Plain of Jars. The French had transformed their main position on the plain into a fortified camp bristling with barbed wire and protected by heavy artillery and tanks. They quickly beat back the invaders. In anticipation of new assaults, forty to fifty small forts were constructed at strategic locations on the plain. Four colonels from the GCMA were dispatched to Laos to meet with Touby and his second in command, a remarkable young Hmong officer by the name of Vang Pao. The agreement was that Touby and Vang Pao would station their Hmong on the crests of the mountains to report on enemy movements and, when feasible, to conduct guerrilla raids and ambushes while the Expeditionary Corps concentrated on protecting the Plain of Jars.

Smarting from the earlier encounter and defeat, the communist forces did not attempt another assault on the Plain of Jars but pushed on to link up with the other five battalions heading for Luang Prabang, the royal capital of Laos, where the forty-nine year-old Laotian king, Sisavang Vong, was in residence. By April 28, the combined communist forces were on the edge of the city. The population of Luang Prabang was thrown into a panic. The French urged the king to flee. He refused, partly out of a stubborn defiance of the invaders, and partly because of the prophecy of a blind monk who claimed that the Vietminh would not set foot in the royal capital. The blind soothsayer was correct. Fearing the prospect of his twenty battalions becoming bogged down and cut off from their supply lines, Giap ordered a general withdrawal to the safety of Vietnam. Like Ho Chi Minh, Giap was a patient man. There would be other invasions and one day Vietnamese troops would remain for good and fulfill Vietnam's destiny to rule all of Indochina, a grand design that had been only temporarily thwarted by the imposition of French colonialism on Indochina nearly a hundred years earlier.

Such is the weakness of objectivity in even the keenest minds. Giap perceived no inconsistency between his hatred of French colonialism and his own vision, shared by his comrades in Hanoi, of a "free" Indochina, united by force of arms if necessary, under the ironfisted rule of the Vietnamese Communist Party.

CHAPTER 10

Vang Pao

*W*ITH THE FALL OF Dien Bien Phu in May of 1954, France's days in Indochina were numbered. Later in the year a Geneva agreement divided Vietnam at the 17th parallel and recognized North Vietnam as a fully independent state. The convention required France to withdraw its military forces from North Vietnam and Laos. The u.s. refused to sign the agreement. President Eisenhower pledged to turn back communist aggression in Southeast Asia, whatever the cost. The u.s. immediately expanded military aid to Thailand, South Vietnam, and Laos, providing military advisors and funds to enlarge their armies to combat communist insurgency. In Laos the aid subsidized the entire cost of the nation's armed forces and became the principal source of revenue for the government. u.s. advisors worked diligently to steer the nation's politics to the right. cia agents bought votes and rigged elections.

Like France, the North Vietnamese were supposed to withdraw their troops from Laos, but many remained to support the buildup of the Pathet Lao, the military arm of the Laotian communist party. The Neo Lao Hak Sat (NLHS) was locked in a struggle with Laotian royalists for control of the country. The contest remained a stalemate until 1957 when, over the protests of the United States, Laotian communists gained representation in a new coalition government. The coalition lasted only eight months. Its collapse was precipitated by the North Vietnamese Army (NVA) occupation of border provinces near the Ho Chi Minh Trail. Pro-u.s. rightists captured power and imprisoned NLHS representatives, a move that prompted the NVA to step up military support for the Pathet Lao. In mid-1959 fighting broke out between units of the Royal Laotian Army (RLA) and Pathet Lao forces, plunging Laos into a civil war. The scale of the fighting was magnified by the involvement of foreign powers. The U.S. supplied the royalists with arms and military advisors, and the NVA supported the Pathet Lao with arms and personnel.

In late 1960, Kong-Lê, a captain in the RLA, led units into Vientiane and took over the government. Declaring himself a neutralist, he sought to end the civil war by banning all foreign troops from Laotian soil. Within a few months he was ousted by CIA-backed rightists, forcing the neutralists into an uneasy alliance with the Pathet Lao. Though the rightists controlled the city of Vientiane, they suffered repeated defeats on the battlefield and, in July 1962, agreed to form a new coalition government that included both communists and neutralists. This coalition, too, was doomed to failure. Frustrated by U.S. efforts to diminish the influence of the leftists in the National Assembly, the communists pulled out of the coalition and took to the battlefield.

The NVA and Pathet Lao launched offensives during the dry season, which stalled to a halt with the first monsoons. Once the rainy season was in full swing, government forces cut communist supply lines and pushed the enemy back. It remained a seesaw war until 1968, when the U.S. employed massive air power on the Plain of Jars to break the deadlock. Between 1968 and 1972, the number of bombs dropped on the plain was greater in total tons than all the bombs dropped by the U.S. in both the European and Pacific theaters during World War Two.

In late 1972 the U.S. informed Laotian Prime Minister Souvanna Phouma of its intention to settle the war in Vietnam and urged him to come to terms with the Pathet Lao before the U.S. pulled out of the region. With the prospect of a cut-off of all U.S. aid, Souvanna Phouma hastily concluded negotiations with the Pathet Lao, conceding nearly everything to bring the fighting to an end. On February 21, 1973, a new government was formed and the next day a general cease fire was officially declared. Unofficially, the communists hedged their bets by continuing their military buildup and engaging in sporadic fighting to expand the territory directly under their control.

In the following year the Pathet Lao maneuvered to take control of the government while continuing to consolidate their forces in

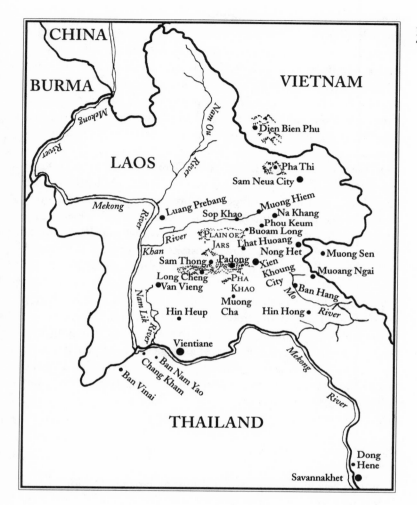

CHINA

BURMA

Mekong River

LAOS

Nam Ou River

VIETNAM

Dien Bien Phu

Pha Thi

Sam Neua City

Mekong

River

Luang Prebang

Muong Hiem

Na Khang

Sop Khao

Phou Keum

River

PLAIN OF

Buoam Long

JARS

Lhat Huoang

Khan

Nong Het

Muong Sen

Sam Thong

Padong

Xien

Muoang Ngai

Long Cheng

Khoung

PHA

City

Van Vieng

KHAO

Ban Hang

Nam Lik

Muong

Mo

Hin Heup

Cha

Hin Hong

River

River

Vientiane

Ban Nam Yao

Chang Kham

Ban Vinai

Mekong

THAILAND

River

Dong

Hene

Savannakhet

the field. Fighting broke out in earnest again in 1974 and an undeclared civil war continued into 1975. On March 27th of that year, Pathet Lao forces accompanied by NVA regulars launched a massive offensive against what was left of the RLA on the southern edge of the Plain of Jars. By the end of August the Pathet Lao had captured Vientiane and organized a "revolutionary committee" to serve as an interim government until something more permanent could be arranged.

In December 1975, the Lao People's Democratic Republic (LPDR) was established, less than a week after the forced abdication of the king. Souvanna Phouma was permanently retired from Laotian politics; his half-brother, Prince Souphanouvong, who had helped found and organize the Laotian communist party, became President of the new communist state. Three divisions of NVA regulars remained on Laotian soil to insure it would not be an independent communist state.

Laos would have fallen to the communists much earlier had it not been for the Laotian Hmong who did most of the fighting for a free Laos and, one must add, most of the dying. Nearly one third of the Laotian Hmong, almost half of all males over fifteen, perished during the conflict. All through the struggle the Laotian Hmong placed their fate in the hands of one man, Vang Pao, the first and only Hmong to rise through the ranks of the RLA and achieve the rank of general.

FROM COURIER TO GENDARME

Vang Pao was fourteen years old when the Japanese invaded Laos. Too young to serve in the maquis as a guerrilla, he nevertheless itched to be part of the war effort. With Touby's help he landed a job as a messenger and interpreter for the French. Though he had only a few years of schooling, starting late and ending early (to paraphrase his own description), Vang Pao was a quick student and, like many Hmong, mastered foreign languages with relative ease. Much of Vang Pao's time during this period was spent as a courier carrying messages between different units of Touby's maquis. On occasion he led French officers, when they parachuted in from India, to the safety of Hmong villages or to hideaways deep in the mountain grottos. By the time the Japanese capitulated he was accompanying French officers on military missions, including the retaking of Xieng Khouang city.

Vang Pao performed his duties with distinction and Touby was eager to reward him with a position in the Xieng Khouang provincial bureaucracy. Restless and always on the move, Vang Pao balked at the idea. He simply did not have it in him to become a career bureaucrat. What he wanted instead was to be assigned to the newly formed provincial police force under Lieutenant Ticot who had recently arrived from Pakistan to take command of the paramilitary unit.

Beginning as a recruit in late 1947, Vang Pao was promoted to corporal in March 1948 and sent a month later to the noncommissioned officer school for corporals of the gendarmerie at Luang Prabang. No doubt it helped his cause that the Xieng Khouang gendarmerie did more than merely keep the peace, for Vang Pao's unit often engaged Laotian rebels and the Vietminh units supporting them in the field, providing many occasions for him to reveal his natural aptitude for command. Vang Pao graduated first in his class. In January 1949, he was promoted to chief-corporal and sent to the National Gendarmerie School where he again graduated first in his class and was promoted to Sergeant-Major. He received two more promotions, achieving the rank of adjutant in October 1950. If Vang Pao was to advance further in rank, he would have to become a commissioned officer.

It was during 1950 that Vang Pao's company of gendarmes participated in a joint operation with a battalion of Laotian riflemen against two enemy battalions, one Vietminh and the other Pathet Lao, operating southeast of Xieng Khouang city. The Pathet Lao battalion held a position near the Mo River, while the Vietminh occupied the village of Ban Hang. Vang Pao's mixed group of gendarmes and riflemen assaulted the Vietminh at Ban Hang; another group of Laotian riflemen attacked the Pathet Lao near the Mo River.

The assault on Ban Hang lasted through the night and into the early morning when the Vietminh retreated toward the border, leaving many dead behind. However, repeated ambushes accompanied by heavy casualties frustrated Vang Pao's pursuit of the fleeing enemy. The French officers in charge argued over what to do next. Lieutenant Casteri, who commanded the forward position, stubbornly refused to lead his men into any more ambushes. Vang Pao, commanding a contingent of his gendarmes, attempted to gain control of the pass used by the Vietminh to launch ambushes, and hold it until the rest of the battalion advanced and linked up. Vang Pao's unit was already well dug into defensive positions when the first Vietminh appeared on the trail. There were six of them. Three were killed, and three escaped, two of them with wounds.

The next day the rest of the battalion caught up and hounded the Vietminh across the border to the Vietnamese village of Muong Sen, a Vietminh stronghold, which they overwhelmed. Their forces broken and scattered, the Vietminh were obliged to adopt guerrilla tactics, operating in small units and using hit-and-run tactics. Accustomed to conventional warfare, the Laotian riflemen performed poorly against these assaults.

The French turned to Vang Pao who was eager to help, so long as he was given a free hand in the matter. He had formed some ideas on how to deal effectively, although unconventionally, with Vietminh guerrillas. Moreover, he intended to rely heavily on Hmong soldiers who, accustomed to guerrilla fighting, did not warm to strict army discipline.

Vang Pao correctly assumed that the key to gaining the upper hand over the Vietminh lay with winning the trust of the civilian population in Vietminh-occupied areas. They were the best source of military intelligence, for they knew the exact deployment and strength of Vietminh units in their locale. It would be necessary to infiltrate enemy territory without being detected. Laotian riflemen were always spotted quickly because they kept to the beaten path. Vang Pao intended to lead his Hmong off the trails up into the dense mountain forest where they would be invisible.

Vang Pao's Hmong unit operated undetected, and the civilian

population proved to be very cooperative. Unlike the Vietminh who often impressed civilians into *corvée* labor and robbed them of their food and livestock, Vang Pao's Hmong never accepted food or shelter from villagers unless it was freely offered. And civilians were never mistreated. Vang Pao avoided situations where attacks on the Vietminh might involve civilian casualties. His most successful operation during this period might have been aborted had the villagers in the Vietminh-occupied town of Hin Hong not been away in the fields harvesting their poppies. The attack came early in the morning when the Vietminh, sleeping contentedly in the village chief's home, were just beginning to stir. Vang Pao's Hmong surrounded the house and on his signal opened fire. Only one Vietnamese escaped, but he was wounded. Vang Pao followed the blood trail into a mountain grotto. He asked the Vietnamese man to surrender, but he refused. Two grenades lobbed into the grotto changed his mind, and he was taken prisoner.

The man carried important documents which were turned over to Captain Fret, the French officer overseeing Vang Pao's operations. One of the documents revealed the meeting place where couriers from the Hin Hong Vietminh (whom Vang Pao had just liquidated) exchanged weekly information with their comrades at Muong Phanh near the Vietnamese border. Captain Fret suggested that Vang Pao and a few of his Hmong take the place of the departed Viets and surprise their Muong Phanh confederates. There were two of them. Vang Pao shot them both, killing one and wounding the other who scurried up a hill and took a position at the base of a large tree. Vang Pao rushed him and was nearly struck by a grenade that exploded a few yards behind him. He tossed his own grenade which found its mark. The courier carried papers detailing the organization and operations of the Vietminh units in the region.

OFFICER MATERIAL

Captain Fret was thoroughly impressed with Vang Pao's military prowess and insisted that the Hmong adjutant apply for candidacy to officer training school. The written exam was parachuted into the military camp at Muong Ngan. Vang Pao took the exam in the military barracks with Captain Fret looking over his shoulder. When Fret realized that Vang Pao could write almost no French at all he remarked, "it is a pity you will damage your career because you do not have a command of grammar or tenses," and proceeded to dictate the correct answers. After passing the oral exam at Vientiane, Vang Pao traveled by dugout canoe down the Mekong River to the officer training school at Dong Hene near Savannakhet.

Vang Pao's studies at the school lasted fourteen months, from the beginning of 1951 until March 1952. He graduated seventh in his class. Despite the traditional training he received at the school, he persevered in his conviction, confirmed by his encounters with the Vietminh in 1950, that only unconventional tactics would prove effective against the Vietnamese communists. This explains his lack of interest in all the gadgetry of the French High Command at Hanoi during a mandatory two week postgraduation tour. Organization charts, complicated chains of command, and set-piece battles had not defeated the Vietminh in the past, and it would certainly not defeat them in Laos in the future.

THE 14TH INFANTRY

Three months after his graduation, Second Lieutenant Vang Pao was assigned to the 14th Infantry company stationed at Muong Hiem on the eastern border of Luang Prabang province, close to communist strongholds in neighboring Sam Neua province. The gendarmerie had been absorbed into the regular military and Vang Pao was now an officer in the RLA. As the only Hmong in the company, his job was to establish contacts with area Hmong who had not been forthcoming with information about communist forces in the province. Their reluctance was understandable. Laotian authorities had abused them for years, and it would take some persuading to get them to cooperate with their former oppressors. Not only was Vang Pao successful in gaining Hmong cooperation in gather-

ing intelligence, he also was able to recruit seventy-one of them into the 14th. Shortly afterward he was promoted to first lieutenant.

In late March of 1953, the Vietminh invaded Laos with seven thousand regulars. The French command ordered the post at Muong Hiem to fortify its position and hold it at all costs in order to receive the French and Laotians retreating from their overrun positions in Sam Neua province. Nearly three hundred French and Laotians made it to Muong Hiem, leaving many dead and wounded behind. When it was learned that fifteen battalions of Vietminh were preparing for a major assault on Muong Hiem, RLA headquarters in Vientiane sent orders to evacuate. Vietminh were already swarming in the hills. The plan was to sneak out at night before the enemy had a chance to launch an attack. To mask the retreat, the post's commander, Captain Cocostequy, had torches placed all around the post and ordered buglers to sound the call for the evening meal. With the enemy convinced that the camp was settling in for the night, the entire camp population departed shortly after dusk. After a five hour march to the top of one of the mountains overlooking the post, the evacuees paused to watch the fireworks below. Before leaving they had stockpiled the post's artillery and ammunition that could not be carried out and set explosives to detonate once they were well away.

The explosion alerted the Vietminh to the escape. Since Vang Pao was familiar with the countryside, Cocostequy placed him in charge of the retreat. Along the way, Hmong villagers provided information which repeatedly saved the column from ambush by the Vietminh. The same villagers also provided food. Vang Pao kept the column off the main roads and trails and traveled the mountain crests where the enemy was unlikely to go. Unused to clambering up steep slopes over rough terrain, the French and Laotians were soon exhausted by the pace Vang Pao set.

Early one morning several days into the march, a wild goat wakened Vang Pao. He took it as an omen from his ancestors that it was unsafe to remain camped in the area. He roused the column to push on, against the protests of the French. They considered talk of omens and messages from ancestors pure nonsense, but they had no knowledge of the terrain and were at Vang Pao's mercy.

By early morning the column had descended the mountain and entered a river valley. All seemed innocent enough, but Vang Pao suspected a trap. It was precisely the sort of terrain he would choose for an ambush: an open field surrounded by thickly wooded hills with the way out of the valley partially blocked by a large butte. If the enemy was deployed as Vang Pao suspected, they would all be drawn into a murderous cross fire. But Cocostequy was not about to leave the valley and return to the mountains. He intended to do the rest of his retreating over flat valley trails. Realizing Cocostequy would not listen to reason, Vang Pao left the column and started up the mountain the way they had come. Other soldiers began to follow, among them some French officers. At that moment enemy soldiers, stationed just where Vang Pao had suspected, opened up with machine guns and mortars. The Laotians panicked and threw away their rifles so they could grasp the bushes with both hands as they desperately clawed their way up the mountain. Only the Hmong held on to their rifles, a habit drilled into them from childhood.

Again Vang Pao led the column to the crests, where it remained until Cocostequy collapsed from exhaustion. Cocostequy transferred command of the Hmong soldiers to Vang Pao, and turned over the Laotians to one of their own officers. Convinced he was going to die, he ordered both groups to leave him behind. The Laotians set off for Luang Prabang while Vang Pao led the remainder of the column, including several French officers, southwest toward Sop Khao, a town on the edge of the Khan River. Before departing he placed Cocostequy in the care of one of his Hmong who was to hide him in a Hmong village until someone could be sent to retrieve them both.

When Vang Pao reached Sop Khao, he learned from Hmong there that the unarmed Laotians had been easily captured by Vietminh and marched back to Muong Hiem, which had become the communist headquarters in the region. He also learned that the Vietminh had been spreading rumors in Hmong villages that he had also been captured in hopes that the Hmong would lose heart and cease providing the French intelligence and sanctuary.

During the second week of May, Vang Pao reached the fortified French camp on the Plain of Jars. The Vietminh assault had bogged down. One cause of the stalled offensive was Touby's maquis who had harassed the communists' supply lines and provided excellent intelligence to the French regarding Vietminh movements and force levels.

FIRST COMMAND

The 14th artillery was gone. However, Vang Pao was at last given his own command: a special commando unit of more than seventy men. A few months later he was brought into the GCMA, sharing responsibility with Touby for the Hmong maquis whose guerrilla network encompassed Xieng Khouang and Sam Neua provinces. Until May of 1954, Vang Pao conducted guerrilla operations around Nong Het on the eastern border of Xieng Khouang province. With the fall of Dien Bien Phu imminent, the French gave him new orders.

As early as April of 1954, it was clear to the French that Dien Bien Phu would fall to the communists unless they could persuade the U.S. to employ massive air power against Vietminh artillery on the mountain slopes overlooking the French garrison. Military analysts in Washington worked out the air assault on paper. Code-named Vulture, the plan included the option of using nuclear weapons. President Eisenhower considered the idea ridiculous and canceled the operation. The French High Command substituted Condor for Vulture, a rescue operation involving four infantry and four airborne battalions who would approach Dien Bien Phu from the south by way of Laos. They would break through the Vietminh forces, blocking the besieged fortress's southern escape route, and attempt to evacuate survivors. As it turned out, the French could not lay their hands on enough transport planes to supply the mission with air drops in the field. Only the four infantry battalions were brought into play. They advanced no further than the bend of

the Nam Ou River at the Vietnam/Laos border where they met
stiff enemy resistance.

With Condor bogged down and Dien Bien Phu ready to fall, it
was decided at the last moment to substitute another plan. In keeping with the bird motif, the plan was named Albatross. It had the
more modest goal of using guerrilla units to infiltrate the area around
Dien Bien Phu and help escapees find their way back to safety.

Touby's guerrillas were to play a pivotal role in the operation,
that is if Touby could be persuaded to go along with the plan. There
must have been some trepidation in this regard, for General Navarre,
Commander-and-Chief of the French forces in Indochina, authorized Colonel Trinquier of the GCMA to offer each of Touby's soldiers a silver bar for undertaking the mission. As it turned out,
doubts about Touby's loyalty to the French were utterly groundless.
He refused any payment for the mission and reminded Trinquier of
his past loyalty, which he had presumed was beyond question.

French commandos and Hmong guerrilla units in Phong Saly
province were closest to Dien Bien Phu and assumed major responsibility for infiltrating the border region near the doomed garrison.
A second group of Hmong guerrillas left Xieng Khouang province
to serve as a rear guard. Touby assigned Vang Pao to lead over three
hundred Hmong north through Sam Neua province toward Dien
Bien Phu. On the way Vang Pao paused long enough for Colonel
Trinquier, who had not seen him for some years, to inspect his
troops. Trinquier was struck by the change in the Hmong soldier.
As the French officer later recalled: "He now had an extraordinary
radiance; he was a leader of the highest order."

CAPTAIN VANG PAO

Vang Pao had just entered Sam Neua province when he learned
Dien Bien Phu had fallen to the communists. He was too far from
the fallen garrison to be of any help to escapees who, as it turned
out, numbered only seventy-eight. Hmong villagers saved the majority by hiding them from the enemy until they were well enough
to travel to the nearest French post.

In December 1954, Vang Pao was promoted to captain and, in 1955, assumed command of the 21st volunteer battalion. In February of the next year he took charge of a battalion at Vientiane and, in June 1958, he was appointed director of the noncommissioned officers school at Khang Khay, but Vang Pao yearned to get back in the field. In 1959 he assumed command of the 10th infantry battalion encamped on the Plain of Jars, close to the headquarters of the Pathet Lao 2nd battalion.

At that time the 2nd battalion was targeted for full integration into the RLA in conformity with the provisions of the 1957 coalition agreement, but it was suspected that the 2nd was instead preparing for an assault against the RLA 10th infantry. Colonel Xang, the commander of Military Region II, ordered Vang Pao to visit the Pathet Lao camp and assess the situation. Vang Pao found it armed to the teeth and battle-ready. When he reported this to his superiors, his battalion was immediately ordered into position on a hill overlooking the Pathet Lao camp, while another battalion took up a position on the main road nearby. That same night the enemy camp went up in flames. The Pathet Lao had put the torch to their own headquarters and fled.

When Vang Pao learned from his scouts what had happened, he naturally expected the battalion guarding the road to launch an ambush against the retreating communists and was astonished to learn that it had never materialized. The Laotian commander guarding the road had refused to fire on his own countrymen. The incident reaffirmed Vang Pao's growing conviction that the war against the communists would never be won if the Laotian government relied exclusively on the ethnic Lao to do the fighting.

Not wanting to let the Pathet Lao 2nd battalion go, Vang Pao headed for a narrow mountain pass near the Vietnamese border. He was certain the fleeing Pathet Lao would use it to reach the NVA post at Muong Sen, just inside Vietnam. When Vang Pao reached his destination, he discovered that a unit of NVA had linked up with the fleeing 2nd battalion. It was these veterans rather than the cut-and-run Pathet Lao who were guarding the pass. The Laotians under his command wanted nothing to do with the NVA who were nicely positioned to pick them off should they try to rush them. Vang Pao and another Hmong, a noncommissioned officer from the Ly clan and a superb marksman, undertook the mission alone.

The two worked their way up the mountainside, dashing and ducking behind boulders, until the NVA were within range of their rifles. The sentries were strung out in pairs. Vang Pao and the Ly clansman cut down the first two in quick succession, then the next two and so on until they had picked off an even dozen. The remaining guard, no doubt feeling a bit like the last bird in a turkey shoot, ran for his life but was finally shot.

By this time another company of RLA soldiers had caught up with Vang Pao's group and the two units pushed on through the pass, routing the NVA who followed their Pathet Lao brothers into Vietnam, leaving a large cache of food and weapons behind.

KONG-LÊ

On August 9, 1960, Kong-Lê, a neutralist, wrested power from the rightists in a successful coup. Though Vang Pao had a grudging admiration for the young Laotian colonel, he was convinced the neutralists were playing into the hands of the communists. A month prior to the coup, Pathet Lao and NVA troops had attacked Royal Army posts in Sam Neua province and launched another campaign to the south along the Ho Chi Minh Trail in the Laotian panhandle. It was no small operation. The NVA threw three regiments and a battalion into the Sam Neua campaign and sent four more regiments and another battalion to support the Ho Chi Minh Trail maneuvers. By the time Kong-Lê declared a new government, they were well on their way to taking over all of Sam Neua province. Meanwhile, Prince Souvanna Phouma, the neutralist prime minister, did nothing but talk of conciliation.

The rightists, led by Phoumi Nosavan, shared Vang Pao's perspective and sought him out as an ally. Though Vang Pao was reluctant to become involved in the intrigues of Vientiane politicians they did have the king's backing. There were two other considerations. The NVA gave every evidence of preparing for a push to occupy the Plain of Jars and use it as a staging area for the conquest of Laos. Thousands of Hmong lived on the plain and surrounding mountains. Because of their past support for the French, Vang Pao believed they would become prime targets for communist "reeducation;" it was in their interest to defend the plain. The other consideration was nationalistic. Vang Pao was convinced that only a revival of the old Hmong guerrilla network on a much larger scale could halt the communist takeover.

With the blessings of the rightists, Vang Pao began organizing a Hmong army at Lat Houang on the southeast edge of the Plain of Jars. It was the first step in a much larger undertaking, that of building a network of nearly seventy thousand Hmong from two hundred villages throughout the highlands surrounding the plain. Once the communists moved to occupy the plain, Vang Pao would give the signal and thousands of Hmong would relocate at seven preselected mountaintops strategically located to cut enemy supply lines.

Although Vang Pao believed this task was manageable from a military standpoint, it required the support of Vientiane politicians. This was Touby's element. Unfortunately, Touby had settled on Souvanna Phouma as his mentor and was firmly allied with the neutralists. To bring Touby over to the rightists, Vang Pao turned to Ya Shao. Considered the most powerful of shaman in Xieng Khouang province, Ya Shao was famous for his ability to contact the spirits and learn where people had left lost articles or, if they were stolen, identify the culprit. Some Hmong claimed they witnessed him remove imbedded shrapnel from the legs and arms of Hmong soldiers, using nothing more than a leaf, which he placed on the wound of the victim and crumpled into a wad to which the metal fragments were miraculously transported. Ya Shao was also one of the few shamans able to combat Ku magic. Originally practiced by the Chinese, Ku caused excruciating abdominal pains, followed by death. While poison or the power of suggestion likely worked this "magic," the Hmong believed it was accomplished by magically reducing the hide of a cow to the size of a mustard seed and then flicking it toward the victim, whose body it entered; the hide then slowly grew back to its original size, causing an agonizing death. Ku magic struck terror in the hearts of most Hmong, and anyone able to combat it was thought to possess enormous powers.

Ya Shao sacrificed two steers to Vang Pao's ancestors for their help in alerting Touby to the communist threat. A short time later, Souvanna Phouma sent Touby to Xieng Khouang city to persuade Vang Pao to abandon the idea of a Hmong maquis. After listening to Vang Pao's arguments for raising a Hmong army, Touby consulted with village chieftains throughout the province; like Vang Pao, they were worried by the communist buildup and favored Vang Pao's plan. As the chieftains were Touby's power base, he could hardly ignore their wishes. Touby endorsed Vang Pao's project and moved into the rightists' camp.

In short order, Vang Pao had more than three hundred Hmong volunteers marching with him to the RLA camp on the Plain of Jars. By the time he arrived the rightists had already taken over the government at Vientiane. Vang Pao distributed weapons to all his men and took command of the camp. The neutralist commander of Military Region II arrived by plane to take charge of what he presumed were his own troops. Vang Pao placed him under house arrest, then flew him to Vientiane.

Meanwhile the rightist commander, General Phoumi, was making a botch of things. After retaking Vientiane, he let Kong-Lê's forces escape to Vang Vieng. Not only had Kong-Lê left most of his heavy armor behind, but Vang Vieng could not be easily defended. In Vang Pao's opinion, if Phoumi had given pursuit and launched a major attack, the neutralists would have been out of the picture for good. Instead Phoumi took three days off from the war to celebrate his Vientiane victory: time enough for Kong-Lê to be resupplied by Soviet cargo plans and joined by NVA advisors. By the time Phoumi was ready to again take up arms, Kong-Lê was already engaged in a diversionary action toward Luang Prabang. Phoumi panicked and sent six battalions against him only to see the neutralist quickly change course and make a dash for the Plain of Jars, supported along the way by Soviet airdrops and Vietnamese paratroopers.

All that stood in Kong-Lê's way was Vang Pao, newly promoted to lieutenant colonel. But he was without his company of Hmong whom he had dispatched to his home town of Nong Het to beat back a NVA attack. And he was having difficulty getting the panicked Laotians under his command to mount a defense of any kind. One lieutenant who had been trained in artillery in France feigned total ignorance of artillery. Furious, Vang Pao loaded six cases of dynamite onto the side litters of a medivac helicopter and had the pilot fly him to the bridge at Nam Yen, just six miles from the base. With the bridge out, Kong-Lê would have difficulty getting his armor close enough to level the already supine post. The pilot landed the helicopter about a thousand yards from the river and waited while Vang Pao dragged the six boxes of explosives to the bridge, placed the charges, and lit the fuses. The charges went off just as the first armored vehicle loomed into view.

When Vang Pao returned to the base, he was able to find only five soldiers to help him harness the only heavy artillery available, two 105-millimeter Howitzers, to the back of a Dodge truck and drive it, along with another loaded with ammunition, to the main road where they set up the cannons and waited for the enemy's column to appear. The six of them held Kong-Lê off for over four hours until they ran out of ammunition.

When Vang Pao landed in Xieng Khouang city, he found the population in a panic and preparing for a mass evacuation south toward Savannakhet, the site of Phoumi Nosavan's former military headquarters. Vang Pao reluctantly joined the evacuees but soon left them to again organize a resistance.

He established a small air base south of the Plain of Jars and made radio contact with Vientiane to inform them that he was prepared to make a stand and needed supplies and munitions. One of Phoumi's staff flew in, accompanied by a u.s. officer who asked Vang Pao what he needed, wrote everything down and, without making any promises, unceremoniously departed. Meanwhile, after decimating one of Phoumi's airborne battalions, Kong-Lê advanced on Vang Pao's position. The first artillery rounds were exploding when Vang Pao led his soldiers and the civilian population in the area to

Padong, a plateau surrounded by Hmong villages.

Every day supplies and arms were parachuted in to equip new Hmong recruits. Vang Pao set women and children to work constructing a makeshift airfield. Volunteers arrived daily from the countryside, mostly Hmong but also Kha and even a few Laotians. Capitalizing on the rising enthusiasm, Vang Pao resumed the organization of his Hmong resistance network begun earlier at Lat Houang. He rapidly organized ten resistance zones, each of which encompassed twenty or thirty villages. The ten zones formed a ring encircling the Plain of Jars. Soon Vang Pao had eighty-four companies of Hmong infantry under his command.

CHAPTER 11

A Hmong War

*B*Y MID-1961, THE U.S. government had seen enough of Phoumi's bungling to conclude that the RLA was incapable of holding back, let alone defeating, the communists. The U.S. diverted nearly all ongoing military support to Vang Pao and his Hmong. Experience with corrupt Laotian officials, both in and out of the army, who were not beneath selling U.S. arms on the black market, convinced the U.S. to bypass the normal supply channels and deliver arms and supplies directly to Vang Pao's troops. The defense of Laos was rapidly becoming an all-Hmong operation, and deliberately so. On recommendation from advisors in the field, who witnessed the contempt Laotian officers had for Vang Pao simply because he was a Hmong, it was decided that all efforts to mount joint operations between the Royal Army and Vang Pao's forces were bound to end in disaster.

Hmong civilians living on the mountains surrounding the Plain of Jars were made to suffer for Vang Pao's greater role in the war effort. Pathet Lao and NVA units regularly raided their villages, beat and executed their village chiefs, and burned their homes, turning thousands of Hmong into refugees. In time, nearly all the Hmong in the region would become refugees and the logistics of relocating them to protected areas and supplying their material needs would turn out to be as difficult to manage as the war itself. Touby proved to be crucial in this effort. In 1962, under the new coalition government, he was appointed to the upper house of the Laotian legislature, the King's Council, which formed the nucleus of the prime minister's cabinet. As Minister of Health, Touby administered U.S. funds for refugee relief and insured that they went to the refugees instead of lining the pockets of Vientiane politicians and army officers.

A retired Indiana farmer was also instrumental in the success of the refugee program. Edgar "Pop" Buell arrived in Laos in 1960 as a volunteer with the International Voluntary Services (IVS). By mid-1961 he was working with Touby to organize a massive relief program that would eventually serve nearly two hundred thousand displaced civilians, most of them Hmong. Buell also created an unofficial Hmong school system that brought one-room school houses to hundreds of mountain villages, and was later expanded to include nine junior high schools, two senior high schools, and a teacher training school. By 1969 three hundred Hmong were attending the most prestigious high school in Vientiane, and twenty-four Hmong went on to attend universities in Australia, France, and the United States.

Toward the middle of 1961 there was another attempt to reestablish a coalition government. To facilitate negotiations, an official cease-fire began on May 3, 1961. The Pathet Lao and Kong-Lê's neutralists celebrated the occasion with an all-out assault on Vang Pao's headquarters at Padong. During the night Vang Pao, assisted by several American Green Berets attached to his headquarters, evacuated everyone. The civilians were led to Yat Mu where nearly nine thousand Hmong refugees, displaced by earlier communist maneuvers, were already camped. Vang Pao relocated his military headquarters at Pha Khao on another mountain south of Padong.

While the loss of Padong was a setback, it did little to dampen Vang Pao's eagerness to engage the enemy, though the makeup of the communist forces he opposed was rapidly changing. At first Vang Pao's volunteers faced only Pathet Lao and neutralist units, but over the months NVA soldiers began to appear among their ranks. It was not long before the Hmong were facing fully equipped battalions and divisions of NVA regulars. Shortly after the evacuation of Padong, a combined force of nine hundred NVA regulars and five hundred Pathet Lao laid siege to Vang Pao's mixed company of Hmong and Kha at Muong Ngat near the Vietnamese border. The defenders were finally forced to abandon the post, but not before killing nearly a third of the enemy.

The NVA sent waves of a hundred men at a time against machine guns and over land mines. This aggressiveness and willingness to

suffer loss exposed the Achilles heel of Vang Pao's army in a protracted war. Ho Chi Minh once pointed out to a French official that
France was doomed to lose a long war with his communists. It was
simple arithmetic. He was willing to sacrifice ten of his Vietminh
for every French soldier killed. It was a high cost, but one which the
Vietnamese could pay and the French could not. The commander
of Ho's army, General Giap, shared this view. He had long ago
adopted a philosophical attitude toward death, which he used to
justify the heavy sacrifices he repeatedly asked of his troops: "Every
minute, hundreds of thousands of people die on this earth." What
then is "the life or death of a hundred, a thousand, tens of thousands of human beings, even our compatriots."

Early in 1962 Vang Pao relocated his headquarters. The new site
was thirty-five miles southwest of Xieng Khouang city at Long
Cheng, an immense high plateau ringed by limestone mountains.
The location had two features to recommend it. The vast plateau
made an ideal location for a large airstrip, and the protective barrier
of the limestone mountains made it a difficult place for the communists to attack.

The CIA immediately set to work laying a four-thousand-foot
landing strip that could accommodate large cargo planes. Power
plants, paved roads, living quarters, and recreational facilities soon
followed. By 1966 Long Cheng had become one of the CIA's largest
field headquarters, second only to the agency's installation at Saigon.
Work on a less grand scale was also underway at Sam Thong, a
village nine miles north of Long Cheng, where a logistics center for
the refugee relief program was established.

The furious pace of the CIA construction crews at Long Cheng
was matched by the Hmong work teams in Vang Pao's ten resistance zones. They built hundreds of mountaintop airstrips that enabled Hmong pilots, trained by the U.S. in Thailand, to routinely
leapfrog from one village to another in small reconnaissance planes
and helicopters, bringing in supplies and gathering information
about enemy movements.

The airfields served another purpose. For the first time opium
merchants (mostly French until 1965) were able to fly in and collect

raw opium from thousands of Hmong farmers living around the Plain of Jars. Later, when Vang Pao's guerrillas gained control of Sam Neua province, they built additional airfields and expanded the network to cover most of the prime opium-growing areas in northeastern Laos. While this breathed new life into opium farming, it was really the last gasp of a dying industry. Within a few years the best opium-growing areas would come under communist control, and this, coupled with u.s. saturation bombing of enemy-held territory, forced thousands of Hmong to leave their fields for crowded refugee camps around Long Cheng.

Vang Pao was a grateful but wary recipient of cIA largess, for he could not help but wonder whether it might stop as quickly as it had started. It was inevitable that the enemy would seek an end to all support for the Hmong army in any negotiations on a new coalition government. To hedge his bets before the new Geneva Conference finished its deliberations, Vang Pao ordered his guerrillas to begin stockpiling arms and ammunition. It was a wise move. The final agreement at the conference, reached in June 1962, mandated a cutoff of all military aid to his army.

Vang Pao had to scale down his operations. Predictably, the communists stepped up theirs. NVA convoys traveling down highway 7 from Sam Neua province brought new troops and munitions to the Plain of Jars. For the moment, the most Vang Pao could do was send out commandos to blow up passes and bridges, reducing the momentum of the buildup. There was one bright spot. The alliance between the Pathet Lao and neutralists was finally coming completely unraveled and most of the fighting on the Plain of Jars was between their forces. This diversion permitted Vang Pao's self-defense units to mount repeated ambushes and employ hit-and-run tactics against communist positions in Xieng Khouang province without fear of a major retaliation. By the spring of 1963 Vang Pao had gained control of nearly seventy five percent of the province.

The relentless Pathet Lao assault on neutralist positions convinced Souvanna Phouma that the so-called coalition government was doomed and that the communists meant to capture power by force of arms. He turned to the u.s. for support. cIA cargo planes once again landed at Long Cheng, and Vang Pao received enough arms and ammunition to mount a new offensive. This time he pushed into Sam Neua province and advanced to within a few miles of the Pathet Lao general headquarters at Sam Neua city.

Pha Thi was one of the targets of the offensive. Situated northwest of Sam Neua city and within a stone's throw of North Vietnam's border, the small Hmong village of Pha Thi sat like a bird's nest atop the 5,680 foot limestone mountain that shared the village's name. More aptly described as a giant wedged-shaped promontory than a mountain, Pha Thi was an unlikely site even for a Hmong village. To reach the flattened top of what the locals aptly called the "Rock," one had to trudge through thick underbrush up narrow, nearly vertical trails. Only a Hmong, or a goat, could have considered Pha Thi inhabitable.

The "Rock's" close proximity to North Vietnam, coupled with the obvious difficulty of mounting an offensive against troops stationed on its crest, was of some strategic significance to the u.s. military. The Joint Chiefs of Staff were already developing contingency plans for the bombing of North Vietnam by mid-1964. The village of Pha Thi was an ideal spot for radar to guide American bombers to targets in North Vietnam. Toward the end of 1964, construction on a radar installation was underway. With the commencement of u.s. air raids on North Vietnam in early 1965, Pha Thi assumed strategic importance for the NVA. As subsequent events revealed, they were willing to invest enormous amounts of time, supplies, and lives to destroy it.

This was all in the future, however. For the moment Vang Pao basked in the glory of his army's achievement. His Hmong now controlled most of northeastern Laos. But capturing so much territory so quickly was a double-edged sword. His guerrillas were mobile assault units, highly skilled at hit-and-run. Now that they had actually forced the communists out of their strongholds, Vang Pao's troops would be obliged to switch roles and become defenders. Vang Pao attempted to adjust by consolidating his commandos into battalion-sized units. But if they were restricted to defending fixed positions, even these battalions would be no match for a division of

NVA regulars. The precarious situation was not immediately apparent because of a new element introduced into the war—U.S. air power. In May 1964, the U.S. began bombing enemy-held positions. The plan was not only to limit the communists' ability to mount major offensives against Vang Pao's forces but also to shatter the social and economic infrastructure of enemy-held territory. In plain language, the aim was to kill and terrorize civilians under communist control, forcing them to abandon their homes and leave the communists masters of depopulated zones; without farmers to feed their troops, coolies to transport their munitions, or laborers to construct their roads, the communists would be obliged to do more with less.

The deadly implications of this larger goal were not immediately apparent to the enemy or the civilians living under their rule. The first bombing sorties were in propeller-powered planes and numbered only a few per day. Only later, when the daily sorties numbered in the hundreds and fighter bombers guided by radar planes saturated villages and fields with napalm, antipersonnel bombs, and high explosives, did the object of the air raids become brutally clear.

Even in the early, less murderous, stages of the bombing, major communist advances against positions held by Vang Pao's troops were few in number. Except for the Plain of Jars itself, where the communists held their ground with bulldog tenacity, Vang Pao's montagnard army controlled nearly all of Xieng Khouang and Sam Neua provinces.

COMMANDER OF THE 2ND MILITARY REGION

In December 1964, Vang Pao was called to Vientiane for a meeting with Souvanna Phouma. In an attempt to impress the Hmong commander with his patriotism, the prime minister showed him a thick account ledger indicating the millions he had socked away in Parisian banks. And why wasn't he back in Paris spending this money and having a good time, the prime minister asked? It was because he was a dedicated patriot who placed the welfare of his nation above his own happiness. As Vang Pao later recalled, the first thing that crossed his mind when Souvanna Phouma finished answering his own question was how a true patriot was able to amass such a fortune on a prime minister's salary.

Souvanna Phouma appealed to Vang Pao's own patriotism. He must take command of Military Region II, encompassing Vientiane, Xieng Khouang, and Sam Neua provinces, and save the country from the communists. It was, the prime minister reminded him, his duty to his country.

Actually, Vang Pao already controlled most of Military Region II. And as long as the Americans continued to be committed to a free Laos, their military support would remain solidly attached to his army. What the prime minister offered was the legitimation of fact. And, of course, for heeding the call to duty, Vang Pao would at last be made a general of the RLA.

Whether the reason for Vang Pao's slow advancement was due to Laotian prejudice against his race or, as reported, because of his attempted assassination of a Laotian commander who upbraided him for manhandling one of his recruits, or because he had meddled in politics by getting Touby to prevent a planned repression of some rebellious Sam Neua Hmong, the fact remained that he was held back and it cut him to the quick. The chance for promotion was therefore enticing.

Yet it was the larger issue of long-term Hmong interests that finally led Vang Pao to agree to the legitimation of his command. It meant a public recognition that the Hmong, as well as the other tribal minorities like the Yao and Kha who were now represented in significant numbers in Vang Pao's army, were bearing the full burden of the national defense. If they succeeded in saving the country from the communists, they might at last be treated as equals by the Laotians.

Recent events highlighted how far the Hmong had yet to go to achieve this nominal equality. Just two months prior to Vang Pao's audience with Souvanna Phouma, a general strike of the Royal Government's court officials shut down the Laotian court system. The strike was in response to the appointment of Touby's brother, Tougeu, to the post of general director of the Justice Department.

Tougeu had worked in the Justice Department for nearly four years before his promotion without encountering such hostility. But, of course, he was only an official, not a director. It is likely many Laotian jurists conceded that the rising military importance of the Hmong necessitated a certain number of Hmong political appointees. That was politics. But to actually grant a Hmong authority over the Laotian court system implied that the Hmong had a right to share real power over the lives of Laotians. The Hmong, the strikers complained, were too ignorant to be given authority over ethnic Lao. They are not real Laotians. They are foreigners. Even though Tougeu did not resign his position, and the strikers returned to work, the "Tougeu Affair" revealed the depth of Laotian racism toward the Hmong.

After assuming formal command of Military Region II, Vang Pao established a forward headquarters at Na Khang on the edge of Sam Neua province. Happily for his soldiers, the fighting slowed to a snail's pace during 1965 because North Vietnam was preoccupied with other matters. The joint operations of the Army of the Republic of Vietnam (ARVN) and U.S. forces were causing problems for North Vietnam's guerrilla network in South Vietnam, the Viet Cong. Over ten thousand NVA regulars were diverted from other operations and sent to the rescue. Even more troublesome, on February 13, the U.S. began operation Rolling Thunder. For the first time North Vietnam was subjected to saturation bombing, although at first the air attacks were restricted to strategic targets in unpopulated areas. The aim was to provide an incentive for the communists to enter negotiations for a peace settlement. When this muzzled approach did not bring the desired effect, napalm and cluster bombs were added to the arsenal and more targets, some quite populated, were chosen.

Attempting a peace initiative, President Johnson called a halt to all bombing in North Vietnam on Christmas day. The bombing pause lasted thirty-seven days, just long enough for the North Vietnamese to rush troops into Laos in an attempt to retake lost ground. Vang Pao's forward headquarters at Na Khang came under repeated attacks. During one of them, Vang Pao was shot in the left arm.

The bullet from a Soviet AK-47 shattered the humerus just below the shoulder. Vang Pao was flown to Honolulu for reconstructive surgery. After a brief recuperation and quick tour of Waikiki Beach, he returned to the field.

A TASTE OF THE MODERN LIFE

From 1966 to 1968, increased air support from U.S. fighter bombers enabled Vang Pao to hold on to the territory he had won and even extend it. The intensive bombing made life in many areas precarious at best, and thousands of residents chose migration to safer areas as the prudent course. They joined the swelling population in and around the two towns of Long Cheng and Sam Thong which had remained safe havens from enemy attacks. As early as 1964 the two towns had grown to thirty thousand and fifteen thousand respectively, with perhaps another thirty thousand living in small villages in the surrounding hills. In the next two years, thousands more were added to these numbers.

The congestion inevitably altered the traditional Hmong lifestyle. Because of the unsuitability of the available land, opium farming diminished in importance. On the other hand, because corn and rice were in high demand in the crowded towns of Long Cheng and Sam Thong, Hmong farmers began raising these staples as cash crops. The town people had the money to buy their produce because nearly every family had sons and brothers serving in Vang Pao's army, receiving nearly four times the monthly pay of their Laotian counterparts in the RLA.

Against their wishes, Vang Pao's soldiers were paid in Laotian kip. By tradition, Hmong used silver as a medium of exchange. The high value of silver, especially in the form of bars, made it suitable only for large transactions: the purchase of a horse or buffalo, or the payment of a bride price. For smaller transactions, barter was the rule. Despite this inconvenience, Hmong preferred silver because it held its value. However, their reservations about the inflation-prone kip were partly dispelled by the decision of the U.S. government to back the kip with dollars. The kip was also more liquid than silver.

It could be used for small purchases: an important condition for a commercial economy. In former times, Chinese or Vietnamese merchants would have rushed in to take advantage of the situation, but the war excluded them from the area. Hundreds of tons of manufactured goods were transported each month on trucks and planes from Vientiane to Long Cheng. There they were received by Hmong merchants who hawked their goods in the expanding markets of Long Cheng and Sam Thong or carted them by truck or jeep over the newly improved roads to surrounding villages.

Some of these merchants, like Neng Vu, enjoyed considerable prosperity. He opened a general store at Long Cheng in 1967. For ten years before his entry into the business world had he worked in the Ministry of Information and Tourism in Vientiane. It was a good job, but his income did not increase fast enough to meet the needs of his growing family. The career change solved his financial problems. Within three years he had saved enough money to purchase a new family home in Vientiane.

Some enterprising Hmong built an ice factory at Long Cheng, while others opened restaurants. Hmong also took up new professions. There were Hmong photographers and Hmong dentists; others became tailors, bakers, cobblers, and radio repairmen. A new cottage industry, the fabrication of brooms, blossomed in the outlying villages and provided employment to more than two hundred Hmong families. Road traffic between Sam Thong and Long Cheng picked up as well, and not all of it consisted of trucks carrying goods to villages. Many vehicles were military jeeps converted into taxis, transporting Hmong over distances that would have taken days to travel by foot.

The Hmong were also emerging as a political force in Laos. After the evacuation of the civil administration of the Royal Laotian government from Xieng Khouang and Sam Neua provinces during the 1961 communist offensive, Vang Pao assumed full responsibility for establishing an interim, and unofficial, civil bureaucracy that provided the Hmong with self-government for nearly fifteen years.

Hmong officials in the new refugee settlements coordinated the ongoing relief effort, maintained law and order, and recruited soldiers for induction into Vang Pao's army. With so many different clans thrown together, they learned new skills in conciliation and compromise. At Long Cheng, for example, to prevent charges of favoritism in the court, no clan was allowed to have more than one representative on the panel of judges. The secrets of urban politics and the governing of large numbers of people were no longer the sole preserve of the ethnic Lao.

These remarkable gains would only translate into lasting improvements if the North Vietnamese were prevented from turning Laos into a puppet state. Should the Hmong fail to frustrate North Vietnamese imperialism, they would lose their bargaining position with the dominant ethnic Lao. They could also expect the Vietnamese to exact a terrible price for their persistent opposition. Certainly the Hmong would be perfect scapegoats for the defeated Lao as well as the conquering Vietnamese and their Pathet Lao collabora-tors. Both sides could point a finger at the Hmong as agents of u.s. imperialism and the cause of all the bloodshed. The Lao would be off the hook for resisting the communist takeover, and the commu-nists could employ terrorism against the Hmong as an object lesson to the Lao should they prove uncooperative citizens.

THE FALL OF PHA THI

Such dark foreboding may have seemed out of place in early 1967 when NVA operations were at a standstill and their Pathet Lao were on the run. But by the end of that year, pessimism once again seemed in order. The NVA put thousands of coolies to work constructing a road from Sam Neua city to Pha Thi. It was the first stage in the preparations for a major assault on the radar installation.

There was only one way for the enemy to get a sizable force to the top of Pha Thi. Troops would have to work their way up a nar-row pass and then use grappling hooks to negotiate a sheer cliff. In anticipation of this possibility, the Hmong at Pha Thi placed land mines in the pass. Unfortunately, the North Vietnamese sent in teams of specialists who worked patiently for two months removing most of the mines.

The assault on the radar station followed a diversionary action. In January 1968 the Pathet Lao and NVA launched an offensive against Vang Pao's positions throughout Sam Neua province. With the Hmong in retreat and unable to mount a relief operation for their comrades at Pha Thi, the NVA began their assault on the "Rock" in early March. Heavy artillery bombarded the Hmong defenders and the thirteen American technicians who were dug in on the summit, while the communists moved in force up the pass offering cover fire for suicide squads using ropes to scale the cliff. The Hmong picked them off one by one, until all the ropes dangled free in the wind. The artillery attack continued, however, and at one point it became so intense that the defenders dared not even raise their heads out of their trenches. Food and water were tossed from trench to trench, though there was little to go around. Helicopters attempting to drop in supplies were repeatedly driven off by enemy anti-aircraft guns. By early June Vang Pao conceded the impossibility of his men holding out any longer. After blowing up what was left of the battered radar installation, the Hmong and the one surviving American technician abandoned the summit.

Three months later Vang Pao led five battalions in a vain effort to retake Pha Thi. The Hmong general faced two divisions of determined North Vietnamese regulars. After three weeks of heavy fighting, only one company of Hmong had advanced far enough to secure a tenuous foothold on one of the mountain's main slopes. Another week passed and Vang Pao lost an additional three hundred men. He finally conceded it had been a mistake to lead his guerrillas into a set-piece battle where fire power and the ability to sustain high casualties determined the outcome.

In February 1969 Vang Pao's forward headquarters at Na Khang came under attack. Heavy cannon, rocket launchers, and mortars pounded the base. After three days the headquarters was reduced to rubble and the Hmong were dug into ground that resembled a moonscape. Five thousand NVA advanced in waves against the Hmong trenches. Hundreds were cut down and still they came tumbling over the piles of their own dead. Vang Pao's losses were high, too, and his men were running out of ammunition. He ordered a retreat and left Na Khang as a cemetery for the North Vietnamese.

The communists continued their advance, reoccupying territory that Vang Pao had wrested from them during his 1964-65 offensive. In April they captured the post at Phou Koum, south of Vang Pao's former advance headquarters at Na Khang. The communists moved down Highway 6 toward the Plain of Jars and Vang Pao's redoubt at Long Cheng. The only Hmong outpost blocking their route was at Bouam Long, situated just off the main highway and an easy mark for the enemy's heavy artillery.

Again assault waves followed on the heels of an artillery attack. Dead Vietnamese draped the barbed wire around Bouam Long's perimeter until the weight of the bodies caved in the fencing, allowing fresh troops to stream through. Vang Pao directed his small Hmong air force of prop-driven T-28s against the crush of NVA soldiers. The post held out for twelve days before the enemy withdrew to lick their wounds. Vang Pao immediately dispatched an airborne battalion against Phou Koum and recaptured the fallen post. Phou Koum held out against a last ditch effort by two communist battalions to retake the liberated post.

Having momentarily halted the enemy's advance, Vang Pao began a counterattack with three of his battalions. One captured Dong Dane on Highway 4, giving the Hmong control over the main route to the Plain of Jars from the communist stronghold at Xieng Khouang city, the provincial capital. A second battalion assaulted communist positions northeast of the city, and a third marched on Xieng Khouang city itself. The fighting continued for two weeks.

Watching from the sidelines, and by now thoroughly disillusioned with the communists, an airborne battalion of Kong-Lê's neutralists suddenly switched sides and joined the Hmong assault just in time to share in the victory. The intense fighting had reduced Xieng Khouang's capital to piles of shattered stones and masonry. Instead of establishing a base on the site, Vang Pao withdrew his forces to the surrounding hills. The loss of the city was a major setback in the communist offensive and Vang Pao's intelligence reports informed him that they were gathering for a counter attack. The intelligence was good news. The communists had let their pride rule their reason. By concentrating their forces in an assault on the provincial capital, they left the Plain of Jars unprotected. It was an ideal time to divert troops to the plain and dislodge the communists.

Leaving a portion of his troops dug in near Xieng Khouang city to keep the communists occupied, Vang Pao prepared for a push against the communists on the plain. All through July and early August, American bombers blasted NVA positions on the Plain of Jars. By the time Vang Pao's forces marched out to engage the communists, the saturation bombing had driven most of the larger NVA units to the periphery of the plain where they were unable to offer quick assistance to the Pathet Lao who, for the first time in years, had to face the Hmong alone. Within a few weeks the fighting turned into a complete rout.

MASTER OF THE PLAIN OF JARS

In early October 1969, Vang Pao declared himself master of the Plain of Jars. He was also master of a huge cache of weapons the communists had stored on the plain to support a planned siege of his main headquarters at Long Cheng. There were enough weapons and ammunition to supply a large guerrilla force for ten years, and Vang Pao stockpiled them for just that purpose.

Vang Pao's victory was not celebrated in Vientiane. Anti-war sentiment in the U.S. Congress had resulted in the Cooper Amendment which barred the appropriation of additional U.S. funds for military action in Laos. Vang Pao was ordered to withdraw from the plain or face a cutoff of all supplies. Vang Pao ignored the order. If the U.S. cut off his supplies, he would draw on those captured from the communists.

In late November the NVA threw three divisions at him and entered the plain with newly supplied Soviet heavy artillery and tanks. The Hmong held them at bay but at a high price. When orders were again sent from Vientiane to evacuate the plain, Vang Pao complied. The NVA pursued him toward Long Cheng until the Hmong turned and forced them to retreat back to the plain.

With his army bottled up at Long Cheng, Vang Pao prepared for the inevitable assault on his headquarters. Three elite divisions plus four regiments and a battalion of Dac Cong (suicide forces) were devoted to the capture of the sprawling military base. The incessant attacks forced the evacuation of most of the civilian population to Ban Son just a few miles south of Long Cheng.

The heaviest attacks occurred between December 1971 and April 1972 when eleven thousand rounds of enemy artillery were fired into the base. By early 1972 the NVA had gained a foothold on the limestone mountains surrounding Long Cheng. Though three Hmong battalions were able to retake the mountains, they were soon dislodged by new NVA units. But instead of continuing their assault, the Vietnamese dug in. Vang Pao correctly presumed they were waiting for more reinforcements for the final push. Intelligence reports indicated they would come from the south in an attempted rear guard action. Vang Pao's soldiers encountered them less than a mile from Long Cheng in the Nam Ngum valley, close enough for the artillery at Long Cheng to decimate the surprised NVA regiment.

In early April 1972, after two attempts to drive the NVA off Long Cheng's protective mountain perimeter were beaten back by communist artillery, Vang Pao ordered special units to infiltrate enemy positions. Their job was to identify the location of enemy artillery and direct air assaults against them by U.S. Phantom jets. Within two weeks most of the artillery was put out of commission. This time the Hmong were able to drive the NVA off the mountains.

One of Vang Pao's Hmong officers, Seng Vue, commanded a company of Hmong during one of the assaults. It was rough going through heavy underbrush up a steep trail. When his unit was within a few hundred yards of the summit, it came under heavy fire and his men were slowed to a crawl. Vang Pao was circling overhead in a helicopter, checking the progress of the assault. He radioed Seng Vue to pick up the pace. As an incentive he informed him that if his men did not reach the top within thirty minutes, T-28s would be

HMONG PILOT

ordered to bomb his position. Seng Vue argued with the general. He explained his circumstances and asked for more time. Vang Pao refused to reconsider. Seng Vue argued with him some more, and the more he argued the more enraged he became. He would show Vang Pao what he and his men were made of. This, of course, was exactly the effect Vang Pao intended. Within five minutes Seng Vue's men reached the summit and sent the Vietnamese pell-mell down the other side. Vang Pao was ecstatic when Seng Vue informed him of the achievement.

Ironically, another company attacking dug-in Vietnamese on a different crest transmitted incorrect coordinates to the T-28s crisscrossing the mountains and assaulting enemy positions. Within a few minutes after his conversation with Vang Pao, Seng Vue's men were ducking for cover as a squadron of T-28s began to unload on them. The rocky soil at the summit was so hard packed that the shock waves of the exploding bombs lifted the Hmong several feet into the air. Fortunately no one was killed. Seng Vue concluded Vang Pao had ordered the attack. After checking the condition of his troops, he was back on the radio giving Vang Pao a piece of his mind. Vang Pao was shocked and apologetic. "Any casualties?" he asked. Seng Vue paused and then reported, "There are many dead and wounded." Vang Pao was distraught and promised immediate aid to evacuate the wounded. When Seng Vue thought Vang Pao had suffered enough, he told the relieved general the truth.

Having regained control of Long Cheng's mountain perimeter, Vang Pao's troops drove the NVA back to the plain. Civilians returned to the battered base and rebuilt their homes and shops. The return would not be permanent.

BEGINNING OF THE END

In late 1972 Henry Kissinger informed Souvanna Phouma of America's intentions to withdraw all military support for the RLA once a peace settlement with the North Vietnamese was finalized. By February of the following year, the Laotian prime minister concluded negotiations with the Pathet Lao to begin the process of forming a new coalition government. Both sides agreed to a general ceasefire.

As usual, fighting continued in the field as the Pathet Lao and North Vietnamese hurried to claim more territory for their side. To help improve the position of the rightists and neutralists in the negotiations, the U.S. airlifted five thousand Thai troops to beef up Vang Pao's beleaguered forces. Units of Thai mercenaries already had been integrated into Vang Pao's army. They boasted they would route the NVA and end the war. Most performed poorly. Vang Pao demoted them to conducting local patrols, where they would not endanger the lives of Hmong veterans. The new Thai troops were from the regular army and quickly proved themselves in combat.

A new coalition government was finally formed in April 1974. Though Touby was appointed Deputy Minister for Post and Telecommunications, and two other Hmong were placed on the National Political Consultative Council, Hmong influence over Vientiane politics was near its end. As events soon revealed, the communists had no intention of sharing power with anyone, especially Hmong who had supported Vang Pao. Gestures of conciliation were followed with military aggression.

The fighting heated up in 1975, and in March of that year the communists mounted another major offensive south of the Plain of Jars. When Vang Pao's troops began to make headway against them, he was called back to Vientiane to meet with a worried Souvanna Phouma. The prime minister ordered him to cease all attacks against the communists. Vang Pao inquired what orders he was to follow should his soldiers come under attack. Retreat was the answer. "Retreat to where? To Vientiane? To Thailand?" Vang Pao shouted. He ripped off his general's stars and angrily tossed them on the prime minister's desk.

Souvanna Phouma was later reported to have described Vang Pao's response to the French Ambassador and remarked that "The Hmong have served me well, Vang Pao has fought well for me. The Hmong are good soldiers. It's a pity that peace may come only at the cost of their liquidation."

For Vang Pao the war was over. The NVA and Pathet Lao took advantage of the situation by advancing on Long Cheng while a general evacuation was already underway. At Phou Kang, a few miles away, several thousand Hmong refugees were huddled near a bluff. Those near the front raised their hands to protect their eyes from the dust and debris thrown up by the rotors of a landing helicopter. A dejected Vang Pao emerged and, in a voice choked with emotion, addressed his people for the last time. "My brothers it is with great sadness that I address you today. My greatest desire was to end my days among you. That has become impossible. The political situation has deteriorated so much that my presence is the cause of great damage. One day, if destiny favors me, humbly I will again serve the Hmong people."

Vang Pao surveyed the upturned faces and delivered his final orders. "After I leave, the Pathet Lao will accuse me of a thousand crimes, and ask you to concur. Do so. When in the presence of the communists never say anything good about me; never reveal what is in your heart. Rather, invent wrongs, charge me with all the crimes of the land. Understand me well; I do not say to you: 'have no confidence in the Pathet,' but only defy their methods and their hypocritical proceedings. They will want you to hand over your weapons. Give them to them, but not all. Hide the rest carefully because I fear that you will soon have need of them."

Tears streamed down his face. "Farewell my brothers. I can do nothing more for you. I would only be a torment for you. Remain united, retain your solidarity. May heaven keep you."

The helicopter ferried Vang Pao nineteen miles south to Muong Cha where a plane waited to carry him to the U.S. air base at Oudorn, Thailand. On the way he had a change of mind. Though he was no longer commander of Military Region II, no longer a general in the RLA, he was still a Hmong. And there were five thousand Hmong soldiers still willing to follow him. He would continue the struggle alone.

When Vang Pao stepped out of his helicopter, he ordered the pilot of the waiting plane to fly to Thailand without him. He returned to Long Cheng and immediately set about distributing arms and ammunition to his troops. He was busily reorganizing them into guerrilla units when he received a piece of information that forced him to abandon the project.

The source of the information was Yang Dao, recently returned from a junket to East Germany and Moscow sponsored by the new coalition government. Any illusions Yang Dao may have had about future fair treatment of the Hmong by the communists were shattered when he attended an East German banquet held in honor of their Laotian visitors. One of the speakers paused during the mandatory encomium of the communist revolution in Laos to point a finger directly at Yang Dao and bellow: "It is because of the damned Hmong that it has taken so many years to achieve a communist revolution in Laos." Proof that this was not an aberration was provided by President Podgorny in Moscow when he informed the Laotians that for the good of international communism the Hmong would, of course, have to be liquidated.

There was more bad news when Yang Dao returned to Vientiane. He learned from friends that the Pathet Lao and NVA were preparing for a major assault on Long Cheng, and that no one, not even the rightists, would lift a finger to intervene. What was worse, sensing the end was near, neutralist and rightist troops were joining the communists in droves. Given the drift of events, it would soon be the Hmong against everyone else.

Yang Dao boarded a plane for Long Cheng to apprise Vang Pao of the situation. Vang Pao had no wish to needlessly sacrifice the lives of his men in a futile last stand. And he certainly wanted to avoid anything that might make the Hmong victims of a race war. He had no choice but to disband his army and leave for Thailand.

HIN HEUP

Shortly after Vang Pao's departure, the communists took command of Long Cheng. Thousands of Hmong refugees crowded together in the sprawling tent city of Phou Kang, anxiously waiting to see what the communists had planned for them. Judging by the angry articles surfacing in the Vientiane newspapers, it would not be pleasant. On May 9th the Pathet Lao paper, *Khao Xane Pathet Lao*, intimated the party's position: "It is necessary to extirpate, down to the root, the 'Hmong' minority."

Fearing for their lives, the residents of Phou Kang joined thousands of other Hmong refugees (nearly forty thousand in all) from nearby towns and villages in a long march toward Vientiane with the vague intention of somehow crossing the Mekong and joining their leader in Thailand. Like the great migrations of the past, they carried all their worldly goods on their backs, but this time they did not walk the crests but followed the dirt trails and roads that descended into the Vientiane plain.

At one point in the march the throng paused to watch a helicopter land at the head of the column. A Hmong emerged from the cockpit. It was Touby Lyfoung. "Return to your homes and villages," he pleaded. Touby was now sixty-one. Years of sedentary life in Vientiane had made him fat. When asked if he could guarantee their security if they returned home, Touby responded that they needed none. "Vang Pao is gone, you have committed no crimes. You will be safe." Unconvinced, the crowd announced their intention to push on to Vientiane. With the sad realization that his word no longer carried much weight among his own people, Touby climbed back in the helicopter and departed for Vientiane.

Touby returned the next day in the company of Pathet Lao soldiers in a last ditch effort to convince his people to abandon the march and return to their villages. Using the back of a jeep as a podium, he informed the crowd that he had recently talked to Vang Pao on the phone. Their leader was in the United States and wanted them to remain in Laos. Again Touby was asked if he could guarantee their security if they went home. "Will you come and live among us, Touby," one Hmong inquired. "You could protect us from the Pathet Lao. If you swear to join us we will remain."

"I can't," Touby replied. He told them that he was in contact with Faydang, his former enemy and now a high official in the Pathet Lao. "Faydang," he assured them, "will come and guarantee your safety." When this information did not sway them, Touby suddenly raised his hand. "All who will stay here in Laos with me raise your hand." He counted the hands. Only four were raised. Not without a sense of humor, Touby observed there would be at least five Hmong left in Laos.

Before leaving, Touby promised he would return the next day with assurances from the Vientiane government that the Hmong would come to no harm if they remained in Laos. The marchers never saw him again. As they drew closer to Vientiane, they did see more Pathet Lao soldiers who arbitrarily confiscated their food and valuables. When one exhausted Hmong tried to bargain for space for his family on a passing truck, a Pathet Lao soldier forced him out of the vehicle at gun point and shouted "the war is over and the Hmong have nothing left to do but die!" It was a bad omen.

On the ninth day of the march the Hmong reached the outskirts of Hin Heup, a small town on the edge of highway 13 that led directly to Vientiane. The entrance to the town was barricaded. When some Hmong tried to remove the barriers Pathet Lao soldiers swarmed out and blocked their path. Several Hmong tried to push through the soldiers and were knocked down. Shots rang out. An old woman fell to the ground. Other soldiers began to use their rifles, some as clubs on whomever was in their range, while the rest shot indiscriminately into the crowd. Armored vehicles were used to herd the Hmong down the road to the narrow bridge that crossed the Nam Lik River. Many Hmong simply fell off the bridge into the water and drowned. Others were deliberately tossed into the river by soldiers. Thousands of Hmong sought refuge in the forest, others turned and ran back up the road. Soldiers chased them, shooting or bludgeoning the stragglers.

Most of the survivors of the Hin Heup massacre returned to their villages only to be subjected to repeated interrogations by Pathet Lao soldiers who routinely accused them of having fought with Vang Pao. Many were sent to reeducation camps. A large number never returned. Even Touby, living in Vientiane, was not immune. He was sent to a reeducation camp in Sam Neua province where he reportedly died from malaria in 1978.

Thousands of Hmong were forced into agricultural communes in the lowlands, where they were stricken by tropical diseases. Others were given a bag of rice and a few tools and plopped down in the mountain wilderness where they were expected not only to survive but to become self-sufficient peasant farmers.

Some Hmong were permitted to return to their old villages in Sam Neua and Xieng Khouang provinces where much of the land was barren from the years of u.s. bombing and overgrown with imperata, a form of rugged grass with deep roots against which Hmong hoes were no match. The repatriated Hmong were barely able to produce enough to keep alive. Nor was it much consolation to realize that the ethnic Lao were not faring much better. Within a few years the inefficiencies of forced collectivization coupled with bouts of heavy flooding dramatically reduced the output of Laotian farmers. The LPDR was forced to rely on international aid to prevent famine. There was no revenue to run the state. Desperate for funds, the government encouraged the Hmong to resume opium farming. Following the lead of the "French imperialists," the LPDR established its own opium monopoly, and required Hmong opium farmers to sell their harvests to the state at below-market prices.

After thirty years of more or less continuous fighting and the loss of approximately one third of their population, the Laotian Hmong found themselves back where they had started three gen-erations earlier: poor, repressed, and longing for freedom.

CHAPTER 12

Resisters, Refugees, and Immigrants

RESISTANCE

NOT ALL OF THE HMONG who remained in Laos after the 1975 communist takeover sought accommodation with the new regime. Thousands took to the hills, dug up the rifles they had buried, and organized a resistance. One of these rebels was Yang Shua Sai. The communists sent him to a reeducation camp in the spring of 1975. It is possible he would have died in the camp had he not agreed to return to his village and organize a propaganda campaign highlighting the alleged crimes committed against the Laotian people by Vang Pao and his u.s. supporters. The day Yang Shua Sai returned to his village, he escaped into the forest and began recruiting Hmong guerrillas. Within a few months he returned to his old village and liberated it from the communists.

The major concentration of Hmong resisters was around Phu Bia mountain on the southeastern edge of the Plain of Jars. The area remained impregnable to the NVA and Pathet Lao until 1978 when four Vietnamese divisions, backed by MIG-21s and heavy artillery, conducted a protracted campaign against the Hmong rebels. Though the MIGs and artillery inflicted heavy damage, it was chemical warfare and the use of napalm that broke the back of the rebellion.

Chong Neng Xiong commanded a unit of the Phu Bia rebels. His men enjoyed several victories over the NVA even after their massive troop buildup. Being outnumbered was hardly a new experience. What was new were the rockets fired from Soviet gunships. Chong had seen rockets before, but these were different. Instead of white smoke, these rockets trailed red or yellow smoke and exploded above the ground spraying a fine powder over fields and villages. If the powder got on your skin, or you breathed it in, you got very sick. The major symptoms were bleeding from the nose and mouth, nausea and severe stomach cramps followed by diarrhea. If the powder got into a village stream, it affected nearly everyone. The very old and very young often died, while adults remained sick for several weeks; and, of course, affected rebels were too ill to fight. Just how many Hmong were killed by the chemicals is unknown, though if one can trust the testimony of Pathet Lao soldiers who participated in the chemical warfare, the number was high: nearly fifty thousand killed between 1975 and 1978 in the Phu Bia region alone.

While the deadly effects of the "red" and "yellow rain" seriously weakened the resolve of the Hmong rebels, the napalm effectively broke the back of the Phu Bia rebellion. Though napalm bombs were sometimes dropped on villages, crops were the primary targets. The bombing intensified just before harvest. In many villages the napalm completely destroyed the corn and rice crops, leaving thousands near starvation within a few months

Mass starvation compelled thousands of rebels to abandon the Phu Bia mountains. Many sought refuge in Thailand. A large number did not survive the trek. If they were not shot by Pathet Lao or NVA soldiers, they died of starvation or drowned when they tried to cross an unguarded (often unguarded because the river was presumed too dangerous to cross) section of the Mekong. One group of 2,500 Hmong arrived at the Hong Khai refugee camp in December 1977. The group had numbered almost 8,000 when the march began.

A small number of diehard rebels continued the struggle, retreating further north into the mountain wilderness. Some received help from an unexpected source. Feeling threatened by the partnership between its Soviet nemesis and its historical adversary, Vietnam, China attempted in 1980 to blunt the tip of the Vietnamese sword. Hmong rebels, as well as thousands of other Laotian hill tribesmen, were recruited for guerrilla operations against Vietnamese and LPDR military forces. Most of the fighting occurred in Phong Saly and Nam Tha provinces, usually close to the Chinese border. Though the guerrillas routed LPDR forces in several engagements,

China balked at supporting large scale units, dooming the resistance to a marginal threat.

HMONG IN THAILAND

Nearly forty thousand Hmong fled to Thailand in late 1975. At first Thailand's government allowed the immigrants to settle near established Hmong communities in the provinces of Nong Khai, Nan, and Chiang Rai. But as the numbers began to swell, the nation's rulers in Bangkok had second thoughts. With Laos now a puppet of bellicose Vietnam, the Thai did not want to be open to the charge of harboring rebels who might use Thailand as a home base for guerrilla incursions into Laos. Nor did the Thai government like the prospect of Hmong rebels living in close proximity to existing Hmong communities in Thailand. As recently as 1967, Thai military units had suppressed Hmong revolts in Chiang Rai, Nan, Phetchabun, and Tak provinces. While new aid programs had gone a long way to smooth relations with Hmong communities, worries over new rebellions remained.

To avoid these problems, Hmong refugees were isolated in border camps at Chang Khong, Chang Kham, Ban Nam Yao, Sob Tuang, and Ban Vinai. And as a disincentive for other would-be Hmong immigrants, the government's Department of Interior (DOI) provided less than minimal assistance to the camp inmates. Because of near famine conditions in Laos, the low level of assistance in the camps did not serve as an effective deterrent to continued immigration. By late 1978 the camps held over fifty thousand Hmong.

Many camp inmates would have perished from malnutrition or disease had it not been for the help of private relief agencies and, later, funds from Hmong relatives who had immigrated to France and the U.S. While private aid kept the Hmong alive, it did not raise them out of poverty. For this they needed employment which, from the very start, had been difficult to find. Thailand's DOI prohibited Hmong refugees from moving to urban centers where there were jobs, and there were few employment opportunities close to

215

the camps. Outside of tending a garden plot to augment the family diet, large numbers of Hmong remained unemployed.

To add to their problems, the Thai sometimes victimized camp inmates. At Ban Vinai, for example, Thai bandits regularly preyed on Hmong entering and leaving the camp. On occasion Hmong women working in their fields were attacked and raped. In 1982 Hmong from Ban Vinai armed themselves with axes, hoes, and knives and tracked down the criminals, killing nearly a hundred within a week.

Impoverished and sometimes persecuted, cooped up in refugee centers and denied access to mountain land where they could at least become self-sustaining, many Hmong in the camps turned to the messianism of Pa Chay to lift their spirits; it offered the promise that heaven would intercede to make them victorious over their enemies and one day provide them a homeland.

Hmong messianism had not vanished from Laos with Pa Chay's death. In the late 1920s, a young Hmong woman claiming magical powers, and in possession of a magic flag, led veterans of Pa Chay's campaign on raids against French garrisons. When she was captured and executed, a shaman from Xieng Khouang province named Xay Vang Lo took her place. He preached messianism and urged Hmong in the area to revolt. To attract a larger following, he set out on a pilgrimage to the town of Nong Het, where he intended to build a tower, ascend it, and appeal to heaven for help. The Lo kiatong, Bliayao Lo, ordered the shaman ambushed before he reached Nong Het. During the ambush, the kiatong's agents killed the shaman and a number of his disciples. A second shaman, She Yi Xiong, stepped in to continue the struggle from his home base in the rugged Phu Bia mountains. He claimed to be the reincarnation of an earlier Hmong messiah who had led a revolt against the Chinese. With a small guerrilla force, he assaulted several French garrisons in Xieng Khouang province. His younger sister carried a flag during the raids to magically repel French bullets, made only of lead. The rebels fired silver bullets, melted down from jewelry and silver bars donated by Hmong villagers, for She Yi Xiong believed only silver bullets could kill French souls. French troops captured the shaman and his sister near Xieng Khouang city in an engagement at Lat Boua. The soldiers brutally tortured She Yi Xiong, and reportedly raped his sister, before executing the two.

Messianism surfaced again in Sam Neua province in the late 1950s, though the movement was short-lived and did not involve an organized rebellion. Then, in August 1967, Shong Lue Yang, a war refugee from Vietnam, appeared in Long Cheng with a fully developed Hmong script, which he claimed he had learned from the gods. The shaman announced to war-weary residents of Long Cheng that salvation was near at hand. The Hmong would be sent a king. Shong Lue Yang even specified the date of the messiah's arrival—September 15th.

When the promised king did not appear, Shong Lue Yang explained that the messiah had come but could not find any Hmong and departed. Having abandoned their traditional costume, the Hmong at Long Cheng were indistinguishable from the ethnic Lao. Salvation would only come when the Hmong rejected modern ways and honored the traditions of their ancestors.

Shong Lue Yang's following was sufficiently large to be a matter of concern to Long Cheng's authorities who eventually had him jailed and later executed. The movement did not end with his death. His disciples elevated Pa Chay to the status of a demigod and called themselves the *Chao Fa*, God's disciples. They chose the pig as a symbol of their movement, and new converts were taught to read Shong Lue Yang's script. A contingent of the Phu Bia rebels were Chao Fa disciples. Aping Pa Chay, they engaged in magical ceremonies before battles and carried magic flags to deflect communist bullets.

After 1978 many Chao Fa sought sanctuary in Thailand's refugee camps, where they recruited other Hmong into the religious movement. By 1980 the camp at Ban Vinai had its own Chao Fa temple, replete with religious icons. A ten-foot-high statue of Tzong Patheng, a Chao Fa patron saint, rose before the temple's entrance. A smaller statue of another protector spirit, a two-headed clay incarnation of a creature from Hmong mythology, sat on an altar inside the temple. Off to one side of the temple a gazebo housed a

life-sized statue of a boar, the symbol of the Hmong messiah. The temple courtyard contained a youth center where children were taught the Hmong Chao Fa script, the traditions and legends of their people, and the catechism of the Hmong Chao Fa. The message preached by the Chao Fa at Ban Vinai was simple: only through the preservation of tradition can the Hmong hope for salvation, that is for a nation of their own.

The movement's momentum dwindled after a few years. Many of the Chao Fa in the camps emigrated to the u.s. and there were few new converts. By 1986, the temple grounds at Ban Vinai were turned into a soccer field. Temple buildings still stood, but had become ramshackle; and there was little interest in organizing work crews to refurbish them.

HMONG IN THE U.S.

Approximately half of the Hmong in Thailand's refugee centers chose to migrate to western countries rather than remain in the camps waiting for the day they might safely return to Laos. Several thousand settled in France, Australia, and Canada, but most chose the u.s. because Vang Pao was there.

Granted political asylum in 1975, Vang Pao settled on a 450-acre cattle ranch in the remote Bitterroot Mountains of Montana. Except for the winter snow, the coniferous forests of the Bitterroots were not much different from the mountain forests of Laos. But herding cattle was not the same as commanding men, and Vang Pao became restless. His forced retirement did not last long. Hmong were migrating to the u.s. in large numbers.

Church organizations and small communities sponsored the first wave of Hmong immigrants. With little out-of-pocket expense, these immigrants soon became sponsors themselves, since the federal government provided liberal funding for the resettlement of Indochinese refugees. Another wave of Hmong immigrants from Thai refugee camps swelled after a significant number of Hmong became citizens, for under provisions of the 1965 Immigration Act, naturalized citizens had the "right to bring in members of their extended families through regular immigration channels."

As the size of America's Hmong population grew, Vang Pao's phone began to ring off the hook with appeals for advice and aid. In 1977 he left his mountain ranch for southern California, where he founded Lao Family Community, a self-help organization for Laotian refugees. Funding by the California Department of Social Services a year later enabled the organization to expand its operations into other states and qualify for federal grants. Eventually Lao Family Community established offices in nearly every Hmong community in America. Hmong received aid in finding jobs, obtaining vocational and language training, and advice and representation in their dealings with the wider community.

Even with the support of Lao Family Community, many Hmong had problems adjusting to American society. In rural, and sometimes urban areas, Hmong unaccustomed to fishing licenses and hunting seasons were arrested for taking game illegally. Hmong foraging for mushrooms, and unfamiliar with American varieties, have nearly died from eating poisonous mushrooms. A number of Hmong have been arrested for growing opium for personal consumption—usually for an elderly member of the family suffering from chronic pain associated with arthritis or some other degenerative disease. Other traditional practices, such as marriage by abduction, have landed Hmong in jail. In 1988, a Hmong from Fresno abducted a Hmong woman from her workplace. Ignoring tradition, the young woman called the police. Her abductor was sentenced to four months in jail and fined a thousand dollars. In a similar case in St. Paul, Minnesota, the county prosecutor let the offender off with a fine after learning that Hmong women are expected to protest when abducted or lose face. The prosecutor doubted he could convince a jury the woman really meant "no" when she protested her abduction. In 1993 charges of kidnapping and rape were dropped against another Minnesota Hmong when the prosecutor's office discovered that the girl's family had accepted a bride price prior to the abduction.

The toughest adjustment has been economic. Many southeast Asian immigrants, such as Vietnamese, owned their own business or worked for government before migrating to the u.s., which prepared them for a modern economy. Hmong immigrants knew only war and peasant farming. Poorly educated, and with almost no command of English, they were ill-prepared for even menial jobs. Large numbers have relied on welfare to survive. Of the more than 100,000 Hmong living in the u.s. in 1987, nearly sixty-three percent were still on welfare. In some California communities the welfare rate of Hmong families exceeded eighty percent.

The high rate of welfare dependency was not entirely due to inadequate job skills and low levels of education. The Hmong were dependent on welfare long before they arrived in the u.s. By the late 1960s, most Hmong in Laos had become war refugees, living in resettlement centers south of the Plain of Jars and kept alive by American aid. After the communist takeover, many of these same Hmong escaped to refugee camps in Thailand, where they survived on the largesse of the United Nations and various international charitable organizations. Consequently, many Hmong had already been on welfare for more than a decade before immigrating to America. Not only had welfare become a way of life, few Hmong

considered it degrading. Food Stamps or income from Aid to Families with Dependent Children (AFDC) were viewed as a continuation of the earlier American aid in Laos: support owed to the Hmong for fighting America's secret war. Seen in this way, welfare was hardly disgraceful; it also provided a standard of living only dreamed of in Laos.

Welfare has greatly influenced Hmong demographics. The first Hmong in America located in the cities of their sponsors, usually church organizations. Once on their feet, Hmong relocated to be closer to other Hmong, especially those of their own clan. Soon there were more than fifty Hmong communities spread over thirty states. This broad geographical distribution was sustained by liberal federal grants for Indochinese refugees that augmented state welfare benefits. However, in 1982 the federal government drastically reduced grants to states for income and job training for Indochinese refugees. By 1984 most of this money had dried up. Welfare dependent Hmong began migrating to states with high levels of welfare benefits, principally to Wisconsin, Minnesota, and California.

By 1990 the largest concentration of Hmong was in Fresno, California, making it the unofficial center of Hmong culture in America. Its New Year celebration was the largest in the country, attracting more than forty thousand Hmong from across the United States. The cultural vitality of Fresno's Hmong community masked its inherent fragility. The majority of Fresno's Hmong were dependent on welfare. Recent welfare reforms in California have cut benefits and forced Hmong supported by the state's AFDC to enroll in a modest workfare program. In 1994 nearly two hundred Hmong families in Fresno refused to enroll in the program. Hmong community leaders feared a mass exodus from Fresno. As one leader observed: "The glue that holds the Hmong together is their number. This glue is being weakened and torn apart." The glue may be numbers, but the bonding agent is welfare.

While welfare indirectly sustains Hmong culture, it also subtly undermines it. AFDC is organized to aid nuclear, not extended families. Although many Hmong still live as extended families under one roof, a large number live as nuclear families with grandparents residing in separate homes or apartments. This has weakened traditional authority patterns. Welfare has also enabled some Hmong women to leave their husbands and "strike out on their own," something unheard of in Laos.

Hmong culture has changed in other ways. Access to medical care has undermined Hmong shamanism. Hmong often still turn to a shaman when they are ill, but if the shaman fails to effect a cure, they do not hesitate to seek out a physician. Also most Hmong in America have converted to Christianity, which has no place in its theology for shamanist beliefs.

Ancient rituals have become an amalgam of old and new. Since sacrificing pigs and cattle is difficult in an urban setting, store-bought meat is often substituted. Bride prices are seldom paid in silver bars as dictated by tradition. Traditional costumes are seldom strictly traditional. Inexpensive aluminum jewelry from Thailand has replaced the more expensive customary silver. At the New Year festival women often dress for effect, borrowing elements of clothing from other clans because of their attractiveness, or incorporating more flashy Thai and Lao dresses and sashes. In the larger communities, American-style beauty contests have been added to the New Year festival, as well as music contests that include Hmong rock bands.

Changes in ritual and beliefs have been so marked that a recent survey of Hmong attitudes revealed that few American Hmong continue to link Hmong identity to either orthodox rituals or shamanism. Only preserving the Hmong language was thought essential, and maintaining traditional family roles with men clearly in charge. Even this minimal identity seems threatened. Increasingly, children in Hmong families speak little Hmong, and anecdotal evidence suggests that Hmong women exercise greater independence in the family setting than was common a decade ago.

Some Hmong traditions remain unchanged. Hmong girls who marry outside of their race are generally ostracized. And, as in Laos, Hmong girls marry by their mid-teens, most by the age of sixteen. Many become pregnant and drop out of school, which is unfortunate since Hmong girls are usually top students. Their husbands, not being much older, have bleak employment prospects. The incentive for the family going on welfare is therefore high. And given Hmong birth rates, leaving welfare becomes increasingly difficult over time. A study by the International Population Center at San Diego State University found Hmong birth rates in the u.s. to be one of the highest of any ethnic group in the world.

Still, there is hope for the future. Hmong in America value educational achievement. Encouraged to excel at school, and publicly praised at community gatherings for their academic achievements, large numbers of Hmong children will likely be successful competitors for skilled jobs. Some Hmong are already working as engineers, computer programmers, social workers, and university professors; a Hmong has been appointed to West Point. What is uncertain is the extent to which this growing economic progress will further weaken traditional Hmong culture and erode the solidarity of Hmong communities.

While most Hmong have become American without ceasing to be Hmong, a sizable, though shrinking, minority nevertheless desire to return to Laos. When ties to Hmong in Thai refugee camps were still strong, the vast majority dreamed of repatriation. Letters and audio cassettes were exchanged with relatives in the camps on a regular basis. Stories of the exploits of Hmong freedom fighters operating in Laos and rumors of the impending collapse of the LPDR flowed steadily between Thailand and America. In the late seventies and early eighties, Hmong communities throughout the U.S. contributed huge sums to support Hmong guerrilla operations in Laos. Some American Hmong were even willing to travel to Thailand and organize a resistance army to invade Laos and attempt to bring down the communist regime so that Laotian Hmong scattered across the globe could be repatriated.

It is now two decades since Laos fell to the communists. Until recently, the LPDR ruled the country with an iron fist. Hmong guerrilla activity peaked in 1977, was crushed in 1978, and has since waned to near insignificance. Nearly all of the Thai refugee camps for Hmong have closed, depriving the resistance of its main source of manpower, and a safe haven. This fact, coupled with Laos's impoverished economy, has dampened aspirations for repatriation. Today, only the very old continue to cling to the dream of returning to Laos. For their children, many of whom now have families of their own, Laos is a fading image, still warm but no longer glowing.

It is nothing new for the Hmong to be driven from their homeland and to be forced to start life anew in a foreign country. The difference for American Hmong is that they chose the U.S., a nation of immigrants who shared one dream: to build a society where no one ever has to start over again. Noted for their love of freedom, and oppressed for centuries because of it, the Hmong are a welcome addition to the melting pot called America.

Books

Allen, Nathan. *The Opium Trade.* 13 vols.; London: Longwood Press, 1978.

Beauclair, Inez. *Tribal Cultures of Southwest China.* Taipei: The Orient Cultural Service, 1972.

Bernatzik, Hugo Adlof. *Akha and Miao: Problems of Applied Ethnography in Farther India.* New Haven: Human Relations Area Files, 1970.

Bertrais, Yves. *The Traditional Marriage Among the White Hmong of Thailand and Laos.* Chiangmai, Thailand: Hmong Center, 1978.

Bessac, Suzanne and Jo Rainbolt. *Notes on Traditional Hmong Culture from Montana Hmong Recollections.* Missoula: University of Montana, 1978.

Bhikkhu, Dhammaraso and Virocano Bhikkhu. *The Historical Background and Tradition of the Meo.* Bangkok, Thailand: n.p., 1973.

Bliatout, Bruce Thowpaou. *Hmong Sudden Unexpected Nocturnal Death Syndrome. A Cultural Study.* Portland, Oregon: Sparkle Publishing Enterprises, 1982.

Bonifacy, Auguste. *Cours d'Ethnographie Indochinoise.* Hanoi-Haiphong: Imprimerie D'Extreme-Orient, 1919.

Branfman, Fred (ed.). *Voices from the Plain of Jars.* New York: Harper Colophon Books, 1972.

Burchette, Wilfred. *Mekong Upstream.* Berlin: Seven Seas Publishers, 1959.

Burling, Robbins. *Hill Farms and Padi Fields.* Englewood Cliffs, New Jersey: Prentice-Hall, Inc., 1965.

Chard, Chester. *Man in Prehistory.* 2nd ed.; New York: McGraw-Hill Book Co., 1975.

Chindarsi, *Nusit. The Religion of the Hmong Njua.* Bangkok: The Siam Society, 1983.

Clark, Grahame. *World Prehistory in New Perspective.* 3rd ed; Cambridge: Cambridge University Press, 1977.

Coon, Carelton. *The Living Races of Man.* New York: Alfred A. Knopf, 1965.

Cooper Robert, Nicholas Tapp, Gary Yia Lee, and Gretel Schwoer-Kohl. *The Hmong.* Bangkok: Artasia Press Co., 1991.

Coulborn, Rushton. *The Origin of Civilized Societies.* Princeton, New Jersey: Princeton University Press, 1959.

Daniel, Glyn. *The First Civilizations: The Archaeology of their Origins.* New York: Thomas Y. Crowell Co., 1968.

Dasse, Martial. *Montagnards, Revoltes et Guerres Revolutionaires en Asie du Sud-Est Continentale.* Bangkok: DK Book House, 1976.

De Lajonquiere, Etenne Lunet. *Ethnographie du Tonkin Septentrional.* Paris: Ernest Leroux, 1906.

Diguet, Edouard. *Les Montagnards du Tonkin.* Paris: Challamel, 1908.

Dommen, Arthur. *Laos: Keystone of Indochina.* Boulder, Colorado: Westview Press, 1985.

Donnelly, Nancy. *Changing Lives of Refugee Hmong Women.* Seattle: University of Washington Press, 1994.

Doyle, Edward and Samuel Lipsman. *The Vietnam Experience: Setting the Stage.* Boston: Boston Publishing Co., 1981.

Eberhard, Wolfram. A *History of China.* 2nd ed.; Los Angeles: University Press, 1960.

_____ *China's Minorities: Yesterday and Today.* Belmont California: Wadsworth Publishing Co., 1982.

Fagan, Brian. *Men of the Earth: An Introduction to World Prehistory.* Boston: Little, Brown and Co., 1974.

Fall, Bernard. *The Two Viet-Nams: A Political and Military Analysis.* Rev ed.; New York: Frederick Praeger, 1964.

_____ *Hell in a Very Small Place: The Siege of Dien Bien Phu.* Philadelphia: J.B. Lippincott Co., 1967.

Franke, Wolfgang. *A Century of Chinese Revolution: 1851-1949.* New York, Harper Torchbooks, 1970.

Geddes, William. *Migrants of the Mountains: The Cultural Ecology of the Blue Miao (Hmong Njua) of Thailand.* Oxford: Clarendon Press, 1976.

Girard, Henry. *Les Tribus Suavages du Haut-Tonkin: Man et Meos.* Paris: Imprimerie Nationale, 1903.

Graham, David Crockett. *Songs and Stories of the Ch'uan Miao.* Washington D.C.: Smithsonian Institution, 1954.

Gryaznov, Mikhail. *The Ancient Civilizations of Southern Siberia.* Translated from the Russian by James Hogarth; New York: Cowles Publishing Co., 1969.

International Narcotics Control, Hearings. Committee on Foreign Affairs. House of Representatives. 87th Cong. 2nd Sess. 1982.

Karnow, Stanley. *Vietnam: A History.* New York: The Viking Press, 1983.

Keen, F.G.B. *The Meo of Northwest Thailand.* Wellington, New Zealand: R.E. Owen, Government Printer, 1966.

Knoll, Tricia. *Becoming Americans: Asian Sojourners, Immigrants, and Refugees in the Western United States.* Portland, Oregon: Coast to Coast Books, 1982.

Lancaster, Donald. *The Emancipation of French Indochina.* London: Oxford University Press, 1961.

Langer, Paul and Joseph Zasloff. *North Vietnam and the Pathet Lao.* Cambridge, Mass.: Harvard University Press, 1970.

Larteguy, Jean. *La Fabuleuse Aventure du Peuple du l'Opium.* Paris: Presses de la Cite, 1979.

Le Bar, Frank and Adrienne Suddard, eds. *Laos: Its People, Its Society, Its Culture.* New Haven: Conn.: Human Relations Area Files Press, 1960.

Lemoine, Jacques. *Un Village Hmong Vert Du Haut Laos.* Paris: Editions du Centre National de la Recherche Scientifique, *1972.*

Mason, Linda and Roger Brown. *Rice, Rivalry, and Politics: Managing Cambodian Relief.* London: University of Notre Dame Press, 1983.

McCoy, Alfred. *The Politics of Heroin in Southeast Asia.* New York: Harper & Row, 1972.

Mottin, Jean. *The History of the Hmong (Meo).* Bangkok: Odeon Store Ltd., 1980.

_____ *Elements de Grammaire Hmong Blanc.* Khek Noy: Don Bosco Press, 1978.

_____ *Allons Faire Le Tour du Ciel et de la Terre: Le Chamanisme des Hmong Vu dans les Textes.* Sap Samothot, Thailand: n.p., 1981.

_____ *55 Chants D'Amour Hmong Blanc.* Bangkok: Siam Society, 1980.

_____ *Fetes Du Nouvel An Chez Les Hmong Blanc De Thailande.* Bangkok, Thailand: Don Bosco Press, 1979.

Page, Homer. *The Little World of Laos.* New York: Charles Scribner's Sons, 1959.

Pollard, Samuel. *The Story of the Miao.* London: Henry Hooks, 1919.

Rocher, Emile. *La Province Chinoise Du Yun-Nan.* 2 vols.; Paris: Ernest Leroux, 1879.

Roy, Jules. *The Battle of Dienbienphu.* Translated by Robert Baldick; New York: Harper & Row, 1965.

Savina, F.M. *Histoire Des Miao.* Paris: Societe des Missions-Etrangeres, 1924.

Schanche, Don. *Mr. Pop.* New York: David McKay Co., 1967.

Shaplen, Robert. *Time out of Hand: Revolution and Reaction in Southeast Asia.* New York: Harper & Row, 1969.
_____ *A Turning Wheel.* New York: Random House, 1973.

Shrock, Joanne, et. al. *Minority Groups in Thailand.* Washington D.C.: Department of the Army, 1970.
_____ *Minority Groups in North Vietnam.* Washington D.C.: U.S. Government Printing Office, 1972.

Smalley, William, Chia Koua Vang, and Gnia Yee Yang. *Mother of Writing: The Origin and Development of a Hmong Messianic Script.* Chicago: The University of Chicago Press, 1990.

St. Cartmail, Keith. *Exodus Indochina.* Auckland: Heinemann, 1983.

Stover, Leon and Takeko Stover. *China: An Anthropological Perspective.* Pacific Palisades: Goodyear Publishing Co., 1976.

Stuart-Fox, Martin. *Laos: Politics, Economics and Society .* London: Frances Pinter, 1986.

Sullivan, William. *Obbligato: Notes on a Foreign Service Career.* New York: W.W. Norton & Company, 1984.

Tapp, Nicholas. *Sovereignty and Rebellion: The White Hmong of Northern Thailand.* Oxford: Oxford University Press, 1989.

Terry, Charles and Mildred Pellens. *The Opium Problem.* Reprint of 1928 edition; Montclair, New Jersey: Patterson Smith, 1970.

Thee, Marek. *Notes of a Witness.* New York: Random House, 1973.

The Global Connection: Heroin Entrepreneurs, Hearings. Subcommittee to Investigate Juvenile Delinquency. u.s. Senate. 94th Cong. 2nd Sess. 1976.

The Hill Tribes of Thailand. Chiang Mai, Thailand: Technical Service Club Tribal Research Institute, 1986.

The Hmong in St. Paul: A Culture in Transition. St. Paul, Minnesota: Community Planning Organization, 1980.

Thompson, Virginia. *French Indochina.* New York, Macmillan Co., 1937.

Trinquier, Roger. *Les Maquis d'Indochine.* Paris: Albatros, n.d.

Westermeyer, Joseph. *Poppies, Pipes, and People: Opium and Its Use in Laos.* Los Angeles: University of California Press, 1982.

Whitaker, Donald et. al. *Area Handbook for Laos.* Washington D.C.: U.S. Government Printing Office, 1972.

Wiens, Herold. *China's March Toward the Tropics.* Hamnden, Connecticut: The Shoe String Press, 1954.

Yang, Dao. *Les Hmong du Laos Face au Developpement.* Vientiane, Laos: Edition Siaosavath, 1975.

Zacher, Mark W. and R. Stephen Milne, eds. *Conflict* and *Stability in Southeast Asia.* New York: Anchor Books, 1974.

ARTICLES

Adams, Leonard. "China: The Historical Setting of Asia's Profitable Plague." Appendix to Alfred McCoy. *The Politics of Heroin in Southeast Asia.* New York: Harper & Row, 1972.

Beck, Roy. "The Ordeal of Immigration in Wausau." *The Atlantic Monthly* April 1994.

Beech, Keyes. "How Uncle Sam Fumbled in Laos." *Saturday Evening Post.* April 22, 1961.

Betts, George. "Social Life of the Miao Tsï." *Journal of the Straits of the Royal Asiatic Society*, Vol. 33, 1899.

Bourotte, Bernard. "Marriages et Funeralles Chez les Meos Blancs de la Region de Nong-Het (Tran Ninh)." *Institut Indochinois Pour l'Etude de l'Homme, Bulletins et Travaux.* Vol. 6, 1943.

Branfman, Fred. "The President's Secret Army: A Case Study — The CIA in Laos, 1962-1972." In *The CIA File*, eds. Robert Borosage and John Marks. New York: Grossman Publishers, 1976.

Bridgman, E. C. "Sketches of the Miau-Tsze." *Royal Asiatic Society.* No. 3, 1859.

Bristar, Soul Vang-Choj. "The End of the Hmong." *California Hmong Times.* December 15, 1994.

Burchett, Wilfred. "Pawns and Patriots: The U.S. Fight for Laos." In *Laos: War and Revolution*, Nina Adams and Alfred McCoy. New York: Harper & Row, 1971.

Chagnon, Jacqui and Roger Rumpf. "Dignity, National Identity and Unity." *Southeast Asia Chronicle.* Vol. 73, June 1980.

Clarke, Judith. "The Laotian Dilemma." *Asia Week.* February 2, 1986.

Clarke, Samuel R. "The Miao and Chungchia Tribes of Kweichow Province." *East of Asia.* vol. 3, September, 1904.

Cooper, Robert. "The Hmong of Laos: Economic Factors in the Refugee Exodus and Return." In *The Hmong in Transition*, eds. Glen Hendricks, Bruce Downing and Amos Deinard. New York: Center for Migration Studies, 1986.

Durdin, Peggy. "Soviet Imperialism: The Grim Lesson of Laos." In *The Many Faces of Communism*, ed. Harry Schwartz. Berkeley: Berkeley Publishing, 1962.

Ebihara, May. "Mon-Khmer." In *Ethnic Groups of Mainland Southeast Asia*, Frank Lebar, et. al. New Haven: Human Relations Area Files Press, 1964.

Everingham, John. "One Family's Odyssey to America." *National Geographic.* Vol. 157, No. 5, May, 1980.

Fass, Simon M. "Economic Development and Employment Projects." In *The Hmong in Transition*, eds. Glen Hendricks, Bruce Downing and Amos Deinard. New York: Center for Migration Studies, 1986.

Feldman, Orna. "A New Life for the Hmong." *Boston Magazine.* Vol. 75, April, 1983.

Feng, H.Y. and J.K. Shryock. "The Black Magic in China Known as 'Ku'." *American Oriental Society Journal.* Vol. 55, 1935.

Fink, John. "Secondary Migration to California's Central Valley." In *The Hmong in Transition*, eds. Glen Hendricks, Bruce Downing and Amos Deinard. New York: Center for Migration Studies, 1986.

Foisie, Jack. "U.S.-Backed Laotian General Scorned by Other Army Leaders." *Los Angeles Times*. March 12, 1970.

Garrett, W. E. "The Hmong of Laos: No Place to Run." *National Geographic*. Vol. 145, No. 1, January, 1974.

Grandstaff, Terry. "The Hmong, Opium and the Haw: Speculations on the Origin of their Association." *Siam Society Journal*. Vol. 67, No. 2, 1979.

Gua, Bo. "Opium, Bombs and Trees: The Future of the Hmong Tribesmen in Northern Thailand." *Journal of Contemporary Asia*. Vol. 5, No. 1, 1975.

Hammond, Ruth. "Strangers in a Strange Land." *Twin Cities Reader*. June 15-21, 1988.

Jackson, Larry. "The Vietnamese Revolution and the Montagnards." *Asian Survey*. Vol. 9, No. 5, May, 1969.

Jones, Susan and Philip Kuhn. "Dynastic Decline and the Roots of Rebellion." In *The Cambridge History of China*, eds. Denis Twitchett and John K. Fairbank. Vol. 10. Cambridge: Cambridge University Press, 1978.

Karnow, Stanley. "Free No More: The Allies America Forgot." *Geo*. Vol. 2, 1980.

Langer, Paul. "Laos Under the Gun." *Asia Week*. October 5, 1979.

Lee, Gary Yia. "Culture and Adaptation: Hmong Refugees in Australia 1976-83." *Hmong-Australia Society Newsletter*. Vol. 6, No. 2, June, 1984.

Lee, Gary Yia. "Minority Policies and the Hmong." In *Contemporary Laos*, ed. Martin Stuart-Fox. New York: St. Martin's Press, 1982.

Lemoine, Jacques. "Les Ecritures du Hmong." *Bulletin des Amis du Royaume Lao*. Nos. 7 & 8, 1972.

Lyman, Thomas Amis. "Green Miao (Meo) Spirit-Ceremonies." *Ethnologica*. Vol. 4, 1960.

"Man Pleads Guilty to Abduction in Arranged Marriage." *California Hmong Times*. November 15, 1993.

McAlister, John. "Mountain Minorities and the Viet Minh: A Key to the Indochina War." In *Southeast Asian Tribes, Minorities, and Nations*, ed. Peter Kunstadter. Vol. 2; Princeton, New Jersey: Princeton University Press, 1967.

McCoy, Alfred. "French Colonialism in Laos, 1893-1945." In *Laos: War and Revolution*, Nina Adams and Alfred McCoy. New York: Harper & Row, 1971.

Mickey, Margaret Porcia. "The Cowrie Shell Miao of Kweichow." *Papers of the Peabody Museum of American Archaeology and Ethnology*. Vol. XXXII, No. 1, 1947.

Morechand, Guy. "Notes Demographiques Sur un Canton Meo Blanc du Pays Tai." *Bulletin de la Societe des Etudes Indochinoises de Saigon*. Vol. 27, 1952.

Norindr, Chou. "Political Institutions of the Lao People's Democratic Republic." In *Contemporary Laos*, ed. Martin Stuart-Fox. New York: St. Martin's Press, 1982.

Oliver, Myrna. "Cultural Defense—A Legal Tactic." *Los Angeles Times*. July 15, 1988.

Olney, Douglas. "Opium Found in St Paul: Woman Held." *Minneapolis Star and Tribune.* August 12, 1982.

_____ "Population Trends." In *The Hmong in Transition*, eds. Glen Hendricks, Bruce Downing and Amos Deinard. New York: Center for Migration Studies, 1986.

Papa, Mary Bader. "Police Pounce on Poppy Patch." *The Spokesman-Review.* July 30, 1982.

_____ "Waking up to the American Dream." *Twin Cities Magazine.* May, 1982.

Richburg, Keith. "Cambodia is Turning Out to be Vietnam's Vietnam." *The Washington Post National Weekly Edition.* December 1, 1986.

Roux, Henri and Tran Van Chu. "Quelques Minorites Ethniques du Nord-Indochine." *France-Asie.* Vol. 10, 1954.

Schein, Louis. "The Miao in Contemporary China: A Preliminary Overview." In *The Hmong in Transition*, eds. Glen Hendricks, Bruce Downing and Amos Deinard. New York: Center for Migration Studies, 1986.

Shaplen, Robert. "A Reporter at Large: Survivors." *New Yorker.* September 5, 1977.

Smalley, William A. "Stages of Hmong Cultural Adaptation." In *The Hmong in Transition*, eds. Glen Hendricks, Bruce Downing and Amos Deinard. New York: Center for Migration Studies, 1986.

Smalley, William. "Khmu." In *Ethnic Groups of Mainland Southeast Asia*, Frank Lebar, et. al. New Haven: Human Relations Area Files Press, 1964.

Spigarelli, Asunta. "Rice, Eggs, and GAIN Reform." *California Hmong Times.* Nov. 1, 1994.

Terry, Charles and Mildred Pellens. "The Agony of the Hmong." *Asia Week.* Dec 15, 1978.

Trinquier, Roger. "Temoignage: Les Maquis d'Indochine." *Revue Historique des Arrnees.* Vol. 2, 1979.

Vreeland, Susan. "Future of Laotian Folk Art Hangs by a Thread." *The Christian Science Monitor.* November 19, 1981.

Vreeland, Susan. "Through the Looking Glass with the Hmong of Laos." *The Christian Science Monitor.* March 30, 1981.

Wekkin, Gary. "The Rewards of Revolution: Pathet Lao Policy Toward the Hill Tribes Since 1975." In *Contemporary Laos*, ed. Martin Stuart-Fox. New York: St. Martin's Press, 1982.

Yang, Dao. "Guerre Des Gaz: Solution Communiste Des Problemes Des Minorities Au Laos." *Temps Modernes.* Vol. 30, No. 402, January, 1980.

Yang, Dao. "Why Did the Hmong Leave Laos?" In *The Hmong in the West: Observations and Reports*, eds. Bruce Downing and Douglas Olney. Minneapolis-St. Paul: University of Minnesota Press, 1982.

Yie-Fu, Ruey. "The Miao: Their Origin and Southward Migration." *Proceedings: International Association of Historians of Asia.* October, 1962.

Yun, Lu. "Miao Woman Pioneers Reform." *Beijing Review.* Vol. 29, No 38, September 22, 1986.

Interviews

Her, Thao (1985)
Lee, Bliacher (1985)
Moua, Yao Naotou (1985).
Vu, Fu (1984)
Vu, Fu (1987).
Vu, Tou (1984).
Vu, Tou (1985).
Vue, Cher Sue (1985).
Vue, Nao Yang (1985).
Vue, Nao Yang (1985).
Vue, Neng (1985).
Vue, Seng (1985).
Vue, Shue Long (1985).
Vue, Tong Leng (1985).
Vue, Xia Ying (1985).
Xiong, Katoua (formerly known as
    Xiong Chong Neng) (1985).
Yang, Cher Cha. (1985).
Yang, Nao Ying (1984).
Yang, Nao Ying (1987).

Index